P9-AOV-143

By Robert Metz

Jackpot!

CBS: Reflections in a Bloodshot Eye

How to Shake the Money Tree

JACKPOT!

Everything You Need to Know
About Smart Money Investing
in the New Wall Street

by

ROBERT METZ

SIMON AND SCHUSTER · NEW YORK

COPYRIGHT © 1977 BY ROBERT METZ
ALL RIGHTS RESERVED
INCLUDING THE RIGHT OF REPRODUCTION
IN WHOLE OR IN PART IN ANY FORM

PUBLISHED BY SIMON AND SCHUSTER
A DIVISION OF GULF & WESTERN CORPORATION
SIMON & SCHUSTER BUILDING
ROCKEFELLER CENTER
1230 AVENUE OF THE AMERICAS
NEW YORK, NEW YORK 10020

DESIGNED BY EVE METZ
MANUFACTURED IN THE UNITED STATES OF AMERICA

2 3 4 5 6 7 8 9 10

LIBRARY OF CONGRESS CATALOGING IN PUBLICATION DATA
METZ, ROBERT.
    JACKPOT! : EVERYTHING YOU NEED TO KNOW ABOUT SMART
MONEY INVESTING IN THE NEW WALL STREET.

    1. INVESTMENTS—UNITED STATES.   I. TITLE.
HG4921.M47   332.678   76-52973
ISBN 0-671-22565-0

Charts prepared by John Magee, Inc.

TO MY SON, ANDY, THE DANDY.
AND, OF COURSE, TO LIZ—
WHO MAKES IT ALL WORTHWHILE.

ACKNOWLEDGMENTS

Apart from the individuals cited in the book by name—all of whom I thank—I want to mention a man who insisted that I write this book long after I had decided against it. He is Shelly Wilshinsky of Shearson Hayden Stone, a good friend and an impeccably honest man.

I want to express also my particular thanks to George J. Stassen of Girard Bank in Philadelphia, who helped again and again with wonderful enthusiasm and then gave the manuscript a careful read-through.

Howard Diamond of Fourteen Research backstopped me on the options material, and Frank Henjes, who runs his own shop in Wall Street, contributed heavily to and then read painstakingly all the material on corporate and municipal bonds. Alan (Ted) H. McAlpin of First Regional Securities, Inc., gets less credit in the text than he deserves for help with corporate bonds and preferred shares. Ted filled in many blanks in my knowledge and graciously allowed me to quote his research reports extensively and without constant credit to the source.

Last but by no means least is Sam Skurnick of Bruns, Nordeman, Rea & Company. Sam pored over the manuscript with characteristic care, turning up substantive error and even discovering typos missed by the editors and myself. At several points in the text, I confess that it is Sam speaking and not I. Beyond this, I offer my thanks and apologies to the scores of individuals who contributed and whose names I have neglected to mention. If I have managed to blunder once or twice despite their efforts, I accept sole responsibility.

ROBERT METZ

CONTENTS

12 · CONTENTS

PART IV · *Bonds*

PART V · *Mutual Funds*

PART VI · *Taxes*

Preface

Beyond the Dreams
of Avarice

ONE DAY, A WHILE BACK, as I sat at my desk at the New York *Times* composing a column about a high-technology company, I received a call from the company's public relations man. He was concerned that I might write something that could hurt his company's stock. The shares had been soaring, having practically doubled in the space of a few weeks' time.

The P.R. man was a former science reporter for a major daily newspaper. He assured me that the company's shares were *not a speculation* and added that they *simply could not go down.*

The man was sincere and sophisticated—in matters of science, but not the stock market. The company was a manufacturer of glassy substances commercialized as an annotatable microfilm. One of the nation's largest and most-respected companies had recently paid the microfilm maker a small sum for the right to market the product and related materials and thus caused the gains in the stock market. But it is fair to say that the smaller company was still a thousand-to-one shot in the stock market. Yet the P.R. man saw it as another Polaroid for sure.

That same company's shares had once gained an incredible 88 points interday and closed up 22 in a frenzied trading session on the over-the-counter market. That was during the go-go years of the late 1960s. But for years thereafter, the stock had never broken

10, and as recently as 1975 the shares had traded at a low of 2 and a fraction. I was writing a critique of the current action in the stock. In the piece, I noted that the founder, though self-taught, was believed to be a genius, but I took a jaundiced view of the stock's immediate prospects—and rightly so. The company had lost money in every year of its existence and at the time owed more than it was worth.

The P.R. man was so like the rest of us. He wanted to think that his once-in-a-lifetime opportunity was knocking at the door, and he was ripping off the knob to let it in. I have heard such stories dozens of times in the twenty years I have been doing newspaper work—virtually all of them as a financial reporter. But I have learned that instant gold is like instant coffee. It looks like the real thing, but it isn't.

All smart investors look for gold, but they usually settle quite sensibly for silver and lesser valuables in Wall Street. Once more, they are cautious. Their primary concern is to keep what money they've got by investing conservatively. They may take a flier occasionally, but they won't put a substantial part of their capital into such speculations.

They know that there is a great deal to finding success in the stock market. You'll learn this too—if you don't already know it. Among other things, you'll need to know something about finance —though much less than you might imagine. You need to develop a feel for the stock market and its moods. You need to be properly cynical over that gushing stockbroker who calls late in the week. Chances are his weekend pleasures may depend upon the commissions he earns out of your rash investment. You need, most of all, to learn to think for yourself with regard to your investments.

If this book accomplishes what I set out to do with it, you'll find scores of the right things to do in Wall Street and warnings galore that should help you keep out of trouble. I've tried to distill the best of what I have learned about investing. I've also demonstrated, I think, that there is no single strategy for success—that the market changes and that you must adjust as it does so. I do stress, however, the importance of a long-term approach.

I do believe that the right combination of caution, study, and perspicacity can lead to substantial financial success and, for some, millions. You might ponder the success of my friend Morton Adler. Mr. Adler visited the small and struggling Haloid Corporation photographic paper manufactory on Warner Street in Rochester, New York. He was impressed with the company's patented process for affixing magnetic dust to paper and thought the company's management team dynamic. He bought lots of the shares for next to nothing and made millions of dollars when Haloid succeeded phenomenally as Xerox Corporation.

There are hundreds of individuals in this country who can tell you that Morton Adler's experience, while spectacular, is not unique. I hope at the very least that as a result of reading this book you will become a better investor, and, after a decent interval, richer.

ROBERT METZ

New York City

A Caveat

In this book I paint a grim picture of the competence and of the kinder instincts of stockbrokers. I have done so because in twenty years of following the financial community I have rarely seen or been informed of service above and beyond the call of duty, or, for that matter, of service meeting reasonable standards.

I am referring to Wall Street service standards generally available to individuals of modest means—those with from fifteen to fifty thousand to invest, the individual sometimes called the Little Guy.

My assumption has been that few reps (registered representatives) care a rap about this individual, especially if the individual is smart enough and sensible enough to limit his trading. Remember that for the rep, happiness is a millionaire client with the patience of a small boy on the last day of school.

The commission-hungry rep can't be bothered with genteel manners and caution. If he isn't fresh, he's out of business.

I should point out, however, that there is definitely a different drummer out there in investor land. He's the customer's man who lives in a pleasant commercial backwater far from the crowd at Broad and Wall. Unlike his city cousin, he needs relatively little income to lead the relaxed life he seeks. He's a neighbor to his clients in a small community and thus anxious that they do well. If you live in this man's town—wherever he may be—you can discount some of the starker aspects of the broker story.

If you are extraordinarily lucky, you may even find a paragon of a broker in the city. There are a few, of course. To survive, such a broker has to have scores of clients like yourself; little need or wish for a lofty income; and an uncommon desire to serve others. Unfortunately, such rare individuals do not wear turned collars and are therefore difficult to spot.

If you find this rare bird—or live in that neck of the woods where such birds flock—peace be with you and good luck.

PART I
INVESTING

1 · Lonely Campaign

AN OHIO RAILROAD WORKER who suffered serious injury from falling into one of the road's uncovered manholes was referred to a prominent lawyer with a brilliant trial record. The lawyer took the case and won it handily—the jury awarded the disabled plaintiff $100,000.

When the lawyer received the money, he called his client to his richly paneled offices and explained that his fee would be 25 percent, and that his trial costs were 15 percent. He charged 10 percent more for research and brief preparation and added an additional 10 percent charge for miscellaneous expenses.

The modestly dressed plaintiff hobbled over to look at his $40,000 check and remarked, "Tell me, sir, who in hell fell into that manhole—me or you?"

Many veterans of the killer stock market of the first half of the current decade may feel they were pushed into open manholes, and some of them can be forgiven if they blame their brokers for supplying the shove.

It is fair to say that no one is likely to care as much about your money as you do, and it probably follows that you should not rely on someone else to manage it—certainly not a broker whose interests conflict dramatically with yours.

There may be few brokers who share the view of one cynic who told a conscientious broker I know that he should "screw your clients before they screw you." Nevertheless, careful, dedicated brokers who handle accounts of less than $100,000 with tender loving care are scarce enough that you needn't waste your time looking for one. Someday you may just find one, but in the meantime those you rely on along the way may lose half your capital.

There are two major reasons for this. Remember first that a broker's training is sketchy at best. More than one quick study—to use the show-business term for an actor who quickly commits lines to memory—has crammed for and passed the New York Stock Exchange "registered representative" test in a week. Brokers' on-the-job training was actually reduced from six months to four in 1975, when the new examination was "made considerably tougher" in the words of an exchange spokesman.

Whether a young person just out of school will know and care enough to do that most difficult of all jobs—help you make ends meet and actually lengthen the rope—is certainly doubtful. Unlike the young teacher who is just one page ahead of the class, your young broker may be spotting you years of practical experience in managing money and is thus ten pages behind. The old hands are no different—just better salesmen. You'd best treat them all like the clerks they are. And that brings us to point two: motivation. It is hard to imagine a system with a more diabolical bias against the customer.

While relatively few cases reach the courts concerning "churning"—the purchase and sale of an investor's securities for the sole purpose of generating commissions—it happens frequently, nevertheless. Brokers may even churn accounts convinced that they are doing it for the customer's own good. Such is the subtlety of the commission system.

The most ignorant broker is likely to be aware that the commission system rewards failure more than it rewards success—at least in the short run. (You may remember that the celebrated economist John Maynard Keynes remarked, "In the long run, we'll all be dead!")

It works this way. You pay your broker a single commission if he gets you a stock that goes up. After all, you're no fool. You're going to resist his efforts to get you to sell it. That stock is making money for you. If you've got, say, $20,000 in that account, and paid $5,000 for the stock, he's just allowed you to take 25 percent out of circulation. Where is he if he keeps that up? He's no fool either. Consider where he'd be if he got you four winners at $5,000 a crack. The answer, of course, is working for himself—not for you.

The fact is your broker is *not* that good. Rather, the average retail stockbroker is much more likely to find you a loser right off. What happens next? Don't call him, he'll call you. After a decent interval, he'll be on the phone to say he's sorry about that Penn Central thing . . . "But people a lot smarter than I got hung with that one." Then he'll say something like:

"You're in luck 'cause I've got one that will more than make up for your loss. I may be a fool to tell you this, but I sneaked into our institutional research department and got the name of a stock that's going to double in value in a few weeks. Only our best customers know about it."

You pay your second commission to sell your Penn Central and send a check for your third commission to buy his new pipe dream. There you have it. (Actually *he* has it; *you've had* it.) He gets three paychecks for the wrong answer, only one for the right answer. You were expecting another Johnson & Johnson and all you got was stab wounds and a Band-Aid.

Now this is overstated, of course—but only slightly so, and not at all for some poor brokers' customers. On the other hand, in a roaring bull market, even the worst brokers may look good—or at least not bad.

A while back as the Dow Jones industrial average assaulted the magical 1000 level, I watched fascinated as a broker filmed for the evening news gave a customer advice by telephone as the mini-cam looked over his shoulder: "IBM looks good, General Motors can be bought here, I can recommend Kodak . . ." And he *could* shoot off his mouth with fifty of the best stocks bubbling in a speculative barrel of enthusiasm.

But the problem is that the market goes down too. There are times when it is best to be entirely out of the stock market and collecting 7½ percent in a savings account. But market fever infects

—even in down markets. It is not just the stockbrokers who succumb. Even the professional money managers lose perspective—the men who run your money at the mutual funds. I once sat in the lush boardroom of a billion-dollar mutual fund organization sipping tea out of fine English china while the chief executives there told me why they would be foolish to get out of the market, a market that had devoured nearly a third of their shareholders' capital in three years. It would be foolish to sell stocks and buy bonds, which, after all, weren't even keeping pace with inflation. Losses grew thereafter.

As it happens, then, those most likely to share the responsibility for managing your money—brokers and mutual fund money managers—in one way or another and often as not will be acting against your best interests. The broker does it for commissions, the professional money manager because the organization's charter requires it.

What you must do, then, is to school yourself to be a better investor than your broker—a more effective money manager than the mutual fund professional.

It is not an overwhelming task. This book is designed to help you grasp the important principles of investing and to recognize the difference between a stock tout and a worthwhile piece of advice.

You'll have to make your own decisions. You'll probably surprise yourself with your innate good sense. And, in the unlikely event that you fall into a manhole, you'll know at least that you weren't shoved. With proper precautions, you'll land safely on your feet—and not on your head.

COMMON-SENSE INVESTING

It is hard to overstate the role of common sense in investing. A stockbroker who has made a lot of money both for customers and for himself tells me he once saw a news item that seemed certain to have a favorable impact on a particular company's fortunes. He quickly called the floor of the New York Stock Exchange and learned that he could buy 10,000 shares of the company's stock, then priced at $6. Since he could borrow half the money he needed to make the purchase under the 50-percent-down (margin) rules then in effect, he would have to commit only $30,000. But then he thought, "Hey! If this stock looks so good to me, why doesn't it look equally good to someone else?" He didn't buy the shares. Thirty minutes later, he happened to see 10,000 shares of the stock trade at the indicated price and, shortly after that, the price was up a full point. He had missed an opportunity to turn a quick $10,000 profit because he didn't value his own common sense.

Fortunately, investors need not act with such haste. Speculators must, but not investors. A speculator is out to make a quick buck, often at high risk. Wall Street cynics will tell you that an "investor" is someone who is sitting with his losses. Actually, an investor is someone who has carefully evaluated an opportunity and taken advantage of it. His common sense led him to the investment in the first place and gave him the strength of his convictions when he called his broker to follow through. Frequently, brokers make light of their customer's convictions. Frequently, brokers are wrong. A smart broker is worth hearing out—the general caliber of brokers is up, following a mass exodus of nitwits and dingbats during the five-year (some say six-year) bear market. But if the broker can't come up with a cogent point, clearly expressed, that you neglected to consider when you made your judgment, stick with it.

2 · Sheltered Waters
for Unwatered Stock

THE ABRUPTNESS with which institutional investors dump their stocks—causing them to drop precipitously—has had a stunning impact on the thinking of the small investor. Many have been caught up in such debacles, and the worst of it is that the damage occurs so suddenly that the individual hasn't time to react. By the time he reads the newspaper and becomes aware of the fact that his cherished growth stock has fallen out of bed, he has already lost 15 to 25 percent of his investment.

Some have been unfortunate enough to buy their shares in the doomed stock just days before the bloodshed and thus suffer even greater trauma. After such devastating experiences, many sell all their stocks, convinced that the giant institutions have made the stock market unsafe for democracy.

The long-term holder can adopt a philosophical point of view, reasoning that what goes down must come back, but it is hollow consolation. Frequently, it is years before such stocks begin to approach old levels, and when they do the temptation is to sell them and come out "even." Anyone following this approach with a low-dividend growth stock will lose the income potential of his money and suffer whatever damage inflation does to the dollar in the meantime.

But there is no reason for the individual to be discouraged with the stock market. For the fact is, the institutions' enormous size works against them in highly attractive sectors of the market. And it is just those sectors that offer some of the best opportunities for success.

Basically, there are three factors that the institution must consider to a degree which you need not: "size," liquidity, and fads.

The institution must think about the number of shares needed for a meaningful position—that is, about size. For instance, a $100 million institution that buys 10,000 shares of a $5 stock has committed one two-thousandth of total capital. If the stock were to quadruple so that the institution's $50,000 investment grew to $200,000, the institution has not added significantly to total net worth. The $200,000 still represents just one five-hundredth of total capital.

Imagine your personal elation if you had committed one-tenth as much to the same stock—$5,000 for 1,000 shares at $5 each—and your shares quadrupled in value to $20,000. In all probability, this would be a significant gain for you—unless you had once picked up a disheveled man in tennis shoes out West and delivered him to his Las Vegas penthouse.

Don't worry that the institution may buy up most of the shares of such a company. Under SEC rules, mutual funds may not buy more than a fraction of the shares of any company, and there are similar strictures on other institutions.

This brings us to the question of liquidity. You know what illiquidity is. Illiquidity is owning a $50,000 house in a $25,000 neighborhood and an exciting new job offer in faraway Bermuda. For an institution, illiquidity is the inability to sell in ten minutes—at any price—the 100,000 shares it gradually acquired over a period of six months.

Liquidity wouldn't matter if the institutions hadn't done such a fine job of selling clients on the "total return" concept of investing. That is, the institutions asked to be measured on the basis of income (dividends) plus capital gains—the total return. Clients liked the idea, but asked, "How do we measure that?" The institutions said, "Ask us what we've done for you lately—over the most recent quarter." Now institutions are stuck with it.

One result has been that institutional portfolios are mercilessly culled for bad apples before the quarterly reporting period ends. (That's why institutions B, C, and D sell their shares of XYZ minutes after institution A.)

If a stock isn't liquid it can't be purchased, because it can't be sold quickly. A money manager told me that even if he buys a "perfectly good name" he must be able to get out if it goes sour, to reverse his judgment.

This keeps institutions out of some stocks that have great prospects—but in which liquidity is a problem; stocks like life insurance companies. The working population is still growing, and some 13 million new employables will be joining the work force in the next five years. They'll need life insurance. But the institutions aren't buying some of those stocks because the market for the shares is thin. The same money manager commented on the dilemma which forced him in early 1976 to turn his attention away from certain life insurance stocks and to the auto makers—the then current fad.

"I can see the life insurance stocks picking up dramatically, but I can't park my money there when there isn't a ripple of interest in the group. I would if my clients understood, but they do not. I have to put money into the auto stocks instead—for a quick, cyclical swing—like the other institutions. Our problem in this business is that the focus is too short-term for our own good." And thus the money manager is at the mercy of fads. So are you, but hardly to such an extent; nothing is forcing you to pass up a sound but currently unfashionable stock.

All of this suggests that there are wide areas of the stock market in which the patient student of the market can make money—especially when one considers that the stocks the institutions cannot and will not buy are by and large at or near historic lows. Hundreds of basically sound stocks have not participated in the 1976 bull market.

3 · The Dream Machine

EVERY INVESTOR'S DREAM is to be able to buy stocks when they are cheap—when the whole market is down, not just when a few undiscovered special situations exist.

Count yourself lucky, then. For as this is being written there is widespread agreement in Wall Street—even among the pessimists —that there has rarely been a moment in history over the last quarter-century when there were as many superior values around as there are now.

That may sound strong; after all, the Dow Jones industrial average of 30 key companies' stocks rests near 1000 and is thus within a freckle of its all-time high—1051.70.

Nevertheless, there is impressive evidence that the stock market, like Thursday's child, has far to go; that a generally rising trend could continue for a couple of years and that even thereafter hundreds of out-of-the-spotlight stocks will remain cheap.

But before we consider the many stocks individuals have almost to themselves, let's take a closer look at the 30 Dow industrials. In May, Jay Levy, an economist with a sharp focus on fundamentals, noted that, corrected for inflation, the Dow Jones industrials were no higher than they were in February 1966.

Those 30 Dow stocks are big ones, stocks like General Motors, Swift, and Union Carbide. More widely based market indicators, such as the Value Line composite average of 1,600 stocks, portray an even more attractively priced market. That average is lower than it was ten years ago by at least a third.

Now let's look at what the post-recession earnings recovery is doing to the relative price of stocks. Consider again the 30 Dow issues. When that average first approached the 1000 level in early 1966, the combined earnings of the 30 totaled $55. Nearly three years later—in December 1968—the Dow was on the recovery trail and once again made it to the 1000 level. The 30 stocks again showed earnings of $55.

Oddly enough, the 30 Dow stocks set their record high on January 11, 1973—in mid-bear market—as the institutions sought shelter from the worst market since the Great Depression. At that time, with the Dow Jones industrials at 1051.70, the combined earnings of the shares reached $68.

We all know that stocks are purchased because of the promise of earnings—when higher earnings are anticipated, other things being equal, stock prices go up. What are we to make of the fact that in May 1976 the anticipated earnings for the Dow 30 were close to $100 and rising while the stocks themselves were trading at a bit below 1000?

If you think the market high, remember the high earnings anticipated that have carried stocks to current levels. The stocks that have participated in the bull market so far are by and large those of the nation's largest companies—the ones the institutions can and do hold in their portfolios. Remember that even in the worst year of the recession—1975—the earnings of the largest companies didn't suffer too much. The Fortune 500 companies reported an average earnings drop of just 13.3 percent in 1975.

Small companies, though, suffered egregiously by comparison. Hundreds of small companies failed. Those that survived chewed away deadwood like angry beavers—even gnawing at the solid timbers in a frantic effort to avoid disaster.

A top official of a Philadelphia bank who lives in a suburban community populated primarily by executives said that several neighbors who worked for smaller companies were summarily fired during the slump. "These were bright, highly productive individuals, not ding-a-lings. . . . In a storm, the teak chest goes over the side."

As a result, as the money manager and others have observed, the surviving small companies are tightly run today. Assuming their markets are reasonably intact, many are in a position to score heavily in the recovery. Some are not quite ready to turn around, others are well along the road to economic health, and still others are booming. Many in each category are undervalued at current stock market prices.

Remember that smaller companies draw their shareholders from the ranks of individuals—not from mutual funds and other giant institutions. Remember that small investors left the market by the millions, helping to depress share values in smaller companies. Low stock prices persist among junior issues on the American Stock Exchange and in the over-the-counter market, clearly suggesting that the small investor is yet to return to the market. Even more important, the low prices suggest opportunity.

Price/earnings ratios—the indicator of how many times current (or anticipated) profits the stock sells at—are low. Many sound companies that carried price/earnings ratios in the teens before stumbling in the recession now carry P/Es of 5 to 1. When the values underlying the shares are sound, this is cheap. Prices could go lower—this is always true—but this is clearly an era of cheap stocks.

Let's get down to cases. George J. Stasen, a veteran market observer, money manager and senior vice president of Girard Bank, tapped the computer to back up his contention—and just incidentally mine—that the market is "cheap."

He looked at prices on the New York and American exchanges and at the prices of about 720 over-the-counter stocks. He used stock prices as of the end of the first quarter of 1976—March 31. He thus included most of the gains of the spectacular bull market of January 1976. But he measured those prices against the most recently reported 12 months' earnings results, which was the period ended December 31, 1975. First-quarter results weren't out yet.

Since 1975 marked the nadir of the recession, the earnings shown by most companies for the calendar year were probably the worst in many years. By thus measuring the high stock prices of March 31, 1976, against the low earnings of 1975, he biased his results in terms of the highest price/earnings ratios reasonable under the circumstances. He comments:

"When I examined the data, I found that the average P/E on the New York Stock Exchange was 12.4, the American Stock Exchange average was 10.8, and the over-the-counter market average was 11.9.

"If the market functioned perfectly, investors would pay high price/earnings ratios for earnings that are about to recover or expand sharply, and investors would pay low price/earnings ratios for earnings that are about to contract. Looking at the broad scope of stock market history, investors have paid between 6 and 22 times earnings. Clearly, by this yardstick, investors were acting more as if they believed that earnings would deteriorate rather than that they would recover. Of course, the explanation lies in the fears generated by the six-year bear market.

"Furthermore, there is trouble with averaging large numbers of anything in that some worthwhile intelligence is glossed over. Take the 3,276 issues that were covered by the preceding group and eliminate from them all the stocks reporting no earnings. This leaves a total of 2,808. On March 29, of this group, four out of ten (1,123 stocks) were selling at less than 8½ times earnings, three out of ten (842 stocks) were selling at less than 7 times earnings, two out of ten (562 stocks) at less than 6 times earnings, and one out of ten (281 stocks) at less than 5 times earnings.

"Undoubtedly, many of these companies have problems and their earnings' streams are in jeopardy. But I find it hard to believe that so large a list would not contain many bargains which are available to any investor willing to do the homework and exercise the required patience.

"If these numbers impress you, consider a finer screen, also done at the end of the first quarter, but set to catch those companies with a P/E of 4.0 or lower. Sometimes it is difficult to imagine what a P/E of 4 represents."

Every year a company selling at a price/earnings ratio of 4 generates earnings equal to one-fourth the value—25 percent—of the stock. Invest in a company which maintains its latest 12 months earnings for four years and it will have earned what you paid for it. As George Stasen puts it:

"On the NYSE on March 31, there were 19 such companies. The ASE had 22 and the OTC had 14 [using only the large OTC companies from Mr. Stasen's sample]; that is a total of 55 companies.

"Additionally, I would expect to find the thousands and thousands of smaller issues trading in the OTC market to be an even more fertile field."

Mr. Stasen took another look at the companies selling at a P/E of 4 and under. At the end of September, he commented that he expected to find fewer such companies since the economic recovery had continued and investors seemed to be less fearful than they had been. To his surprise, the number of companies with a P/E of 4 or under, jumped from 55 to 146. As of the latter date, there were 24 companies on the NYSE, 80 on the ASE, and 42 on the OTC. He also commented that investors tend to assume that stocks with low P/E's represent the flotsam and jetsam of the stock market. In many cases that is all true, but consider some of these companies.

For instance, on the NYSE there is a company that sells at 3.8 times 12 months' reported earnings. What distinguishes this company is that its annual earnings have grown at a rate of 43 percent for the past five years and its annual dividend growth has been 9.3 percent for the same period. Lest you think that the wolf is at the door, the company's current ratio is 3.1 to 1.

Perhaps a more extreme example can be found in a company whose price/earnings ratio is 1.2. For the past five years the annual earnings growth rate has been 112 percent. Four years ago, this company reported earnings of 13 cents per share, but the latest 12 months report is $4.39 per share.

I would like to return to the theme that averages tend to hide a lot from the investor. For instance, if one were to look carefully at the 1,512 major companies covered by the *Financial Weekly IndustriScope*, published by Media General Services Inc., of Richmond, one can develop a conviction that opportunities abound in the marketplace.

For example, over half of these companies grew faster than 19 percent a year during the past five years—recession notwithstanding. Furthermore, one-third of this group yields more than 4.8 percent, which would be competitive with a passbook savings return. In addition, the record indicates that more than one-third of these companies have increased their dividends at better than 9.6 percent for each of the past five years. On average, this has been accomplished by paying out little more than 40 percent of earnings and reinvesting the balance in the business. Over one-third of the market is reporting earnings on the common stock equity of in excess of 15 percent. One-third of these companies have an interest coverage on debt of better than 7.1 times—telling us how healthy they are—and one-third have current ratios of in excess of 2.4 to 1.

The diligent investor can find one-third of this group that are selling at discounts from book value of 17 percent or much more. All told, this overview suggests that there is more than enough reason to do homework on the values available in the marketplace.

These statistics are exciting, but distressingly unrevealing for the investor seeking names of companies. You want to know about specific companies that carry low price/earnings ratios—companies that may (and may not) be bargains.

Financial Weekly has released some statistics that may help. This newspaper strives to provide the kind of computer analysis for small investors that professionals like George Stasen generate internally. The journal recently provided a list of 280 low P/E issues. In the list are many good names. Some of the good names may be bargains and some not. Even some of the not-so-good names may be bargains. Things change rapidly in the corporate world. The screening is, of course, up to you.

Now that you've seen the list you may be tempted to conclude that finding cheap stocks in this or almost any market is like shooting fish in a barrel—to be salted away for later harvesting. Almost, but not quite.

For every stock of excellent potential there are scores with no prospects whatsoever. Your problem is to find the wheat; winnow out the chaff. Junior professionals at leading banks are embarked on such a search—on their own behalf. The shares, as we've already implied (more on this later), are too small to be included in institutional portfolios. But you can compete with these professionals. As a studious amateur, you must apply yourself well.

Company	Price	Earnings	
	Close (12/31/76)	Latest Reported 12-Mos EPS	Price/Earnings Ratio
—	$	$	—
New York Stock Exchange			
Alison Mtg Inv	2¼	35.75	.1
Ames Dept St	11⅝	2.50	4.7
Bangor Punta	11¼	2.52	4.5
Cadence Indus	3¾	.96	3.9
Chrysler Corp	20⅜	4.62	4.4
ConAgra	12⅝	3.27	3.9
Cone Mills	25½	5.48	4.7
Cooper Tire	15⅜	4.41	3.5
Craig Corp	15⅛	3.76	4.0
Dan River Inc	9½	1.96	4.8
Diamond M Dril	17	3.76	4.5
Edwards AG	14¾	3.94	3.7
Electron Mem	3½	.92	3.8
Fedl Company	24½	5.14	4.8
Gateway Ind	6⅜	1.77	3.6
Grt Lks Dredge	23¼	4.78	4.9
Hazeltine Corp	9⅛	3.46	2.6
Holly Sugar	30¼	13.65	2.2
Hutton, EF	17¼	3.66	4.7
Iowa Beef Pro	21⅜	6.17	3.5
Kane–Miller	10	2.46	4.1
Lockheed Air	9¼	2.92	3.2
Lowenstn Sons	14¾	3.51	4.2
Mad Sq Gard	6⅛	1.25	4.9
Manh Indus	7⅞	1.83	4.3
Marathon Mfg	13⅛	3.37	3.9
Massey–Ferg	21¾	6.04	3.6
MBPXL Corp	11⅝	3.19	3.6
McDermott	46⅜	11.02	4.2
Mohawk Rub	22⅜	4.59	4.9
Morse Shoe	12⅝	2.73	4.6
Natl Indus	7⅜	1.49	4.9
Natomas Co	36⅜	7.37	4.9
Paine Webber	8½	1.90	4.5
Palm Beach	10⅛	2.14	4.7
Readg & Bates	17¼	4.07	4.2
Rowan Cos	28½	6.55	4.4
Sabine Royalty	52⅛	13.03	4.0
Service Cp Intl	5	1.27	3.9
Shearson Hayd	9¾	2.28	4.3
Tonka Cp	12⅛	2.71	4.5
US Rlty Invest	2⅝	1.30	2.0
Varo Inc	8¾	1.86	4.7
Witter, Dean	14⅞	3.41	4.4
Zapata Corp	13	2.77	4.7
Zayre Corp	7⅝	1.72	4.4
American Stock Exchange			
AAV Cos	5½	1.34	4.1
Acme Precision	2¼	.47	4.8
A & E Plastik	5¾	1.40	4.1
Affil Cap Corp	3½	.95	3.7
Alaska Airlines	5	1.21	4.1
Allian Tire Rub	5⅛	1.12	4.6
Allied Thermal	14⅞	4.17	3.6
Am Intl Pict	4¼	1.19	3.6
Am Safety Eq	5⅜	1.46	3.7
Anthony Indus	7⅝	1.59	4.8
Armin Corp	7⅛	2.07	3.4
Atalanta Corp	4⅜	1.95	2.2
Autom Rad Mfg	5⅛	1.51	3.4
AVC Corp	9½	3.09	3.1
Banister Contl	9⅝	2.26	4.3
Big V Supmkt	7½	1.77	4.2
Brascan Ltd	11¾	3.63	3.2
Buell Indus	12⅛	2.59	4.7

Company	Price: Close (12/31/76)	Earnings: Latest Reported 12-Mos EPS	Earnings: Price/Earnings Ratio
—	$	$	—
Butler Intl	9⅞	2.08	4.7
Cagle's Inc A	3⅜	1.09	3.1
Calif Life Cp	3¼	.90	3.6
Capital Reserve	2	.43	4.7
Caressa Inc	4⅞	1.08	4.5
CHB Foods	6¾	1.94	3.5
Coachmen Inds	16⅝	3.97	4.2
Compac Corp	5	1.14	4.4
Computer Inv	1½	.80	1.9
Concord Fab	5⅞	2.11	2.8
Cosco Inc	2⅜	1.64	1.4
CRS Design As	6¾	1.55	4.4
Damon Creatn	2⅞	.79	3.6
Donnkenny	6¾	1.89	3.6
Drug Fair Inc	11⅛	2.38	4.7
Dunlop Holding	1½	.35	4.1
Eazor Express	5⅜	1.23	4.4
EDG Inc	16½	4.38	3.8
Esquire Radio	9⅝	2.03	4.7
Etz Lavud Ltd	1¾	.64	2.7
Fab Indus	5¼	1.43	3.7
Family Rec Pl	2¼	.60	3.8
Film Cp Am	1⅝	.45	3.6
Ford of Can	89¼	18.22	4.9
Garland Corp	3¼	.67	4.9
Gates Lrjet	8¾	2.19	4.0
Gaylords Natl	4⅛	1.51	2.7
Gen Houseware	2⅜	.49	4.8
Gen Research	3⅝	.82	4.4
Gloucester Eng	12⅛	3.10	3.9
Gorin Stores	3⅞	.80	4.8
Grt Amer Ind	5⅝	1.54	3.7
Greenman Bros	3½	.81	4.3
Greer Hydraulic	5⅝	1.21	4.6
Guilford Mills	5	1.55	3.2
Gulf Rep Finl	9⅝	2.06	4.7
Hampton Ind	6¼	2.05	3.0

Company	Price: Close (12/31/76)	Earnings: Latest Reported 12-Mos EPS	Earnings: Price/Earnings Ratio
—	$	$	—
Hannaford Bros	12¼	2.63	4.7
Hanover Shoe	10⅜	2.26	4.6
Harvey Group	⅝	.17	3.7
Hasbro Indus	8	1.83	4.4
Health – Mor	6⅛	1.52	4.0
House of Ron	5⅛	1.06	4.8
Howell Indus	4¼	1.27	3.3
Huntington Hlth	3⅛	.71	4.4
Integrated Res	1⅝	.37	4.4
Intl Funeral Sv	2⅛	.45	4.7
Intl General	13	2.90	4.5
Intl Seaway	7¼	2.52	2.9
Intl Sys Cont	18½	4.40	4.2
Interway Cp	12⅝	3.76	3.4
Irvin Indus	5⅜	1.29	4.2
Jaclyn	7⅞	1.63	4.8
Jamesway Cp	9⅜	1.90	4.9
Jetronic Ind	3⅜	.70	4.8
Kenwin Shops	6⅞	1.45	4.7
Kleer – Vu Ind	3½	1.43	2.4
Kuhn's – Big K	7	1.55	4.5
Laneco Inc	3⅝	.95	3.8
Liberty Fabrics	7½	2.28	3.3
Macrodyne Ind	¾	.26	2.9
Marlene Ind	7⅛	2.19	3.3
Marshall Ind	6⅞	1.53	4.5
Masland, CH	9⅜	2.00	4.7
Masters Inc	3½	.78	4.5
Medfield Cp	5⅝	1.50	3.8
Mego Intl	12¾	2.67	4.8
Meridian Ind	⅝	.29	1.9
Metex Corp	10½	2.79	3.8
Mich General	3⅜	.76	4.4
Mich Sugar	11⅜	2.54	4.5
Mickelberry	6¼	1.55	4.0
Modern Maid	7¼	1.64	4.4
Morton's Shoe	5¼	1.51	3.5

Company	Price	Earnings	
	Close (12/31/76)	Latest Reported 12-Mos EPS	Price/Earnings Ratio
—	$	$	—
Natl Distrib Co	5½	1.50	3.7
Natl Spinning	3	1.12	2.7
Newpark Rsrcs	4⅞	1.10	4.4
Newbery Enrgy	9½	2.32	4.1
Niag Fron Svc	13¾	3.00	4.6
Nichols, SE	4⅛	1.05	3.9
Noel Industries	3	.76	3.9
Offshore Co	16⅝	3.63	4.6
Ohio Brass Co	44¾	9.75	4.6
Olla Industries	7⅛	2.02	3.5
Ozark Air	3⅝	.89	4.1
Pandel Brad	5	1.43	3.5
Pat Fashions	2⅞	.75	3.8
Pato Cons Gld	6⅝	2.00	3.3
Pemcor Inc	6½	1.62	4.0
Penobscot Sh	4½	1.13	4.0
PepCom Indus	16⅝	3.50	4.8
Perini Corp	8⅛	2.11	3.9
Philipp LD Tel	6⅞	1.90	3.6
Piedmont Indus	2	.48	4.2
Pitts Des Mo	23½	4.95	4.7
Richton Intl	6⅞	1.44	4.8
Roblin Indus	4⅝	1.05	4.4
Ruddick Corp	4⅞	1.09	4.5
Russell Corp	7⅝	1.85	4.1
Salem Corp	13	2.65	4.9
San Carlos	6½	1.86	3.5
Saunders Lsng	9⅜	2.35	4.0
Schenuit Ind	9⅛	1.92	4.8
Scope Indus	24	5.79	4.1
Seabd Alld Mil	8⅛	1.84	4.4
Seaport Cp	¾	.16	4.7
Servo Cp Am	4⅞	1.04	4.7
Sifco Indus	10½	2.23	4.7
SMD Indus	2¼	.57	3.9
Spectro Indus	3⅞	1.02	3.8
Spencer Foods	7¼	3.01	2.4
Std Alliance	15⅛	3.24	4.7
Std Container	6	1.71	3.5
Std – Coosa	16⅛	3.78	4.3
Std Products	24⅝	5.90	4.2
Star Supermkts	12	2.67	4.5
Steelmet Inc	8⅛	1.68	4.8
Stevcoknit Inc	4¼	1.06	4.0
Supercrete Ltd	3⅝	1.15	3.2
Technical Tape	3⅛	.69	4.5
Technitrol	4⅛	1.20	3.4
Three D Depts	3	.91	3.3
Tiffany Ind	7	1.62	4.3
Treadway	3⅜	.72	4.7
Tubos Mexico	2⅛	.85	2.5
Tuftco Corp	5½	1.13	4.9
U & I Inc	15⅛	4.34	3.5
Unit Asbestos	3⅞	1.16	3.3
US Nat Resour	3⅞	.95	4.1
Univ Cigar	3⅛	.70	4.5
Univ – Rundle	8⅝	1.96	4.4
Valmac Indus	11⅝	4.28	2.7
Vishay Inter	2⅝	.61	4.3
Vulcan Inc	9½	2.50	3.8
Wards Co	4	.98	4.1
Weiman Co	2⅛	.63	3.4
Wstn Fincl	7⅝	1.88	4.1
Wilson Bros	4⅛	.89	4.6
Winkelman Strs	7¾	1.58	4.9

Over the Counter

Alberts Inc	7¾	1.59	4.9
Alton Box	16¾	3.44	4.9
Atwood Oceanics	7¾	2.31	3.4

Company	Price Close (12/31/78) $	Earnings Latest Reported 12-Mos EPS $	Price/Earnings Ratio
Berkline Corp	4⅛	.99	4.2
Black Hills P&L	20⅜	4.68	4.4
Buckeye Intl	10	2.07	4.8
Chem Leaman Tnk	11	2.97	3.7
Conwed Corp	11¾	2.49	4.7
Cullum Companies	10¼	2.24	4.6
Debron Corp	12¾	3.47	3.7
Delwood Furn	6	1.28	4.7
Diamond Crys Salt	15½	3.50	4.4
Donovan Cos	7¾	1.58	4.9
Dynascan Cp	10⅞	3.71	2.9
Elder Beerman Str	5¾	1.43	4.0
Executive Ind	14⅛	3.04	4.6
Flexsteel Ind	12	2.44	4.9
Fredrk & Herrud	6⅛	1.24	4.9
Gen Health Svcs	4	.82	4.9
Heath Tecna Cp	18½	3.75	4.9
Hess Inc	8¼	1.90	4.3
Hunt Bldg Corp	1⅝	.34	4.8
Hy–Gain Elec	10⅜	3.20	3.2
Hyatt Intl Corp	3⅝	.86	4.2
Int Bank Wash A	4⅝	1.17	4.0
Jacobson Stores	8¼	2.14	3.9
Kaman Corp A	20½	4.39	4.7
Kennington Ltd	5¼	2.39	2.2
Kewaunee Sci Eqp	8	2.34	3.4
King Kullen Groc	8¾	2.21	4.0
Krueger WA	13	6.10	2.1
Liberian Iron Ore	14¾	4.22	3.5
Lyon Metal Pds	11¾	2.39	4.9
Manitowoc	34	6.87	4.9
Manor Care Inc	4	1.29	3.1
Marsh Supmkts	9	1.85	4.9
Maui Ld & Pineapp	11	2.23	4.9
McDowell Ent	7	1.69	4.1
Mid–America Inds	4½	1.04	4.3
Mor–Flo Inds	5¼	1.15	4.6

Company	Price Close (12/31/78) $	Earnings Latest Reported 12-Mos EPS $	Price/Earnings Ratio
Morgan's Rests	⅝	.15	4.2
Mosinee Corp	18¾	4.67	4.0
Myers Industries	4⅝	.96	4.8
Na–Churs Intl	5⅞	1.46	4.0
NWn State Port	15	4.08	3.7
Ohio Ferro Alloys	16¼	4.49	3.6
Olga Co	6	1.39	4.3
PVO Intl Inc	12	3.56	3.4
Penn Corp	7½	1.54	4.9
Piedmont Aviation	4⅞	1.23	4.0
Pott Industries	22⅛	5.22	4.2
Progroup	1⅝	.38	4.3
Regency Electro	13¼	2.79	4.7
Robbins Myers	17¼	3.79	4.6
Savannah Fd & Ind	19½	7.99	2.4
Schulman, A Inc	8¾	1.80	4.9
Scripps How Brdc	31½	33.15	1.0
Seaway Food Town	9¼	2.59	3.6
So Airways	3⅞	1.81	2.1
Spang Industries	3¾	1.04	3.6
Sterling Stores	5	1.45	3.4
Strawbrd & Cloth	25½	5.22	4.9
Textiles Inc	14	4.30	3.3
Tyson Food Inc	12½	6.70	1.9
Valmont Indust	19½	4.03	4.8
Victory Markets	3⅞	.82	4.7
Wadsworth Publish.	8	1.83	4.4
Waldbaum Inc	9	2.59	3.5
Wehr Corp	15	4.13	3.6
Weingarten J Inc	6¾	1.70	4.0
Wilson Freight	7¼	1.89	3.8
Wisc Centrl	15	3.78	4.0
Wolverine Alum	7½	1.61	4.7
Ziegler Company	6⅜	1.31	4.9
Hawthorne Fin	12⅞	2.63	4.9
Nationwide A	9½	1.95	4.9
Unicoa	25	5.32	4.7

4 · Where, Oh Where Has My Little Dog Gone?

WE HAVE SEEN that there is a vast horizon of forgotten stocks out there in investorland. Let me stress again that the problem you face is to make sure that you buy good stuff—not the cats and dogs.

If you're going to succeed, you must become a kind of stock market detective. But like *real* detective work, you'll find that there is actually little mystery involved. Besides, there are lots of clues. Common sense plays a major role. Patience does too.

Consider: Years ago a Wall Street secretary became intrigued with a camera her boss brought to the office. She decided to give one to her husband.

A couple of weeks later, the young woman told her boss, a broker, that her husband really liked the camera, took it with him everywhere, and drew a lot of inquiries from people who were equally fascinated with the way that it would take and develop a picture in a minute. Would the broker please buy her 100 shares of Polaroid? The stock was cheap then—dirt cheap, as it turns out. It has never been as cheap since.*

Another stock market detective is Morton Adler. A retired businessman, Mr. Adler was fascinated years ago to discover that an unexciting Rochester company had the rights to a method of affixing iron dust to plain paper in the image of a printed page. He visited the upstate New York company, liked what he saw, bought stock, and became one of the first Xerox millionaires.

---

* Polaroid did take a terrible tumble many years later. It was late in the bear market of the 1970s after the individual's nemesis, the institutions, had gotten carried away with Polaroid's undebugged SX-70 electronic camera. The stock, still heavily recommended at 149½, quickly dropped to 15 for a 90-percent loss. We'll learn later how to abandon ship *before* the institutions.

Where is your Xerox? Your Polaroid? Think about those items advertised on TV or seen in department, hardware or grocery stores. Ask a few questions: confirm their popularity with merchants and friends. This may be a first clue to a good stock.

Your chances of discovering a spectacular company like Polaroid or Xerox are, of course, slim. For every unique product that makes the grade, thus enriching the maker's shareholders, there are dozens that are shot down by a disinterested or even misinformed public.

But you don't have to find a super winner to succeed as an investor; to make profits several times your investment. It has been done in hundreds of stocks in the past. As we have already indicated, there are more such opportunities around today than there were ten years ago.

You don't need a spectacular product, either. In fact, unless a company is heavily protected by patents, as were Polaroid and Xerox, a unique product will attract the toughest kind of competition. Remember the Bowmar Brain? The competition from Texas Instruments and Japanese makers forced this innovative company into bankruptcy.

Even once stodgy companies like Amphenol Corporation,* a maker of knitted deep-pile fabric and auto clocks, can do well in their time. The father of an experienced market analyst years ago held a minor position at Amphenol. During World War II the company supplied electrical and electronic connectors for the war effort. Peacetime transition proved difficult. But the employee looked at the price of the company's shares and concluded that the stock was cheap. He bought some. The shares sank dramatically. Patient enough to hold the stock for many years—no stock table reader he—he didn't sell until the value of his holdings had increased by more than ten to one.

Let's put it this way: In Wall Street, the bluebird of happiness is more likely to be found under a rock than high in the skies. The

---

* During the bull market of the late 1960s, Amphenol at management's behest was taken over by Bunker Ramo to prevent a corporate raid by Solitron Devices.

critical problem is to find a company, however lacking in glamour, that is undervalued in terms of its assets and grow power. Choose carefully. That price/earnings ratio of 2 could just represent the market's hard-headed evaluation of a mediocre company's true prospects.

Sam Skurnick, who runs his own shop within Bruns, Nordeman, Rea & Co.'s big branch at 625 Madison Avenue in New York City, is a member of the New York Stock Exchange who specializes in what he calls "true low-priced stocks."*

Price alone is an incomplete measure, he points out. (I might add that most British stocks sell for pennies a share. But there are hundreds of British shares outstanding for every share of the average American stock.) At however low a price, then, shares may be high-priced in terms of *underlying values.* Mr. Skurnick says that most investors in stocks priced at under $10 a share—his own particular favorite range—lose money because the underlying values don't justify the price.

Mr. Skurnick generally limits his search for value to stocks that are priced well below book value and shares of companies that have current ratios of 2, or even 3 or 4, to 1.

Book value can generally be determined by looking at Standard & Poor's *Listed Stock Reports,* to be found in any well-stocked business library. If the figure is not shown, simply subtract from total assets the total liabilities and the par value of any preferred stock that may exist. Divide the result by the number of shares outstanding. The stock is below book value if the resulting figure is higher than the current market price.

The current ratio, a critical measure of the company's financial strength—its ability to withstand normal business setbacks—is derived as follows: You simply divide current assets by current liabilities.

The above are key *balance sheet* factors. You should pay more attention to the balance sheet than to the income statement. Antennaes clinkers as well as winners.

* We hasten to note that Mr. Skurnick has clinkers as well as winners.

other expert on low-priced companies, Ralph P. Coleman, Jr., who runs the successful Over-the-Counter Securities Mutual Fund, comments:

"Most contemporary broker reports on individual corporations are built around an examination of the company's earning power, translated into earnings per share, past, present, and future. The emphasis is almost exclusively on the income statement, with no more than passing attention to the balance sheet. We suggest that brokers are doing their clients a disservice when they fail to give proper weight to a thoroughgoing examination of a company's balance sheet, to determine its strengths and weaknesses and to factor this analysis into the overall judgment of the corporation, along with analysis of the income statement. If more analysts had paid attention to balance sheets rather than income statements during the 'go-go' years, there would be much less investor disenchantment with common stock investing today."

Here are a number of other guidelines to cheap stocks:

1. The company's earnings are depressed, but there is a record of high earnings in good years. Earnings can be expected to recover when the economy improves.

2. The stock is cyclical and/or highly leveraged. It now sells at a significantly lower price/earnings ratio than it did in good years.

3. The company is not cash-poor and thus vulnerable in the event of unexpected business reverses.

4. The company has other salable assets, readily converted into cash, thus enhancing its resistance to setbacks.

5. The company has substantial depreciable assets—factory and equipment. Heavy depreciation expense means a large cash flow. That is, a company that earns $1 a share and writes off $3 a share in depreciation expense actually generates $4 a share in cash. The depreciation expense is a bookkeeping item that reduces reported earnings without reducing cash. Look at it this way. The company buys a truck for $5,000. The value will drop to almost nothing in, say, five years. The company will charge off $1,000 a year as depre-

ciation expense and decrease its reported earnings accordingly. The cash coming into the company—cash flow—should be increased by the $1,000 annually in truck depreciation expense plus whatever other depreciation expense on plant and equipment the company has. The cash so generated will be available for expansion. Depreciation will have reduced book value of the assets to well below their real market value—what it will cost to replace them in an inflated environment. For example, storage tanks installed by Leon Hess of Amerada-Hess Corporation many years ago would, he frequently points out, cost several times the original price to replace today. The chief executive of Amerada-Hess regards his investment in such tanks as one of his proudest accomplishments. Polaroid, by the way, carries its patents—its most valuable possessions, apart from the talents of Dr. Land—at $1 on the balance sheet. That's conservative accounting.

6. The company pays a dividend that is well covered by earnings. The company should have a history of having increased dividends when earnings have improved.

Let's look at a specific situation—one that Mr. Skurnick has been interested in for many years: Marquette Company. Marquette is the old Marquette Cement Manufacturing Company, the sixth-largest cement company. Nashville-based, it serves 29 states in the East and along the Mississippi River.

Marquette's book value was $31.70 at the end of 1976. As this chapter was written, the stock was selling at 10, or one-third the asset value. As for its value relative to recent years, Marquette earned $1.51 a share in 1975. Thus, the stock is selling at 6.6 times earnings—10, the price of the stock, divided by $1.51, the earnings on the stock. In the past ten years Marquette's price/earnings ratio has averaged in the teens.

Mr. Skurnick strongly believes that, barring special circumstances, a company should pay a dividend. It is the only way a company can reward the shareholder. In the absence of a dividend, the company should have the ability to pay a dividend within the foreseeable future. (Even rapidly growing companies pay dividends —quality companies, that is.)

Marquette paid a 50-cent dividend in 1975, which, at the current price of 10, provides a 5 percent yield—not too far from what a saver would receive from a bank.

For companies serving the construction industry, 1975 was practically a depression year. A substantial resumption of construction activity could result in rising income and dividends for Marquette shareholders.

Marquette has plenty of cash—$22 million at the end of 1975 and working capital of about $35 million. The company's current ratio is almost 4 to 1. Thus, we see a company with an unusually strong balance sheet. The strong financial condition of the company makes it possible for Marquette to acquire other profitable businesses for cash—without diluting the common shares.

In fact, Marquette changed its name to Marquette Company because of management plans to diversify into areas outside of cement through the takeover of profitable companies.

Marquette is itself attractive to larger companies as a takeover candidate. In such takeovers, it is common for the acquiring company to pay a substantial premium over market price. This can result in sudden profits for the shareholders. However, Marquette is more attractive in its own right since it amended its charter at the 1976 annual meeting with changes specifically—and effectively —designed to discourage a takeover by another company.

Marquette's cash flow per share in 1975 was $3.60. Subtracting earnings of $1.51 a share from that figure, we find that Marquette generated $2.09 a share in cash through depreciation charges. Ironically, if the company's fixed assets were substantially less valuable, Marquette would have reported higher earnings. On the other hand, its plants would cost an estimated $280 million to replace today. The original cost of these plants, which produce 4 million tons of cement annually, was considerably less than a third of replacement cost. This does not mean that the company is limping along with inefficient tools. At the annual meeting, Marquette's president told shareholders that half the company's capacity—specifically, 49 percent—was substantially more efficient than the industry average.

But mark this. At this writing, Marquette represents a personal loss for Mr. Skurnick—particularly so on the shares he purchased six years ago when Marquette first came to his attention.

He is holding his Marquette shares as all true investors must be prepared to do. It sometimes takes years for an undervalued stock to reach a market price that reflects underlying values. *Some never do.* Others move up quickly—sometimes within months. As this was written, Gulf & Western Industries bid the equivalent of about 15 a share—a whopping 50 percent premium over the pre-bid price.

Mr. Skurnick's own most profitable holding matured with surprising speed. He recommended Allis Chalmers to clients on Christmas Eve in 1974—at 6⅜. As of mid-1976, the stock had quadrupled to 25½.

Don't be fooled. *The name of the game is patience.* As Louis Rukeyser of Educational Television's *Wall Street Week* says: The object is not to get rich quick, but to get rich slowly.

You are not a giant institution. You do not have to answer to an army of impatient investors. Take your time and your profits will come—perhaps when you least expect them.

Remember that you will be dealing in shares that for the most part sell at under $10 each.* This means that with $5,000 to $10,000 you can diversify into several promising situations. You may have a loser or two in time, but your chances of good profits over the years will be excellent.

---

* Ralph Coleman loves to tell of the institutional representative who was unable to interest the institutions in a stock because at $5 a share, it was "too low," for their portfolios. A year went by, and the stock was then selling at $20. The rep revisited the institutions and found them happy to buy. In their view, the stock had become "seasoned." That is to say, it was in the price range the institutions prefer. A $5 stock would look like a dog, a $20 stock looks like an investment. So they paid four times more than they needed to.

NYSE AND ASE VS. OTC

Mr. Skurnick restricts his purchases to stocks that are listed, preferably those listed on the New York Stock Exchange. He notes that in the speculative boom of early 1976, practically every stock on the Big Board was carried forward—at least to a degree—in the general momentum of the rising market.

"This even included the Real Estate Investment Trusts, many of which were skirting bankruptcy." He adds that if you buy a listed stock that turns out to be a lemon, market conditions over time may nevertheless allow you to get out with limited losses—even with a small profit.

While good undervalued situations undoubtedly exist in the over-the-counter market, Mr. Skurnick takes the position that the man who buys there has to be prepared to take a bath if he picks a lemon.

No doubt about it. Balance-sheet factors are even more important in the over-the-counter market than they are when a stock under consideration is listed on the Big Board or Amex. Experienced investors and those who are learning rapidly through their successes—and losses—in listed issues can dip their toes into the cold waters of the OTC. Others should listen to sage counsel from an investor with considerable experience:

"This is no place for the amateur. You've either got to have a long purse, or you've got to know what you're doing."

A RELATED TEST FOR VALUE

Every once in a while—and particularly after bear markets such as the one that dominated trading in the first half of this decade—there are stocks that sell for less than their break-up or liquidation values.

The advocates of purchasing such stocks reason that some day another company will become aware of the situation and acquire the company at prices far above the current market price. The idea is to find companies that sell at a discount from what the accountants term the net net working capital. (That's right, Mary Hartman, Mary Hartman, net net working capital.)

Mark A. Boyar, a security analyst for Moore & Schley, Cameron & Company explains that net net working capital will usually represent the minimum break-up value:

"This value is determined by subtracting from current assets all liabilities senior to the common stock, including current liabilities, long-term debt, preferred stock, capitalized lease obligations, and certain pension liabilities."

In January 1975, while flipping through the pages of that most necessary of brief corporate portraits, Standard & Poor's *Security Owner's Stock Guide*, he noticed Londontown Corporation, maker of the popular London Fog rain coats.

The stock was then selling at $5 a share on the Big Board. Doing further research, he discovered that Londontown had cash equal to $3.07 a share and was selling at less than a third of its net net working capital of $15.31 a share.

It wasn't long after Mr. Boyar recommended the stock to clients that Interco, Inc., another Big Board company, became interested. Those who bought Londontown shares at $5 and held on until the takeover got $27 for their shares.

There are still a number of companies whose shares are selling at less than net net working capital. Two of Mr. Boyar's more recent discoveries: Salant Corporation, a clothing manufacturer that sells about a quarter of its production to Sears; and Ehrenreich Photo Corporation, also selling at less than net net working capital as this was written. The company distributes the quality Nikon camera from Japan.

Chances are that the circumstances with regard to these two companies will have changed by the time you read this book. There is, of course, no guarantee that such companies' shares will soar—that they will be acquired at high prices by other companies. Lots of investors in such companies wait for years and for nothing. If all such situations worked out, Mr. Boyar and others who do what he does would have all the money.

CHARTING THE CHARTISTS

There are two basic approaches to investing in stocks. One deals in fundamentals—the financial strength of the company, its earnings trend, its ability to retain or increase its market share. The other approach is called technical analysis and deals in graphs of a company's stock on which weekly and daily price ranges and volume are plotted.

The technician believes that when a stock breaks out of an established pattern on a chart, the move has significance and can be "played" for profit. Breakouts sometimes result at resistance points. For example, suppose that some years ago a company increased its capitalization by selling new shares at $20 each. Assume further that the stock thereafter dropped to 15. There is a common tendency for investors to try to break even on their unsuccessful investments. Thus as the market for the shares in the company improved and the price reached $20 a share, selling would probably ensue by those who had bought the new shares at $20. Some resistance to moving above 20 would result. It would probably persist—at least until all those anxious to sell for a break-even at 20 had been accommodated. If the stock suddenly moved to, say, 21 or more, the technicians would assume the selling was over and claim a "breakout on the chart" and would then predict further gains.

Technicians also believe charts sometimes reveal significant buying and selling by insiders and their friends—prior to a news announcement. The theory is that, SEC to the contrary notwithstanding, those greedy insiders will somehow manage to find a way to profit in advance.

While there are obviously many factors that go into a stock's movement, the technicians believe that the market distills them all and that careful analysis of the chart offers profound insight. Many chartists also chart the market as a whole. Most are beholden to Charles Dow, a founder and the first editor of *The Wall Street Journal*, and his associate, William Hamilton. The two men developed the Dow Theory of the market and pegged it to the movements of 35 (now 30) stocks—those of the then leading companies in the nation's major industries. In that pre-computer era it was necessary to choose a representative sample of the market if daily and hourly rundowns of the market's movements were to be calculated and published. The 35 carefully chosen stocks were bellwethers, to be sure, and were believed to reflect the accumulated knowledge, opinion, and foresight of all the industrial, financial, and political brains in the world.

To the Dow theorist, the daily movements of the DJI were less important than the secondary movements lasting weeks to months and the long-term trends that often lasted several years. All three movements were studied simultaneously, though, for clues as to things to come.

Chartists following individual stocks are ready to buy or sell—or at least tell clients to buy or sell—whenever price changes in combination with rises in trading volume change the basics in a chart. At times the approach is arcane. Complex pictures emerge in the charts.

One appealing pattern is the head-and-shoulders tracing. Chartists will tell customers that the pattern is complete except for the right shoulder—as though it were ordained in heaven that the price changes in the stock would sketch in the right shoulder.

While I am not a great believer in the usefulness of charts in profit strategies, it doesn't pay to ignore the charts completely—especially if you are planning a speculative short-term investment. We've seen that resistance points can reflect efforts by shareholders to accomplish certain objectives—to break even—and charts can certainly isolate such resistance points. But the problem is that there is money to be made by powerful interests who trade *against* breakout points. They know that decisions are sometimes made on chart action, and they use their influence to make chart patterns conform to the expectations of the chartists—at least, they have done this in the past from time to time. When they succeed, they can take market action to suit their selfish objectives—at the expense of the chart followers. They chart the chartists for fun and profit.

Technical analysis appeals to the hopes of the average investor or speculator who, by virtue of chart analysis, believes that he is acting in step with insiders and knowledgeable financial interests. He hopes for a quick, rich profit on a sudden move. But to win at this game is probably as difficult for you as winning at one-on-one basketball with Wilt the Stilt. He may not be at his best when you play him, but he'll shut you out anyway.

5 · Backyard Investing

FOR THE SMALL INVESTOR seeking undervalued stocks, the daily newspaper may be regarded as the forum of first resort. There is an equally important forum in your backyard—regional companies. The advantage of buying shares in companies in your region is just that there is more basic information available to local residents like you than there is to the occasional visitor from New York—the analyst for a brokerage firm. Several years ago, everybody locally knew that one town's new hardboard plant had exploded and was a total loss. It was days before the first Wall Street analyst saw—quite by chance—a regionally circulated Associated Press item carrying the news. The Wall Streeter knew that the owner, Masonite Corporation, was counting on the new plant for increased sales and earnings. He quickly told clients of the firm to sell the stock. This is not exactly the kind of news that will make stock market profits for a resident of the town with the demolished plant—unless that resident shorted the stock—but it was a vital piece of information, nevertheless, and news that Wall Street didn't get for some time.

There is considerable upbeat information about local companies that is not exported for weeks. What's more, you're looking at relatively small companies, by and large, and Wall Street is covering fewer and fewer of these every week. Recently this reporter wrote a column about the nation's *second-largest* wholesale drug distributor—Bergen Brunswig—and only one analyst could be found who followed the stock of this company.

What regions are promising? Almost any region with a strong industrial base. In a column several years ago I told how well residents of Westchester County would have done had they invested in local companies.

The resident-investor with a gallon of gas and a library pass can quickly rule out some local companies as unpromising. The rest of the legwork is more direct. Talk to the neighbors. Ask what it is like to work for company A, B, or C. Is the company well run? How's the product? Is it as well made as it appears to be? Are there lots of returns from dissatisfied customers? What are labor relations like? If there are frequent strikes you'll know that. But a surly, disgruntled work crew sometimes doesn't strike. Your neighbor who works there will know about this. Don't expect too much of management. All human institutions have their frailties, and some very well-run companies appear to be badly run on the surface. Sears is one of the best-run companies in the world, yet an employee once threatened to throw me off the loading platform because he believed, erroneously, that I had been leaning on the bell, impatient for my parcels.

If you think you are on to something, try to get an appointment with a company executive in a relatively high position. Even relatively small companies maintain executives who handle investor relations, and this individual should be willing to talk to you if you are about to make an investment.

From your vantage point you may have difficulty finding out

what the competition thinks about the company you like, but try. Find a salesman who works for a competitor—the sales manager, if available to you—and ask whether it is easy or tough to compete with the company you want to invest in. Salesmen are on the firing line constantly; they'll tell you whether or not you've picked a tough company. Remember, the more they put your choice down, the more likely you've found a goodie.

Use your ingenuity. Talk to suppliers, if you can find them, and see if the company is regarded as a top customer, a slow payer, or whatever. Ten years ago, meat suppliers could have told you that McDonald's was growing by leaps and bounds. Not only were they deluged with orders, they had a clear idea of the quality and quantity of meat the successful hamburger chain was buying.

By this point, you already may have done some cursory work at the library. Go back. You don't have to subscribe to an expensive stock advisory service—and, sheeplike, buy what the customers of that particular publisher are reading and buying. You can get much important general information and lots of specifics from Standard & Poor's *Listed Stock Reports* and from Moody's thick paperback quarterly digest of leading companies. Value Line publishes a beautifully organized book of loose-leaf notebook size with a page of information on each of some 1,600 companies—among them many of the best prospects for solid market performance in the years ahead.

Next you'll want to look at the latest information from the company itself. An expert on undervalued companies suggests that you get the annual report and read it—backwards.

"The first thing to look at is the footnotes," he said. "That's where the problems are buried. The next place to look is at the management analysis—how well the company did last year compared with the year before and the year before that.

"A trend may well emerge. The investor will at least discover whether there is current growth. The president's letter that leads the annual report ought to be left for last. It is likely to powder-puff the company's problems."

The analyst added that the prospective investor should also read the accountant's statement for exceptions to management's representation of the company's financial condition.

Remember to pay attention to the balance sheet. You should demand a current ratio of 2 to 1 or higher. Remember also that the less debt a company has, the better chance it has to survive in a pinch. Less debt may mean less growth, but it will probably mean more staying power.

If the investor has gone this far and is still impressed, he is still faced with the difficult problem of evaluating the company's stock in relation to shares of other companies in the same industry and in terms of the stock market as a whole.

Remember our major premise: We are looking for companies with relatively low price/earnings multiples—say 2 to 8. Those high price/earnings companies tend to be volatile, and they are usually well-peopled by your natural enemy, the mercurial, never-to-be-trusted institutional investor.

Since you are dealing with regional companies, you might as well visit a local broker for an opinion. In recent years, regional brokers have grown more important in the investment firmament—everybody knows they know the local companies better than the brokers in New York. If you have good rapport with a good man at a leading local brokerage firm—the one with the best reading on the local companies—you may have forged a link with the best "tipster" you are ever likely to find.

6 · The Trouble with the Nifty Fifty

ASK ANY SHAREHOLDER, Avon Products is not a ding-dong company. Those shrewd enough to put a $10,000 bet on Avon's stock and its door-to-door cosmetics women before 1960 would have been worth

$200,000 in 1972. By that time, Avon Products was a coveted possession of most trust departments of the top banks in the land—one of their so-called Nifty Fifty holdings. These super growth stocks could be counted on to show 12 to 15 percent earnings gains quarter by quarter. They numbered roughly 50 and were the so-called "one-decision" stocks any bank or individual would be proud to own.

Once you made the decision to own Avon—or Xerox, IBM, Johnson & Johnson, to name a few others—you could forget about them. Like perennials, they blossomed constantly—each quarter a new and pleasant confirmation of the same old story.

Even years after the five-year bear market of 1970 arrived, the wisdom of holding shares in the Nifty Fifty was confirmed. While the bulk of the stock market was headed due south, the Fifty—sometimes called the Vestal Virgins—proved a remarkable haven.

The fuel for their continued gains was a mix of two high-octane ingredients. First, they were clearly superior enterprises. Not only did they grow faster than the rest of the nation's business, but they also benefitted from the success syndrome. To wit, they became ever more popular with the banks and other institutions, which reasoned, "We can't go wrong here!" With gay abandon, the institutions pulled billions of dollars out of the slowpokes—contributing unconscionably to their problems—and socked proceeds into the Fifty.

The result was not only foreordained—it was beautiful. Obviously, when the demand for something rises and the supply remains constant, Adam Smith's law prevails. The stock goes up. The Nifty Fifty traded at ever higher price/earnings ratios.

Avon's experience was typical of the group. The company's average price/earnings ratio, a lofty 38 between 1960 and 1966, rocketed even higher. Between 1967 and 1972, the P/E averaged 51. In the last year of the second series, shares traded at a median price/earnings ratio of 55.4. It was to be the highest multiple the shares would achieve.

For Avon, like many of the other Nifty Fifty stocks, was riding for a fall. How many women could you send door-to-door with a cheery, revenue-producing "Avon Calling"? The market was not unlimited; not completely insensitive to an unwinding economy.

The earnings faltered—just a teensy bit. A tremor shook the hearts of trust department managers. Mutual fund executives had trouble sleeping. Would some communicant break the faith? It was like the classic confrontation in the Old West. Nobody really wanted a fight—the stakes were too high. But to draw second might be fatal. (You can thank higher powers that Wall Streeters don't run for president. If a money manager controlled the Button, we'd all go to hell fast—just like Avon Products shareholders.)

At first there was disbelief. The shares had reached 140 in 1972, when the company earned $2.16 a share. And earnings were to reach an acceptable $2.34 a share in 1973. But that was a slip from prior gains. Worse yet, analysts began to conclude that Avon in 1974 would show a decline—both unheard-of for Avon and unforgivable for any stock with a 55 multiple. The selling was reluctant at first. Avon held to the 130 range through mid-1973. Then disaster struck.

It became increasingly obvious that Avon was to be a proper shoot-out victim. Soon nobody, it seemed, wanted the shares—not even Avon's executives, who sold heavily when the stock was still above the 115 level. Between mid-1973 and Christmas, the stock plunged to 57. The year 1974 was an even more frightening nightmare. In the fall, the stock touched 18⅝. This meant that many of those who had discovered the stock as early as 1963 were back to ground zero.*

There is no question but that the institutions had overreacted. Or perhaps it is more correct to say that they had underreacted earlier. Their reaction should have been to the ridiculous 40-plus price/earnings ratios Avon had reached. Obviously, the company couldn't continue to grow at accustomed rates forever. Few women are like Queen Elizabeth I, who, at her death, reportedly had layered over an inch of makeup onto her sunken features.

* See Part III for how and when to sell 'em.

There were some terrible days for Avon holdings when the stock just dropped like a rock, just as there were terrible days for such institutional favorites as Disney, Holiday Inns, Handleman, Curtiss-Wright, Wang Laboratories, Syntex, Cooper Laboratories, and Clorox. They all got bombed by the institutions.

Leon Levy, a principal of Oppenheimer & Co., has said that when an institution sells 100,000 shares of a stock in a lump, it's as though 1,000 investors each decided to sell 100 shares on the same day. But oh the impact of that one trade! Let's look at a different instance on a smaller scale.

Wrigley was a solid performer but not a Nifty Fifty stock—not yet, anyway. Rather, Wrigley was a Steady Eddie—suitable, as they say, for the widows and orphans; a dividend stock. No high-flyer, Wrigley was about as safe as any equity investment could be.

That is, it was safe until the institutions got hold of it and concluded that there was gold in them thar cavities. The wholesale price of gum, always sticky, was going to go up substantially, and Wall Street, sensing bubbling profits, reasoned rashly that the company had Nifty Fifty potential.

Then came that day in October 1971. Shortly before 1:00 P.M., trading in Wrigley stock was halted on the New York Stock Exchange. When the shares reopened at around 2:30, there was no pleasure and no fun. Wrigley was off 27 points—an almost 20 percent drop. Just like that.

What had happened was that Wrigley's third-quarter earnings, though well above those of the similar quarter of the prior year, were nowhere near Wall Street's expectations. Professional investors—like children denied their Doublemint—bailed out, selling more than 20,000 shares. That relatively small package of selling dynamite was all that it took to bomb Wrigley's.

But never forget it. Whatever selling it takes in a given stock to bring disaster—whether 20,000 or 2,000,000 shares—the institutions can be counted on to supply the explosives on the slightest disappointment.

Not only is disaster imminent at the drop of a cent per share, the worst thing about the Nifty Fifty is that the action is—and was in the mid-1970s—mostly over. Most professionals, pushed to the wall, will admit that many great companies make lousy long-term investments—even some cherished names like Xerox.

Ralph Coleman, the over-the-counter ace, explains:

"When an investor buys the big boys of business—the industry leaders—he's usually buying a fairly mature company which may have to add literally hundreds of millions of dollars or even billions of dollars to achieve a significant sales growth which translates—maybe—into a significant profit growth. Certainly most of these companies have the explosive early stages of their growth behind them and future gains will not be as dramatic or sweeping."

Before we close this subject let's consider the institutions and their impact on the stock market in broader terms. Whenever a company's shares have become favorites of the institutions, there is likely to be trouble for the individual who buys in. The institutions, as I've explained in Chapter 3, are among the first to buy fad stocks—stocks of companies which may never show the kind of growth anticipated for them. Look at fairly recent history—the go-go years of the late 1960s. Ninety-nine percent of the computer leasers, the nursing homes, the data processors, and the franchisers never delivered. Someone once wrote that if all the chicken franchisers had made it, there'd have been room for hardly anything else in the national diet. There should be no room in your portfolio for fads—or any other institutional biggie. Remember, when the institutions are in there grasping at feathers, you're likely to get plucked.

7 · Having Said All That . . .

HAVING SAID ALL THAT, the question arises, "What is the Little Guy to do?" Some of the biggest individual fortunes have been made in stocks like the Nifty Fifty. In fact, some believe that the best method of investing is to pick out the shares of several promising institutional-grade companies and sock 'em away for your future annuity.

Consider the man who bought just three stocks in 1958. All three, it then seemed, were likely winners, especially United States Steel and Jersey Standard, now Exxon. He paid $80 a share for his 100 Big Steel and $60 per for his Exxon round lot. He also bought 100 shares of a well-known drug company—Johnson & Johnson at $76 a share. *The company was then considerably smaller than it is today.* Fifteen years later, in the fall of 1973, his steel shares were worth less than half what he paid for them, and he was $3,000 ahead on his Exxon shares. But Johnson & Johnson, after multiple splits, had become 2,200 shares worth a quarter of a million dollars. Johnson & Johnson has since survived institutional bombing attacks quite well, and the 2,200 shares were still worth $210,000 at the end of September, 1976.

Well, then, can you buy growth stocks or not? The answer to that question is, yes, you can buy growth—if indeed you find stocks that are presently growing faster than the national average, that will continue to show superior growth, and that carry reasonable price/earnings multiples. Even with such stocks as these, P/E multiples in the high twenties should be a warning.

As for the Nifty Fifty, many are still growing at somewhat higher than average rates. But in the bull market of 1976 a number of them have begun, once again, to sell at higher than reasonable price/earnings ratios.

If you buy them—and I'm not suggesting that you can't make

money in some of them—you've got to be prepared for disappointment. And, your disappointment is bound to follow on the heels of disappointment in institutional circles. They'll get out before you are even aware that there is trouble on the horizon.

If you are really unlucky, you may buy shares of Xerox the day before the next bombing raid. If you should do that you could sit with losses for years—just like Julius Westheimer.

GROWTH STOCK PERFORMANCE
JUNE 30, 1965—FEB. 27, 1976

	Close 6/30/65*	Close 2/27/76	Point Change	Percent Change
AMP, Inc.	5⅝	30¼	+ 24⅝	+ 438%
American Home Prods.	11¼	33⅛	+ 21⅞	+ 194
American Hospital Supply	8½	34¾	+ 26¼	+ 309
Ampex	15	6⅞	− 8⅛	− 54
Avery Products	4¾	28⅛	+ 23⅜	+ 492
Avon Products	55½	39¼	− 16¼	− 29
Becton, Dickinson	13½	40½	+ 27	+ 200
Bristol-Myers	37¾	68½	+ 30¾	+ 81
Burroughs	8⅛	101⅝	+ 93½	+1151
Coca Cola	38½	84½	+ 46	+ 119
Control Data	39¾	24½	− 15¼	− 38
Corning Glass Works	75	60⅛	− 14⅞	− 20
Disney (Walt)	5	59⅞	+ 54⅞	+1098
FAS International	6¾	¾ †	− 6	− 89
Hewlett-Packard	14	107⅜	+ 93⅜	+ 667
Honeywell	60⅞	52¾	− 8⅛	− 13
Int'l. Bus. Machines	119⅝	255⅝	+136	+ 114
Int'l. Flavors & Frag.	6	23¼	+ 17¼	+ 288
Int'l. Tel & Tel.	27¼	28⅞	+ 1⅝	+ 6
Merck & Co.	27⅛	67½	+ 40⅜	+ 149
Minnesota Mining & Mfg.	28¾	57¼	+ 28½	+ 99
Motorola	21¼	47¼	+ 26	+ 122
NCR Corp.	40⅞	27⅝	− 13¼	− 32
Polaroid	28⅝	37¾	+ 9⅛	+ 32
Rank Organisation	1½	3	+ 1½	+ 100
Revlon	26⅝	74	+ 47⅜	+ 178
Southland Corp.	7⅝	23¼	+ 15⅝	+ 205
Texas Inst.	26⅛	119½	+ 93⅜	+ 357
Warner-Lambert	17⅞	31¾	+ 13⅞	+ 78
Xerox	46⅝	66½	+ 19⅞	+ 43
Average of 30 Growth Stocks				+ 98%

* Adjusted for stock splits, stock dividends, etc.
† Adjusted for a 1 for 20 reverse split.

30 DOW JONES INDUSTRIALS
JUNE 30, 1965–FEB. 27, 1976

	Close 6/30/65*	Close 2/27/76	Point Change	Percent Change
Allied Chemical	48½	43½	− 5	− 10%
Alcoa	47¾	47¼	− ½	0
American Brands	36	40¾	+ 4¾	+ 13
American Can	45¼	34⅝	− 10⅝	− 23
American Tel. & Tel.	66½	55¾	− 10¾	− 16
Anaconda	30½	19¾	− 10¾	− 35
Bethlehem Steel	35⅜	44⅝	+ 9¼	+ 26
Chrysler	46¼	17⅞	− 28⅜	− 61
duPont	235½	152¼	− 83¼	− 35
Eastman Kodak	39⅞	108	+ 68⅛	+170
Esmark	23¼	37⅞	+ 14⅝	+ 63
Exxon	78	87⅛	+ 9⅛	+ 12
General Electric	47⅞	53⅜	+ 5½	+ 11
General Foods	39½	28⅝	− 10⅞	− 28
General Motors	95⅝	65⅞	− 29¾	− 31
Goodyear Tire & Rubber	25	22¼	− 2¾	− 11
International Harvester	36½	27⅛	− 9⅜	− 26
International Nickel	28⅜	31⅞	+ 3½	+ 12
International Paper	30¼	74	+ 43¾	+145
Johns Manville	28⅜	29⅜	+ 1	+ 4
Owens-Illinois	54½	59⅛	+ 4⅝	+ 8
Procter & Gamble	36⅛	84⅞	+ 48¾	+135
Sears, Roebuck	68⅛	71½	+ 3⅜	+ 5
Standard Oil Calif.	30¾	30	− ¾	− 2
Texaco	38¾	25	− 13¾	− 35
Union Carbide	60½	74⅛	+ 13⅝	+ 23
United Technology	47⅜	57⅜	+ 10	+ 21
U.S. Steel	48⅜	79⅛	+ 30¾	+ 64
Westinghouse Elec.	23⅞	16⅜	− 7½	− 10
Woolworth (F. W.)	29¼	24⅛	− 5⅛	− 18
Dow-Jones Ind. Average	868.02	972.61	+104.59	+ 12%

* Adjusted for stock splits, stock dividends, etc.

When I called Baltimore stockbroker and analyst Julius Westheimer in February 1976 to ask about his growth stocks, Mr. Westheimer was sheepishly apologetic. His stocks included many that had been bombed heavily during the Nifty Fifty bear market. Nevertheless, he would tote up his prices and his losses and give me the bad news for a "Market Place" column.

Two days later, I received an excited telephone call from Mr.

EARNINGS PER SHARE RECORD OF 30 GROWTH STOCKS

	1965*	1975	Percent Change
AMP	0.34	0.75	+120%
American Home Prods.	0.32	1.58	+393
American Hosp. Supply	0.36	1.48	+311
Ampex	0.90	0.05†	− 94
Avery Prods.	0.29	0.51	+75
Avon Products	0.83	2.40	+189
Becton, Dickinson	0.52	2.00†	+284
Bristol-Myers	1.57	4.44	+182
Burroughs	0.59	4.14	+601
Coca Cola	1.33	3.78†	+184
Control Data	1.06	2.44	+130
Corning Glass Works	2.26	1.76	− 22
Disney (Walt)	0.62	2.13†	+243
FAS International	NA	NA	NA
Hewlett-Packard	0.56	3.02	+439
Honeywell	2.61	3.96	+ 51
Int'l. Business Machines	3.52	13.35	+279
Int'l. Flavors & Frag.	0.21	0.66	+214
Int'l. Tel. & Tel.	2.04	3.05†	+49
Merck	0.92	3.03	+229
Minn. Mining & Mfg.	1.09	2.29	+110
Motorola	1.31	1.46	+ 11
NCR Corp.	1.67	2.90	+ 73
Polaroid	0.93	1.91	+105
Rank Organisation	0.10	0.48†	+380
Revlon	2.24	4.35	+ 94
Southland Corp.	0.43	1.91	+344
Texas Instr.	1.23	2.71	+120
Warner-Lambert	0.80	2.08	+160
Xerox	0.63	4.29	+580
Total	31.28	78.91	+152

NA Not applicable.
* Adjusted for stock splits, stock dividends, etc.
† Latest 12 months.

Westheimer and he was anything but sheepish. To his surprise, he had discovered that the bull market had more than repaired the worst ravages of the 1970–1975 bear. Over a ten-and-a-half-year period, when the Dow Jones 30 industrial stocks had managed a gain of merely 12 percent, his stocks had, on average, doubled in value.

In view of the bear market carnage—and Congressional orders to institutions to diversify more*—this was quite wonderful. Mr. Westheimer's own shaken faith in the growth stocks was restored.

Readers should keep in mind that Mr. Westheimer is wealthy enough to be able to make 100-share investments in each of his favored growth stocks—and he has done so. Most of us must concentrate on fewer stocks—perhaps as few as three or four of these stocks are all most can afford in round-lot purchases.

Anyone who buys, say, three of the stocks in the Westheimer list —or three of any of the Nifty Fifty stocks—is going to have to consider the fact that interim disappointments set Mr. Westheimer's personal investment program back years. For an individual with three such stocks, two such disappointments would mean real trouble.

I think that if you are leaning toward the Nifty Fifty you'll have to agree that the risks are considerable. My advice is to concentrate on the noninstitutional growth stocks which you can ferret out yourself. If you are correct in your analysis of an obscure company like this, someday you may be a proud owner of the Johnson & Johnson of tomorrow—and you can decide then whether to sell out at a fat profit, before the institutions bomb your prize holding. For they are bound to catch up with you someday and inflate values beyond reason.

Let's look at Mr. Westheimer's list (page 59) and compare his success with the results indicated for the 30 Dow Jones industrial stocks.

WHICH GROWTH STOCK

Look at Mr. Westheimer's list carefully. There are some extraordinary gains—particularly those of Burroughs, up 1151 percent; Disney (Walt), up 1098 percent; and AMP, Inc., up 438 percent. Just as interesting—and perhaps even more instructive—are the

* The Pension Reform Act of 1974 carries implicit penalties for professional investors who do not diversify sufficiently, and this has been read as a warning against a Nifty Fifty investment policy.

losers. FAS International, a fad stock of the go-go years whose popularity reflected the uneven success of Famous Artist Schools, is off 89 percent, while Control Data is down 38 percent. NCR Corporation—which is more like Burroughs than any other company—is off 32 percent. Ampex, the innovative high-tech company which introduced the world's first practical videotape recorder in 1966, chalked up a stunning 54 percent loss, and did so in an era of explosive growth in communications.

Mysterious? Definitely. Unless you develop a flair for security analysis. But with a few basic ideas to work with, you should be able to tell which of these companies are clearly past their prime. Thomas W. Phelps, a distinguished security analyst and author of the excellent McGraw-Hill book *100 to 1 in the Stock Market*, liked to show people a chart of a blue chip Big Board stock, plotted in terms of its price relative to that of the Dow Jones industrial average. In so doing, Mr. Phelps did not identify the company and those who saw the chart usually remarked, "Yeah, that's Xerox."

As Mr. Phelps explained in his book:

"What the chart shows is the market price of this stock divided by the Dow Jones industrial average, month by month. If the stock had risen 20 percent when the Dow rose 20 percent, and fallen 25 percent when the Dow fell 25 percent, the relative price would be a horizontal straight line. For example: Stock price 10, Dow 100, stock price divided by Dow price *10 percent*. Stock price 12, Dow 120, stock price divided by Dow price *10 percent*. Stock price 9, Dow 90, stock price divided by Dow price *10 percent*. As you can see for fifteen years, month in and month out, this stock went up more or declined less than the Dow, with the result that its relative price steadily rose."

But the stock was *not* Xerox. It was American Can, for the time period beginning January 1, 1921, and closing at the end of 1935.

Mr. Phelps went on to point out that since 1935, American Can stock adjusted for all stock dividends and stock splits had fallen by 1971 from more than 25 percent of the Dow to less than 4 percent. At the 1971 *high*, the investor had stock worth about what

AMERICAN CAN
RELATIVE PRICE, 1921-1935

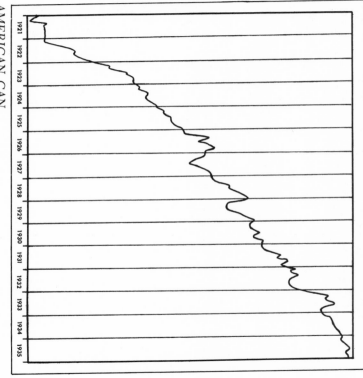

Monthly postings on this chart show how American Can's price compared with the price of the Dow Jones industrial average. Each month the price of American Can was divided by the corresponding price of the Dow Jones industrial average. The resulting figures were posted on a scale that gives equal percentage changes the same size. That is, an advance from 5 percent to 10 percent appears as large as an advance from 50 percent to 100 percent. American Can outran the Dow throughout 1921-35.

he could have sold it for, forty-two years before. Meantime, the Dow had increased about 2½ times in price.

Yet American Can's price/earnings ratio was about 50 percent higher than the Dow's in 1936—because investors still expected

American Can's earnings to increase relative to the Dow's. But by 1940, because of new competition—paper frozen-food wrappers and plastic containers—American Can's earnings had fallen to 37 percent of the Dow, and by 1970, just 27 percent of the Dow.

Yet it was long after careful analysis would have clearly suggested the direction of American Can's future—in 1959—that investors finally stopped putting a premium value on the company's earnings.

Small wonder the glow lasted. From its 1903 low to its 1929 high, Mr. Phelps reports, American Can rose 369-fold. But from its 1929 high to its 1971 high, the rise was zero.

Mr. Phelps comments:

"Even for those who buy right, as Cinderella did, fine carriages turn to pumpkins if one stays too long."

Your problem—if you choose to buy the big winners of the past —is to figure whether, say, Xerox is the American Can of tomorrow. That is, you must determine which stocks offer fast growth and which offer past growth.

Once you find fast growth, you should be determined to hold your selection for many years, though you will continually have to weigh the future for signs of "maturity." Over the next 20 years there may be 100 stocks that will increase in value tenfold, thereby tempting those who hold them to sell.

But some will continue to grow—possibly by 100 times the value at which you—lucky you—purchased them. Since it is much harder to find a new growth stock than it is to hang onto one that you have, you should go slow in deciding to sell out.

In reckoning whether growth has slowed, ground to a halt, or moved into reverse, remember that bigness works against you.

Mr. Phelps sums up:

"To grow at the rate of 20 percent compounded annually for fifty years, a company must be 9,100 times as big at the end of the period as it was at the beginning. If you project that kind of growth for a company with $100 million of annual sales, you must expect those sales to reach $910 billion annually by the year 2027. If you start with a company whose sales already are a billion dollars a year, to count on 20 percent compounded annual growth for the next half century, you must foresee the sales of 9 trillion 100 billion dollars in the year 2027."

HANG IN THERE, BABY

There is yet another hangup in the new Wall Street. There will be perfectly fine growth stocks that you can discover before the institutions and that will later be bought by the institutions. I've made a strong argument against holding such stocks. If you are tempted—as most people are—to sell your shares once they have doubled, quadrupled, or even increased ten times in price, you'll be even more sorely tried if the institutions bomb your latter-day Polaroid. It will take true grit for you to hang in there. And maybe you shouldn't. There is no easy answer to the dilemma. Avon Products provides the argument that maybe you should sell. Polaroid may not—though its $900-million-plus sales suggest that the game is essentially over. Avon Products is clearly so big that, barring some fabulous new market, it now seems unlikely that the shares will provide the kind of growth to justify it as a holding for the individual.*

Moral: Maurice Chevalier's rule—find 'em when they're young.

---

* Remember that American Can's stock gains occurred between 1903 and 1929 while sales were growing from a small base—$23 million—to a growth-dampening $155 million in 1929.

8 · Commissions: The Ultimate Rip-Off—and Where to Turn

If capitalism were likened to religion, charity would represent the capitalist's most noble instincts, and greed his cardinal sin. And there would be little salvation for stockbrokers.

Anyone with the slightest contact with Wall Street knows that brokers rarely give anything away. Thus when the Securities and Exchange Commission decreed that stockbrokers would have to compete for business without the umbrella of administered commission charges after May 1, 1975, some observers were cynical about the prospects for small investors.

The brokers themselves professed to be panic-stricken about unbridled competition. They dubbed the forthcoming deadline Mayday, the international code word for distress, and pretended in other ways that ruin was nigh. If brokers were to be believed, small investors would gang up on them and force commission charges down to nothing. I could almost have cried. After Mayday many small investors did.

For the inevitable happened. Some weeks before Mayday, brokers acting almost as one jacked up commission charges substantially—for there was never an upper limit on charges, only a *floor* under them. Brokers were then ready for Mayday. When it came, one by one they dropped charges to a more or less uniform base that was nevertheless higher than had prevailed before the pre-Mayday hike. They then proclaimed a new era of slim profits and service to mankind.

It was already clear that the giant institutions that hold stock for pensions, policyholders, and mutual fund shareholders previously had wrestled deep discounts from brokers. (They had threatened to join the stock exchange and transact their business directly.)

In the brokers' defense, it might be said that institutions used their power so effectively that brokers had little choice but to sock it to the small investor. Still, some say the brokers socked the small investor so hard they must have been going for a kill—not a knockout. To paraphrase the late Walt Kelly's cartoon character, Pogo, someone had to subsidize the stockbroker and that someone was us.

Bloated commission charges for the small investor actually date back to the beginning of the terrible bear market that cast a black shadow over the entire first half of the decade. It was a period of shrinking business for Wall Street after one of the most reckless speculative periods in investing history. The sere years of 1970 through 1974 shrank business with the public to almost nothing. Many a fat-cat broker was wiped out, and the Street itself was nearly wrecked in a back-office breakdown that scrambled ownership of tens of thousands of customers' shares.

This happened because the brokerage business had never modernized to meet the challenge of a rapidly changing society in which trading volume exploded to unheard-of levels. Where 2 million shares on the Big Board once offered profitable business, 10-million-share days no longer did. Still, processing of stock orders continued under the stewardship of cadres of careful, dedicated, and underpaid clerks doing it all by hand. Each of these thoroughly professional old-timers knew their counterparts at competing firms by first name and had an excellent rapport with them; they managed to keep things perking without a hitch—until the avalanche. By the late 1960s, these aging men were grappling with a raging bull market that caused trading volume to reach levels of 20 million shares or more. It was unprecedented. Bottlenecks began to develop. The clerks were overwhelmed—some were carried out on stretchers, exhausted.

The massive log jam grew as orders piled up and brokers found more and more orders confused beyond recognition. Lost and disputed orders at the major firm of Goodbody & Co. and several other houses nearly led to an insoluble crisis that many believe would have triggered a depression worse than that of the 1930s.

It is a long, even tiresome, story. Suffice it to say that the inevitable result was that many brokerage firms failed and others were absorbed into stronger houses. The survivors wailed for commission increases to pay for the computers they clearly needed to bring nineteenth-century methods up to twentieth-century standards. But at that point, the stock market was thoroughly demoralized. There was hardly a log jam on Wall Street any more. The bear market had slowed trading to a walk, and brokers didn't help matters by hiking commission charges. It was a novel idea: If you couldn't make money in hard times, why you just charged the customer more. One *vegetable wholesaler* who also buys stocks told the author that if *he* pulled that one, his business would literally putrefy.

But Wall Street got away with it. That is, the survivors did. Business *was* putrid. Scores of firms failed and there were mergers galore, as we've noted. But when stock prices finally began to soar in the phenomenal bull market of 1976 and Wall Street began coining money, nobody talked about lowering commission charges. Brokers chuckled softly all the way to the bank. You had to buy shares in Merrill Lynch and other broker-corporations to make money at a broker's expense. Brokers smugly reasoned that customers don't complain when they are making money. Maybe investors don't complain to brokers, but they certainly complain to newspapers.

Frank C. Johnson of Staten Island wrote that his broker wanted to charge him the firm's standard $25 commission on each of two 100 warrant purchases of Mission Investment Trust. After complaining that this was ridiculous since the warrants cost $\frac{1}{16}$ each or $6.25 per hundred, his broker finally agreed to lower its charge to $8 for the first 100 warrants and $6 for the second 100.

But thereafter, his broker nicked Mr. Johnson the minimum $25 commission on a 300-warrant purchase, a 100-warrant purchase, and a 1,400-warrant purchase—all in Mission Investment Trust. Total commissions: $88. Total value of the warrants at ⅟₁₆ each— 6¼ cents—$125. Can a small investor like Mr. Johnson play the market at these costs? "No way!" he wrote.

But look at the commission imposed on the purchase and sale of stocks themselves. They are ample to say the least. A trade of 100 shares of RCA at $26 a share cost the small investor in March 1976 a big $61.51 at Smith Barney, Harris Upham, and between $61 and $54 at such leading brokers as Thomson & McKinnon, Auchincloss, Kohlmeyer, at Hornblower & Weeks–Hemphill, Noyes Inc., at Shearson Hayden Stone, Merrill Lynch, at Bache Halsey Stuart Inc., at Blyth Eastman Dillon, at E. F. Hutton, at Lehman Brothers, and at Dean Witter.

Those prices compare with the last minimum commission charges on such a trade of $49.94. But regardless of which broker you deal with, the worst of it is that you probably won't know until after you trade how much commission you were charged. Most firms have developed tricky techniques for figuring charges— techniques clearly designed to confuse. Even individual registered representatives complain that they cannot figure their firm's charges without difficulty. Obviously a Truth in Commissions Law is needed.

One prosperous firm offered its salesmen a complex table to use in answering questions from customers about commissions. The calculations required brought commission charges similar to those listed in the New York Stock Exchange schedule before May 1, 1975, the lofty pre-Mayday commission peak, and could easily have been shown in simplified tabular form. Such a table had appeared monthly in the Standard & Poor's Stock Guide and is shown on pages 82–86 of this book. But just to let you know how complicated it can be to figure the charges by the broker's method, here's the formula:

MULTIPLE ROUND LOT ORDERS

Money Involved in the Order	Minimum Commission
$ 100 but under $ 2,500	1.3% plus $ 12.00
$ 2,500 but under $20,000	0.9% plus $ 22.00
$20,000 but under $30,000	0.6% plus $ 82.00
$30,000 to and including $300,000	0.4% plus $142.00

Plus (for each round lot)

First to tenth round lot	$6 per round lot
Eleventh round lot and above	$4 per round lot

PLUS On any order involving an amount not in excess of $5,000, the commission computed in accordance with the foregoing provisions shall be increased by 10% and then 8%, and on any order involving an amount in excess of $5,000, the commission computed in accordance with such provisions shall be increased by 15% and then 8%.

Barney Levy of Highland Park, New Jersey, says that in his experience, commission charges are treated "like a military secret"— and adds that the "bad news" arrives with order confirmation.

"No other business is operated this way. . . . The Little Guy is supposed to be shy and not act like a cheapskate and not ask too many questions.

"Sometimes the cost of a transaction, if unknown in advance, will cause you to hesitate."

Obviously, it would not pay to take a risk if there were a chance that the commissions would eliminate the prospects of profit. But there are ways to trim your commission charges and you should be aware of them.

THE AFTERMATH OF MAYDAY

On May 1, 1975, the Securities & Exchange Commission ordered an end to fixed commissions on the purchase and sale of securities. It was supposed to be a great step forward. The advent of competitive pricing was to ensure all investors the best possible price.

How has competitive pricing worked out? For the institutional investors—who buy and sell equities in size—it's been great. They're getting discounts of up to 70 percent on their brokerage commissions. For most mortals, however, it's hard to tell that anything has changed. The table on page 73, prepared by Dan Dorfman for his "Bottom Line" column in *New York* magazine, shows that, except for the brokerage discounters, such as Source Securities and Quick & Reilly, the public is often paying more now to buy and sell a stock than it did in the days of fixed rates. We show what some leading brokerage houses were charging recently to execute some routine transactions—100 shares of RCA at 26, 200 shares of Westinghouse at 18, and 300 shares of Pan American World Airways at 7.

BARGAINS IN TODAY'S "FREE" MARKET

Unless you spend your day hanging around the boardroom of your favorite broker, you have little use for the plush carpeting, the solid mahogany paneling, and the mini-art museum that characterizes many such establishments.

What you want is the Robert Hall type of broker offering minimum services at minimum charge. This clearly implies minimum overhead on his part.

Even when you find a broker who is down-to-earth, you may need help in determining what his charges should be. The following table should be useful to you in your initial efforts to ferret out a reasonable broker. Don't pay more to a broker who tries to con you into believing that you will get more service from the home team than from anybody else.

He may, for example, tout his firm's research. It is a fact that there is little original or even useful research emanating from Wall Street. In fact, one broker who was complaining about the possibility of having to charge customers less if they didn't want the research was told that he might sell the research separately as well. Without thinking, he said, "Are you kidding? Who would be foolish enough to pay for it?"

If you feel—and you shouldn't—that you need a registered representative and not a clerk, then you'll have to pay whatever the firm

	100 shs. RCA @ 26	200 shs. Westinghouse @ 18	300 shs. Pan Am @ 7
Thomson & McKinnon, Auchincloss, Kohlmeyer	61.00	85.00	73.00
Hornblower & Weeks—Hemphill, Noyes Inc.	55.51	82.00	77.00
Shearson Hayden Stone	55.12	81.32	69.00
Merrill Lynch	54.60	79.60	67.50
Bache Halsey Stuart Inc.	54.10	79.60	69.25
Blyth Eastman Dillon	54.00	79.00	68.00
E. F. Hutton	54.00	81.00	69.00
Lehman Brothers	53.95	78.88	68.07
Dean Witter	53.94	78.88	68.07
Old Maximum NYSE Rate	53.94	78.88	68.07
Wertheim & Company	53.94	78.88	68.07
Drexel Burnham	53.44	77.69	67.18
Oppenheimer & Company	53.00	80.00	66.00
Shields Model Roland	52.56	76.86	66.34
Paine, Webber, Jackson & Curtis	52.00	74.00	70.00
Reynolds Securities	52.00	75.00	66.00
Old Minimum NYSE Rate	49.94	73.04	63.03
Source Securities Corporation	35.00	50.00	42.00
Quick & Reilly, Inc.	32.36	47.32	40.84

of your choice asks, and you may end up dealing with a clerk anyway.

Let's look at a couple of ways in which commission costs can be trimmed.

As a general statement, it is worth noting that brokers quite naturally tend to treat their best customers better than those with whom they do little business. Thus, the individual who runs up a commission bill of $1,000 or more a year can ask for and just may obtain from his broker a 25 percent commission discount.

This particular wrinkle in the fabric of commission charges is probably of little use to you, since you would have to do about fourteen round-lot trades in a $50 stock or twenty round lots in a $25 stock each year to qualify.

On the other hand, several brokers, the biggest of which is Bache & Co., offer a break to the individual who resells shares he purchased less than 40 days prior—depending on the period stipulated by the house. The idea is to let the customer get out of something that hasn't worked and into something better without paying too heavy a penalty. Incidentally, this serves the broker as well as the investor. After all, the broker will nick the customer for another full commission charge when the investor recommits the proceeds.

You should ask for the quick-round-trip concession, usually a half-charge commission on the sale, in any event. However, as far as the small client is concerned, the round-trip break is either offered or not, according to firm policy. A really important client will get a break on one basis or the other if he insists.

Assuming you do get a break on a quick round trip, be sure that your broker's basic commission charges are low enough that the concession is meaningful. You may find that a discount broker—discussed in the next section—will offer an initial rate so good that you will do as well on both buy and sell as you do on the sell side with a broker who gives you a 50 percent discount on a quick round trip.

A DISCOUNT . . . IS A DISCOUNT?

Let's take a close look at those discount brokers. But first, let me point out that it is probably fair to say that the discount brokers have not had an easy time of it.

What stockbrokers need to make a good living—to make enough money to want to be brokers—is high trading volume. They enjoyed more than enough business during most of the first half of 1976 to make satisfying profits even at substantial discounts from their normal charges.

This seems clear from the experience of Jeffrey Casdin, who heads Source Securities Corporation, one of the pioneer discount brokers. Source, while not a member of the New York Stock Exchange, has access to the floor of the exchange. This is possible through an arrangement by which the exchange allows nonmembers to participate under a special modification of the normally strict rules limiting floor access to member firms.

Mr. Casdin frankly admits that his business has begun to thrive since—and only since—the 1976 bull market which began in January. He indicated, however, that if enough new customers could be signed up during the high-volume days of 1976, the firm could be expected to remain profitable even when volume slipped to lower levels. Incidentally, Mr. Casdin predicted that when volume does dry up in the next weak market, the big brokers will begin to slash charges to the Little Guy. No signs of that yet. In fact, quite the contrary. One customer got a commission bill recently for 300 shares at 9. The indicated cost was between $70.73 (at 9) and $73.70 (at 10). The bill was 15 percent higher than the larger of the two figures—$84.88. The customer remarked, "Do you know any industry where the customer just gets a 15 percent tax slapped on, no notice, no nothing?"

The table from *New York* magazine in the preceding section will tell you how much the individual was paying for typical stock transactions early in 1976.

You'll see that Source charged $35 to buy or sell 100 shares of RCA, compared with $54 to $56 charged by most brokers to do the same trade. However, that rate is only for customers who have done at least $250 worth of business with Source. Once you have reached that level, you're on the discount tap. Source asks for the $250 up front as an earnest of your intent—or perhaps we should say as the price of admission, since the sum is not refundable.

Source advertises discounts of from 30 to 75 percent off "previous fixed rates," meaning the last minimum commission charges on which most other brokers based their rates.

The discount firm also offers discounts of "up to" 35 percent off previous option exchange rates. The two provisos entail the $250 "lifetime" minimum mentioned earlier, and the duty of the customer to pick his own stocks.

The true mavericks of Wall Street are Quick & Reilly, who are actually a Big Board member firm. Their charge on the 100 shares of RCA amounted to $32.36—or just pennies more than the standard Big Board commission rate before 1970, when the commission spiral began moving skyward. Here's Quick & Reilly's table, which appears to be, as the firm states in its publicity, "Simple and Clear-Cut":

45 percent discount on market orders placed before 9:45 a.m.
40 percent discount on market orders placed after 9:45 a.m.
35 percent discount on good-till-cancelled and limit orders.

It is worth noting here that Quick & Reilly are favoring the kind of orders you should be placing anyway—at least on the buy side. If you want to buy a promising stock, buy it—don't wait for a price. Many an investor has tried to buy a stock at a lower-than-offered price and has been left at the starting gate before a substantial rally.

The bad news is that Quick & Reilly have a minimum commission charge of $30 per transaction, so that the Mission Development warrant buyer mentioned earlier wouldn't like the Q&R terms on his speculation any better than he liked those of his own broker. Obviously, when minimum charges obtain, it will be worth your while to consider doubling or even tripling your order—if you can manage to do so. The firm also offers commission discounts on options and bonds.

Like Source Securities, Quick & Reilly is just getting under way. The firm has offices at 4 Albany Street in Manhattan and a second office at 230 South County Road, Palm Beach, Florida. Whether they survive will depend upon how successfully they woo clients from the bigger houses, how much volume they are able to do in bear markets, and how much competition they face from bigger brokers in any discount war that develops. It will also depend upon their ability to operate efficiently and at a profit.

There is one other potential disadvantage of dealing with discount brokers. The most efficient firms on Wall Street seldom experience delays in relaying orders to the floor of the New York Stock Exchange, and their representatives there are the most adept at getting the best price—execution—possible at a given moment.

On the other hand, Source, at least, makes an effort to check other markets where Big Board stocks are bought and sold—on the Midwest Exchange, the Pacific Coast Exchange, and the PBW Exchange. Source says it also checks the professional arena known as the "third market," a market in which dealers—as opposed to brokers—buy shares for inventory to be resold to the public. Most customers are institutions, but some trades are with individuals. Some third-market trades offer a break to the customer compared with the exchange price and some do not.

Remember that no matter whom you are dealing with, each quarter-point lost as a result of a poor execution costs you $25 on a 100-share trade.

It is clearly more difficult to check up on your broker with regard to executions these days. The opening prices at which Big Board stocks trade haven't been printed in the daily stock tables for years. And in 1976, the newspapers began printing composite tables—incorporating prices at which stocks trade off-board. Thus the high and low prices in some cases reflect trades between professionals in the third market. They may have taken place at as much as a point above or below the trading range of shares traded on the exchange. The result: confusion—and added difficulty for those who would monitor their brokers.

In early May 1976, Merrill Lynch, Pierce, Fenner & Smith, Inc. sent customers a flyer to explain the confusion and to say that it would be executing customer orders on the Big Board unless the firm received specific instructions from the customers to the contrary. Merrill Lynch also pointed to the impossibility of putting a limited price order on one exchange and taking advantage of a better price on another. Limit orders must be held by the specialist on the exchange that has the order.

There isn't a great deal you can do about apparent discrepancies between the prices you receive and pay and the indicated prices shown in the composite tables. Professionals sometimes subscribe to a special service that details all trades in particular stocks day by day. But the pros are dealing with thousands of shares and really need to know. There may be a lot of money involved—a quarter-point on 10,000 shares is $2,500. Also, many institutional investors are required to get the best execution possible under fiduciary responsibility standards of the Pension Reform Act of 1974. Unless you know someone who takes the service and will check prices for you, you are out of luck. Look for a broker, then, whom you feel you can trust, one who gets you good executions and who offers reasonable commission charges. Some cynics say that the last time all three virtues were found in one individual, he was beatified and left the brokerage business to join St. Peter at the Pearly Gates.

One thing to remember about commissions: They don't have to be important to you. It is the thrust of this book that your success as an investor will turn on your ability to find and hold on to quality, undervalued stocks. Thus, commission charges should be of relatively little moment to you in the purchase and sale of stocks. That is, a fairly sizable commission amortized over, say, five to ten years amounts to a relatively small item.

On the other hand, those who own stocks upon which they write call options—selling the right to "call" the stock to someone else—will be more concerned about commission charges. Unfortunately, brokers have abused customers quite frequently on option commissions. You'll have to shop around for option discounts as best you can. Try the discounters.

YOU CAN BANK ON THIS

If a two-paragraph letter from Citibank, the nation's second-largest bank, to certain of its customers in October 1975 said nothing new about bank policy, why did it create a stir on Wall Street?

What the bank did was to remind those who leave securities in the custody of the bank of its charges for buying and selling stocks and bonds in the customer's behalf. Nothing earth-shaking in that.

But analyzed in the context of the commission discounts brokers have been giving the banks since mid-1974, the letter grew in significance. In effect—and apparently without intention—the bank made a bid to become discount broker for its customers.

Some banks in New York and elsewhere have always been willing to buy and sell securities for customers with custody accounts. At least a few provide the service for customers with checking accounts as well. Until mid-1974, though, the charges for the banks' services, added to commissions imposed on banker and individual alike, discouraged most bank customers. The individual investor was clearly better off doing business with a broker directly. Now, however, things are different. Service charges fade in significance when the bank passes along the scant 10-to-15-cent-per-share commission that brokers charge banks and other institutions for trading stocks.

A trade that cost an individual $84 at his broker's—like the purchase of 100 shares of American Telephone at $50 a share—could cost a bank customer around $40 if the transaction were handled in a bank custody account, and $30 or less if he found a bank that would allow him to do the trade as a checking-account customer.

As Citibank noted in its letter, its custody account service charge would be $12.50 and its normal transaction charge another $12.50. Add 15 cents a share—the broker's commission charge would range from 10 to 15 cents a share—and Citibank's total charge would be $40, or half the normal commission charge on a $50 stock.

Chemical Bank in New York City will do the transaction for checking-account customers. The procedure is perhaps a little messy for the fastidious and for those who do not like to have shares registered in their own names. What the customer does is to go to his home branch and ask for an officer to make the trade. On a purchase, the officer would tell the customer to be sure he has left enough money in his checking account to cover the purchase and he would take instructions as to where the shares were to be mailed. The checking account would then be debited for the cost of the shares and the transaction charge. Chemical Bank's transaction charge is $15. If the bank paid 10 cents a share in commission charges, the total cost to the customer would be $25, and if the bank paid 15 cents a share, the total cost would be $30—roughly a third normal brokerage in either case for the American Telephone shares in the example.

The banks that offer the service will also sell shares for customers. The service is highly refined in custody accounts, less so when the customer has only a checking account. In the latter case, he would have to bring his shares in and endorse them over to the bank. Following the sale of the shares the bank would credit the checking account with the proceeds less costs.

The reader should recognize that the banks' brokerage services save the customer less on lower-priced stocks, since commissions are then relatively less important relative to the banks' charges. Nevertheless, most bank-managed securities transactions will offer sufficient savings to outweigh the inconvenience experienced by pennywise customers.

Some banks have already acted to discourage customers who would use the banks to buy and sell securities. Chase wants to raise charges enough to all but eliminate commission-motivated trades.

Meanwhile, the brokers are grumbling about the publicity the banks have received to date, and they might well go to court to discourage the practice. At this writing, Chemical Bank has positively outraged stockbrokers with an additional and more refined securities trading plan, which Chemical now offers on a test basis. For a $30 annual membership fee, the individual can buy and sell securities for $35 per transaction on one to 500 shares and $55 per transaction on 501 to 1,000 shares, commissions included.

9 · Commissions Today

THE REALLY DIFFICULT QUESTION to answer is what commission charges you are going to pay to trade stocks today. Fortunately, the commission charges of most brokers are derivative of the final listed minimum rates in effect prior to Mayday—May 1, 1975.

Many brokers are said to use the tables as indicated for trades involving more than $5,000. Thus the tables shown on pages 82–86, originally prepared by Standard & Poor's Corporation, should be instructive. For trades involving less than $5,000, you are likely to find that your broker charges 8 percent, 15 percent, or an even bigger percentage increment over the rates in the table. A few brokers have an entirely different means of establishing their commission charges. You might try calling your broker and asking for a series of commission charges on hypothetical trades involving less than $5,000. Use your pocket calculator to determine if there is a set percentage premium added to the table rates.

If so, you can easily determine commission charges before doing trades. Again, if you think your broker's rates are too high, you can go elsewhere. There is also the possibility that your broker may even supply a table of rates so that you won't have to go through this rigmarole.

MINIMUM NEW YORK AND AMERICAN STOCK EXCHANGE COMMISSION RATES

SHARE PRICE	SHARES											
	5	10	20	25	30	50	75	100	200	300	500	1000
$1	*	*	*	*	*	*	*	9.24	18.48	27.72	46.20	92.40
2	*	*	*	*	*	7.04	8.14	11.44	22.88	34.32	57.20	107.80
3	*	*	*	*	*	8.14	9.79	13.64	27.28	40.92	67.65	119.90
4	*	*	*	7.04	7.48	9.24	11.44	15.84	31.68	47.52	74.80	129.80
5	*	*	7.04	7.59	8.14	10.34	13.09	18.04	36.08	54.12	81.95	139.70
6	*	*	7.48	8.14	8.80	11.44	14.74	20.24	40.48	58.74	86.90	168.91
7	*	*	7.92	8.69	9.46	12.54	16.39	22.44	44.88	63.03	91.85	180.09
8	*	*	8.36	9.24	10.12	13.64	18.04	24.64	49.28	67.10	96.80	191.27
9	*	*	8.80	9.79	10.78	14.74	19.69	26.07	52.14	70.73	101.75	202.45
10	*	7.04	9.24	10.34	11.44	15.84	21.34	27.50	55.00	73.70	106.70	213.62
11	*	7.26	9.68	10.89	12.10	16.94	22.80	28.93	57.86	76.67	126.07	224.80
12	*	7.48	10.12	11.44	12.76	18.04	23.87	30.36	60.72	79.64	131.65	235.98
13	*	7.70	10.56	11.99	13.42	19.14	24.95	31.79	63.14	82.61	137.25	247.16
14	*	7.92	11.00	12.54	14.08	20.24	26.02	33.22	65.12	85.58	142.83	258.34
15	*	8.14	11.44	13.09	14.74	21.34	27.09	34.65	67.10	88.55	148.24	269.51
16	*	8.36	11.88	13.64	15.40	22.44	28.16	36.08	69.08	91.52	154.01	280.69
17	*	8.58	12.32	14.19	16.06	23.16	29.24	37.51	71.06	106.69	159.60	291.87
18	*	8.80	12.76	14.74	16.72	23.87	30.31	38.94	73.04	110.06	165.19	303.05
19	*	9.02	13.20	15.29	17.38	24.59	31.38	40.37	75.02	113.40	170.78	314.23
20	7.04	9.24	13.64	15.84	18.04	25.30	32.45	41.80	77.00	116.75	176.36	325.40
21	7.15	9.46	14.08	16.39	18.70	26.02	33.53	43.23	78.98	120.11	181.96	332.86
22	7.26	9.68	14.52	16.94	19.36	26.73	34.60	44.66	80.96	123.45	187.54	340.31
23	7.37	9.90	14.96	17.49	20.02	27.45	35.67	46.09	82.94	126.81	193.14	347.76
24	7.48	10.12	15.40	18.04	20.68	28.16	36.74	47.52	84.92	130.16	198.72	355.21
25	7.59	10.34	15.84	18.59	21.34	28.88	37.82	48.95	86.90	133.52	204.31	362.66
26	7.70	10.56	16.28	19.14	22.00	29.59	38.89	49.94	100.35	136.87	209.90	370.12
27	7.81	10.78	16.72	19.69	22.58	30.31	39.96	50.93	102.59	140.23	215.49	377.57
28	7.92	11.00	17.16	20.24	23.01	31.02	41.03	51.92	104.82	143.58	221.08	385.02
29	8.03	11.22	17.60	20.79	23.44	31.74	42.11	52.91	107.06	146.93	226.67	392.47
30	8.14	11.44	18.04	21.34	23.87	32.45	43.18	53.90	109.30	150.28	232.25	399.92
31	8.25	11.66	18.48	21.89	24.30	33.17	44.25	54.89	111.53	153.64	237.85	404.89
32	8.36	11.88	18.92	22.44	24.73	33.88	45.32	55.88	113.77	156.99	243.43	409.86
33	8.47	12.10	19.36	22.80	25.16	34.60	46.40	56.87	116.00	160.35	249.03	414.83
34	8.58	12.32	19.80	23.16	25.59	35.31	47.25	57.86	118.24	163.70	254.61	419.80
35	8.69	12.54	20.24	23.52	26.02	36.03	47.99	58.85	120.47	167.05	260.20	424.76
36	8.80	12.76	20.68	23.87	26.44	36.74	48.73	59.84	122.71	170.40	265.79	429.73
37	8.91	12.98	21.12	24.23	26.87	37.46	49.48	60.83	124.95	173.76	271.38	434.67
38	9.02	13.20	21.56	24.59	27.30	38.17	50.22	61.82	127.18	177.11	276.97	439.67
39	9.13	13.42	22.00	24.95	27.73	38.89	50.96	62.81	129.42	180.47	282.56	444.64
40	9.24	13.64	22.44	25.30	28.16	39.60	51.70	63.80	131.65	183.82	288.14	449.60
41	9.35	13.86	22.73	25.66	28.59	40.32	52.45	64.79	133.89	187.16	291.87	454.57
42	9.46	14.08	23.01	26.02	29.02	41.03	53.19	65.78	136.12	190.52	295.60	459.54
43	9.57	14.30	23.30	26.38	29.45	41.75	53.93	66.77	138.36	193.88	299.32	464.51
44	9.68	14.52	23.58	26.73	29.88	42.46	54.67	67.76	140.59	197.23	303.05	469.48
45	9.79	14.74	23.87	27.09	30.31	43.18	55.42	68.75	142.83	200.59	306.77	474.44
46	9.90	14.96	24.16	27.45	30.73	43.89	56.16	69.74	145.07	203.94	310.50	479.41
47	10.01	15.18	24.44	27.81	31.16	44.61	56.90	70.73	147.30	207.30	314.23	484.38
48	10.12	15.40	24.73	28.16	31.59	45.32	57.64	71.50	149.54	210.64	317.95	489.35
49	10.23	15.62	25.01	28.52	32.02	46.04	58.39	71.50	151.77	214.00	321.68	494.32
50	10.34	15.84	25.30	28.88	32.45	46.75	59.13	71.50	154.01	217.35	325.40	499.28

MINIMUM NEW YORK AND AMERICAN STOCK EXCHANGE COMMISSION RATES

SHARE PRICE	SHARES											
	5	10	20	25	30	50	75	100	200	300	500	1000
$51	10.45	16.06	25.59	29.24	32.88	47.25	59.87	80.73	156.24	220.70	329.13	504.25
52	10.56	16.28	25.87	29.59	33.31	47.74	60.61	80.73	158.47	224.06	332.86	509.22
53	10.67	16.50	26.16	29.95	33.74	48.24	61.36	80.73	160.71	227.40	336.58	514.19
54	10.78	16.72	26.44	30.31	34.17	48.73	62.10	80.73	161.46	230.76	340.31	519.16
55	10.89	16.94	26.73	30.67	34.60	49.23	62.84	80.73	161.46	234.12	344.03	524.12
56	11.00	17.16	27.02	31.02	35.02	49.72	63.58	80.73	161.46	237.47	347.76	529.09
57	11.11	17.38	27.30	31.38	35.45	50.22	64.33	80.73	161.46	240.83	351.49	534.06
58	11.22	17.60	27.59	31.74	35.88	50.71	65.07	80.73	161.46	242.19	355.21	539.03
59	11.33	17.82	27.87	32.10	36.31	51.21	65.81	80.73	161.46	242.19	358.94	544.00
60	11.44	18.04	28.16	32.45	36.74	51.70	66.55	80.73	161.46	242.19	362.66	548.96
61	11.55	18.26	28.45	32.81	37.17	52.20	67.30	80.73	161.46	242.19	365.15	553.93
62	11.66	18.48	28.73	33.17	37.60	52.69	68.04	80.73	161.46	242.19	367.63	558.90
63	11.77	18.70	29.02	33.53	38.03	53.19	68.78	80.73	161.46	242.19	370.12	563.87
64	11.88	18.92	29.30	33.88	38.46	53.68	69.52	80.73	161.46	242.19	372.60	568.84
65	11.99	19.14	29.59	34.24	38.89	54.18	70.27	80.73	161.46	242.19	375.08	573.80
66	12.10	19.36	29.88	34.60	39.31	54.67	71.01	80.73	161.46	242.19	377.57	578.77
67	12.21	19.58	30.16	34.96	39.74	55.17	80.73	80.73	161.46	242.19	380.05	583.74
68	12.32	19.80	30.45	35.31	40.17	55.66	80.73	80.73	161.46	242.19	382.54	588.71
69	12.43	20.02	30.73	35.67	40.60	56.16	80.73	80.73	161.46	242.19	385.02	593.68
70	12.54	20.24	31.02	36.03	41.03	56.65	80.73	80.73	161.46	242.19	387.50	598.64
71	12.65	20.46	31.31	36.39	41.46	57.15	80.73	80.73	161.46	242.19	389.99	603.61
72	12.76	20.68	31.59	36.74	41.89	57.64	80.73	80.73	161.46	242.19	392.47	608.58
73	12.87	20.90	31.88	37.10	42.32	58.14	80.73	80.73	161.46	242.19	394.96	613.55
74	12.98	21.12	32.16	37.46	42.75	58.63	80.73	80.73	161.46	242.19	397.44	618.52
75	13.09	21.34	32.45	37.82	43.18	59.13	80.73	80.73	161.46	242.19	399.92	623.48
76	13.20	21.56	32.74	38.17	43.60	59.62	80.73	80.73	161.46	242.19	402.41	628.45
77	13.31	21.78	33.02	38.53	44.03	60.12	80.73	80.73	161.46	242.19	403.65	633.42
78	13.42	22.00	33.31	38.89	44.46	60.61	80.73	80.73	161.46	242.19	403.65	638.39
79	13.53	22.22	33.59	39.25	44.89	61.11	80.73	80.73	161.46	242.19	403.65	643.36
80	13.64	22.44	33.88	39.60	45.32	61.60	80.73	80.73	161.46	242.19	403.65	648.32
81	13.75	22.58	34.17	39.96	45.75	62.10	80.73	80.73	161.46	242.19	403.65	653.29
82	13.86	22.73	34.45	40.32	46.18	62.59	80.73	80.73	161.46	242.19	403.65	658.26
83	13.97	22.87	34.74	40.68	46.61	63.09	80.73	80.73	161.46	242.19	403.65	663.23
84	14.08	23.01	35.02	41.03	46.95	63.58	80.73	80.73	161.46	242.19	403.65	668.20
85	14.19	23.16	35.31	41.39	47.25	64.08	80.73	80.73	161.46	242.19	403.65	673.16
86	14.30	23.30	35.60	41.75	47.54	64.57	80.73	80.73	161.46	242.19	403.65	678.13
87	14.41	23.44	35.88	42.11	47.84	65.07	80.73	80.73	161.46	242.19	403.65	683.10
88	14.52	23.58	36.17	42.46	48.14	65.56	80.73	80.73	161.46	242.19	403.65	688.07
89	14.63	23.73	36.45	42.82	48.43	66.06	80.73	80.73	161.46	242.19	403.65	693.04
90	14.74	23.87	36.74	43.18	48.73	66.55	80.73	80.73	161.46	242.19	403.65	698.00
91	14.85	24.01	37.03	43.54	49.03	67.05	80.73	80.73	161.46	242.19	403.65	702.97
92	14.96	24.16	37.31	43.89	49.32	67.54	80.73	80.73	161.46	242.19	403.65	707.94
93	15.07	24.30	37.60	44.25	49.62	68.04	80.73	80.73	161.46	242.19	403.65	712.91
94	15.18	24.42	37.88	44.61	49.92	68.53	80.73	80.73	161.46	242.19	403.65	717.88
95	15.29	24.59	38.17	44.97	50.22	69.03	80.73	80.73	161.46	242.19	403.65	722.84
96	15.40	24.73	38.46	45.32	50.51	69.52	80.73	80.73	161.46	242.19	403.65	727.81
97	15.51	24.87	38.74	45.68	50.81	70.02	80.73	80.73	161.46	242.19	403.65	732.78
98	15.62	25.01	39.03	46.04	51.11	70.51	80.73	80.73	161.46	242.19	403.65	737.75
99	15.73	25.16	39.31	46.40	51.40	71.00	80.73	80.73	161.46	242.19	403.65	742.72
100	15.84	25.30	39.60	46.75	51.70	71.50	80.73	80.73	161.46	242.19	403.65	747.68

NEW YORK, AMERICAN AND OTHER MAJOR STOCK EXCHANGES

MINIMUM COMMISSION RATES
EFFECTIVE NOVEMBER 19, 1974

The rates shown are minimum and are scheduled to be abandoned May 1, 1975 in favor of completely competitive rates. Actual rates currently charged on orders up to $300,000 may be higher than the minimums. In addition, reduced rates are available on certain types of orders of $2,000 or less.

THE NON-MEMBER MINIMUM COMMISSION ON STOCKS AND WARRANTS SELLING BELOW $1.00 PER SHARE

The nonmember minimum commission on stocks and warrants below $1.00 per share on that portion of an order involving $300,000 or less, shall be based upon the amount involved in the order and shall not be less than:

Amount Involved In The Order	Minimum Commission
$0-but under $1,000	8.4% of money involved
$1,000-but under $10,000	5.0% of money involved plus 34.00
$10,000-and above	4.0% of money involved plus $134.00

Plus 10% on orders not exceeding $5,000; a flat increase of 15% and then an additional 8% on any order involving an amount in excess of $5,000

Notwithstanding the foregoing, when the amount involved in an order is less than $100.00, the commission shall be as mutually agreed.

SELLING AT $1.00 AND ABOVE

Commissions on stocks selling at $1 per share and above are to be computed on the basis of the amount of money involved in an order. The schedule of rates should be applied to each single order, as defined.

The Constitution sets forth the minimum commission as follows:

On 100 Share Orders and Odd Lot Orders

Money Involved In The Order	Minimum Commission
$ 100-but under $ 800..............	2.0% plus $ 6.40
$ 800-but under $2,500..............	1.3% plus $12.00
$2,500-and above	0.9% plus $22.00

Odd Lot-$2 Less

Multiple Round Lot Orders

Money Involved In The Order	Minimum Commission
$ 100-but under $ 2,500...................	1.3% plus $ 12.00
$ 2,500-but under $ 20,000...................	0.9% plus $ 22.00
$20,000-but under $ 30,000...................	0.6% plus $ 82.00
$30,000-to and including $300,000..............	0.4% plus $142.00

Plus (for Each Round Lot)

First to tenth round lot.......................	$6 per round lot
Eleventh round lot and above.................	$4 per round lot

Plus On any order involving an amount not in excess of $5,000, the commission computed in accordance with the foregoing provisions shall be increased by 10%, and on any order involving an amount in excess of $5,000, the commission computed in accordance with such provisions shall be increased by 15% and then 8%.

The minimum commission on a 100 share order or an odd lot order need not be more than $71.50/80.73 (based on amount of money involved) The minimum commission per round lot within a multiple round lot order is not to exceed the single round lot commission computed in accordance ⁄ th the rate for 100 share orders.

STOCK TRANSFER TAXES

FEDERAL

Expiration-Security transactions have not been subject to Federal taxes since Dec. 31, 1965.

NEW YORK STATE

A tax imposed by the state when a security is sold or transferred from one person to another. The tax is paid by the seller. Sales by out-of-state residents not employed in New York are taxed at reduced rates as indicated in second table below.

Shares selling at	TAX Per Sh.	SALES BY NON RESIDENTS TAX Per Sh.
Less than $5	1¼ ¢	0.625
$5 but less than $10	2½ ¢	1.25
$10 but less than $20	3¾ ¢	1.875
$20 or more	5¢	2.5

MAXIMUM tax on a 'single Taxable sale' is $350.

The rate on transfers not involving a sale is 2½ ¢ a share.

New York State does not impose a transfer tax on sales or transfers of rights to subscribe or warrants.

FLORIDA

15¢ per $100 par value (or fraction thereof) regardless of selling price.

15¢ per $100 actual value (or fraction thereof) on no par stock, but not to exceed 15¢ on each share.

S. E. C. FEE-TRANSACTIONS ON ANY REGISTERED EXCHANGE

1¢ for each $500 or fraction thereof of money involved.

OPTION COMMISSION CHARGES

It is essential that you know commission charges before you enter into option contracts. The profit margins are so close in many instances that your commission charges can throw a gainful trade into the red. On the next several pages you will find a guide to Chicago Board Option Exchange commission rates, prepared and copyrighted by Herzog & Co., Inc. Harry Snyder, co-manager of the Herzog Options Department, actually designed the booklet from which these tables are taken. On exchanges other than CBOE, add 10% to the CBOE rate on orders up to $5,000 and 15% on orders above $5,000.

HOW TO USE THIS HANDY GUIDE: To find the money amount involved in any specific CBOE trade, turn to the page containing the price of the option. Then go from left to right across the page until you arrive at the column containing the number of options in the trade. The TOP figure in this box is the MONEY AMOUNT. The bottom figure is the MINIMUM CBOE COMMISSION for this trade, as per CBOE prospectus 4/26/74.

Commissions on the CBOE for options under $1 are subject to negotiation and are set according to the policy of the brokerage house you do business with. Determine the commissions before making any commitments under $1.

CBOE trades involving over $30,000 on a single trade are also subject to commission-negotiation. And before making any trades at all on the CBOE, be sure to examine an up-to-date prospectus.

		1	2	3	4	5	6	7	8	9	10
1	Money	100.00	200.00	300.00	400.00	500.00	600.00	700.00	800.00	900.00	1,000.00
	Comm.	25.00	26.60	33.90	41.20	48.50	55.80	63.10	70.40	77.70	85.00
1 1/16	Money	106.25	212.50	318.75	425.00	531.25	637.50	743.75	850.00	956.25	1,062.50
	Comm.	25.00	26.76	34.14	41.53	48.91	56.29	63.67	71.05	78.43	85.81
1 1/8	Money	112.50	225.00	337.50	450.00	562.50	675.00	787.50	900.00	1,012.50	1,125.00
	Comm.	25.00	26.93	34.39	41.85	49.31	56.78	64.24	71.70	79.16	86.63
1 3/16	Money	118.75	237.50	356.25	475.00	593.75	712.50	831.25	950.00	1,068.75	1,187.50
	Comm.	25.00	27.09	34.63	42.18	49.72	57.26	64.81	72.35	79.89	87.44
1 1/4	Money	125.00	250.00	375.00	500.00	625.00	750.00	875.00	1,000.00	1,125.00	1,250.00
	Comm.	25.00	27.25	34.88	42.50	50.13	57.75	65.38	73.00	80.63	88.25
1 5/16	Money	131.25	262.50	393.75	525.00	656.25	787.50	918.75	1,050.00	1,181.25	1,312.50
	Comm.	25.00	27.41	35.12	42.83	50.53	58.24	65.94	73.65	81.36	89.06
1 3/8	Money	137.50	275.00	412.50	550.00	687.50	825.00	962.50	1,100.00	1,237.50	1,375.00
	Comm.	25.00	27.58	35.36	43.15	50.94	58.73	66.51	74.30	82.09	89.88
1 7/16	Money	143.75	287.50	431.25	575.00	718.75	862.50	1,006.25	1,150.00	1,293.75	1,437.50
	Comm.	25.00	27.74	35.61	43.48	51.34	59.21	67.08	74.95	82.82	90.69
1 1/2	Money	150.00	300.00	450.00	600.00	750.00	900.00	1,050.00	1,200.00	1,350.00	1,500.00
	Comm.	25.00	27.90	35.85	43.80	51.75	59.70	67.65	75.60	83.55	91.50
1 9/16	Money	156.25	312.50	468.75	625.00	781.25	937.50	1,093.75	1,250.00	1,406.25	1,562.50
	Comm.	25.00	28.06	36.09	44.13	52.16	60.19	68.22	76.25	84.28	92.31
1 5/8	Money	162.50	325.00	487.50	650.00	812.50	975.00	1,137.50	1,300.00	1,462.50	1,625.00
	Comm.	25.00	28.23	36.34	44.45	52.56	60.68	68.79	76.90	85.01	93.13

		1	2	3	4	5	6	7	8	9	10
1 11/16	Money	168.75	337.50	506.25	675.00	843.75	1,012.50	1,181.25	1,350.00	1,518.75	1,687.50
	Comm.	25.00	28.39	36.58	44.78	52.97	61.16	69.36	77.55	85.74	93.94
1 3/4	Money	175.00	350.00	525.00	700.00	875.00	1,050.00	1,225.00	1,400.00	1,575.00	1,750.00
	Comm.	25.00	28.55	36.83	45.10	53.38	61.65	69.93	78.20	86.48	94.75
1 13/16	Money	181.25	362.50	543.75	725.00	906.25	1,087.50	1,268.75	1,450.00	1,631.25	1,812.50
	Comm.	25.00	28.71	37.07	45.43	53.78	62.14	70.49	78.85	87.21	95.56
1 7/8	Money	187.50	375.00	562.50	750.00	937.50	1,125.00	1,312.50	1,500.00	1,687.50	1,875.00
	Comm.	25.00	28.88	37.31	45.75	54.19	62.63	71.06	79.50	87.94	96.38
1 15/16	Money	193.75	387.50	581.25	775.00	968.75	1,162.50	1,356.25	1,550.00	1,743.75	1,937.50
	Comm.	25.00	29.04	37.56	46.08	54.59	63.11	71.63	80.15	88.67	97.19
2	Money	200.00	400.00	600.00	800.00	1,000.00	1,200.00	1,400.00	1,600.00	1,800.00	2,000.00
	Comm.	25.00	29.20	37.80	46.40	55.00	63.60	72.20	80.80	89.40	98.00
2 1/8	Money	212.50	425.00	637.50	850.00	1,062.50	1,275.00	1,487.50	1,700.00	1,912.50	2,125.00
	Comm.	25.00	29.53	38.29	47.05	55.81	64.58	73.34	82.10	90.86	99.63
2 1/4	Money	225.00	450.00	675.00	900.00	1,125.00	1,350.00	1,575.00	1,800.00	2,025.00	2,250.00
	Comm.	25.00	29.85	38.78	47.70	56.63	65.55	74.48	83.40	92.33	101.25
2 3/8	Money	237.50	475.00	712.50	950.00	1,187.50	1,425.00	1,662.50	1,900.00	2,137.50	2,375.00
	Comm.	25.00	30.18	39.26	48.35	57.44	66.53	75.61	84.70	93.79	102.88
2 1/2	Money	250.00	500.00	750.00	1,000.00	1,250.00	1,500.00	1,750.00	2,000.00	2,250.00	2,500.00
	Comm.	25.00	30.50	39.75	49.00	58.25	67.50	76.75	86.00	95.25	104.50
2 5/8	Money	262.50	525.00	787.50	1,050.00	1,312.50	1,575.00	1,837.50	2,100.00	2,362.50	2,625.00
	Comm.	25.00	30.83	40.24	49.65	59.06	68.48	77.89	87.30	96.71	105.63
2 3/4	Money	275.00	550.00	825.00	1,100.00	1,375.00	1,650.00	1,925.00	2,200.00	2,475.00	2,750.00
	Comm.	25.00	31.15	40.73	50.30	59.88	69.45	79.03	88.60	98.18	106.75
2 7/8	Money	287.50	575.00	862.50	1,150.00	1,437.50	1,725.00	2,012.50	2,300.00	2,587.50	2,875.00
	Comm.	25.00	31.48	41.21	50.95	60.69	70.43	80.16	89.90	99.29	107.88
3	Money	300.00	600.00	900.00	1,200.00	1,500.00	1,800.00	2,100.00	2,400.00	2,700.00	3,000.00
	Comm.	25.00	31.80	41.70	51.60	61.50	71.40	81.30	91.20	100.30	109.00
3 1/8	Money	312.50	625.00	937.50	1,250.00	1,562.50	1,875.00	2,187.50	2,500.00	2,812.50	3,125.00
	Comm.	25.00	32.13	42.19	52.25	62.31	72.38	82.44	92.50	101.31	110.13
3 1/4	Money	325.00	650.00	975.00	1,300.00	1,625.00	1,950.00	2,275.00	2,600.00	2,925.00	3,250.00
	Comm.	25.00	32.45	42.68	52.90	63.13	73.35	83.58	93.40	102.33	111.25
3 3/8	Money	337.50	675.00	1,012.50	1,350.00	1,687.50	2,025.00	2,362.50	2,700.00	3,037.50	3,375.00
	Comm.	25.00	32.78.	43.16	53.55	63.94	74.33	84.71	94.30	103.34	112.38

		1	2	3	4	5	6	7	8	9	10
3 1/2	Money	350.00	700.00	1,050.00	1,400.00	1,750.00	2,100.00	2,450.00	2,800.00	3,150.00	3,500.00
	Comm.	25.00	33.10	43.65	54.20	64.75	75.30	85.85	95.20	104.35	113.50
3 5/8	Money	362.50	725.00	1,087.50	1,450.00	1,812.50	2,175.00	2,537.50	2,900.00	3,262.50	3,625.00
	Comm.	25.00	33.43	44.14	54.85	65.56	76.28	86.84	96.10	105.36	114.63
3 3/4	Money	375.00	750.00	1,125.00	1,500.00	1,875.00	2,250.00	2,625.00	3,000.00	3,375.00	3,750.00
	Comm.	25.00	33.75	44.63	55.50	66.38	77.25	87.63	97.00	106.38	115.75
3 7/8	Money	387.50	775.00	1,162.50	1,550.00	1,937.50	2,325.00	2,712.50	3,100.00	3,487.50	3,875.00
	Comm.	25.00	34.08	45.11	56.15	67.19	78.23	88.41	97.90	107.39	116.88
4	Money	400.00	800.00	1,200.00	1,600.00	2,000.00	2,400.00	2,800.00	3,200.00	3,600.00	4,000.00
	Comm.	25.00	34.40	45.60	56.80	68.00	79.20	89.20	98.80	108.40	118.00
4 1/8	Money	412.50	825.00	1,237.50	1,650.00	2,062.50	2,475.00	2,887.50	3,300.00	3,712.50	4,125.00
	Comm.	25.00	34.73	46.09	57.45	68.81	80.18	89.99	99.70	109.41	119.13
4 1/4	Money	425.00	850.00	1,275.00	1,700.00	2,125.00	2,550.00	2,975.00	3,400.00	3,825.00	4,250.00
	Comm.	25.00	35.05	46.58	58.10	69.63	80.95	90.88	100.60	110.43	120.25
4 3/8	Money	437.50	875.00	1,312.50	1,750.00	2,187.50	2,625.00	3,062.50	3,500.00	3,937.50	4,375.00
	Comm.	25.00	35.38	47.06	58.75	70.44	81.63	91.56	101.50	111.44	121.38
4 1/2	Money	450.00	900.00	1,350.00	1,800.00	2,250.00	2,700.00	3,150.00	3,600.00	4,050.00	4,500.00
	Comm.	25.00	35.70	47.55	59.40	71.25	82.30	92.35	102.40	112.45	122.50
4 5/8	Money	462.50	925.00	1,387.50	1,850.00	2,312.50	2,775.00	3,237.50	3,700.00	4,162.50	4,625.00
	Comm.	25.00	36.03	48.04	60.05	72.06	82.98	93.14	103.30	113.46	123.63
4 3/4	Money	475.00	950.00	1,425.00	1,900.00	2,375.00	2,850.00	3,325.00	3,800.00	4,275.00	4,750.00
	Comm.	25.00	36.35	48.53	60.70	72.88	83.65	93.93	104.20	114.48	124.75
4 7/8	Money	487.50	975.00	1,462.50	1,950.00	2,437.50	2,925.00	3,412.50	3,900.00	4,387.50	4,875.00
	Comm.	25.00	36.68	49.01	61.35	73.69	84.33	94.71	105.10	115.49	125.88
5	Money	500.00	1,000.00	1,500.00	2,000.00	2,500.00	3,000.00	3,500.00	4,000.00	4,500.00	5,000.00
	Comm.	25.00	37.00	49.50	62.00	74.50	85.00	95.50	106.00	116.50	127.00
5 1/8	Money	512.50	1,025.00	1,537.50	2,050.00	2,562.50	3,075.00	3,587.50	4,100.00	4,612.50	5,125.00
	Comm.	25.00	37.33	49.99	62.65	75.01	85.68	96.29	106.90	117.51	128.13
5 1/4	Money	525.00	1,050.00	1,575.00	2,100.00	2,625.00	3,150.00	3,675.00	4,200.00	4,725.00	5,250.00
	Comm.	25.00	37.65	50.48	63.30	75.63	86.35	97.08	107.80	118.53	129.25
5 3/8	Money	537.50	1,075.00	1,612.50	2,150.00	2,687.50	3,225.00	3,762.50	4,300.00	4,837.50	5,375.00
	Comm.	25.00	37.98	50.96	63.95	76.19	87.03	97.86	108.70	119.54	130.38
5 1/2	Money	550.00	1,100.00	1,650.00	2,200.00	2,750.00	3,300.00	3,850.00	4,400.00	4,950.00	5,500.00
	Comm.	25.00	38.30	51.45	64.60	76.75	87.70	98.65	109.60	120.55	131.50

		1	2	3	4	5	6	7	8	9	10
5 5/8	Money	562.50	1,125.00	1,687.50	2,250.00	2,812.50	3,375.00	3,937.50	4,500.00	5,062.50	5,625.00
	Comm.	25.00	38.63	51.94	65.25	77.31	88.38	99.44	110.50	121.56	132.63
5 3/4	Money	575.00	1,150.00	1,725.00	2,300.00	2,875.00	3,450.00	4,025.00	4,600.00	5,175.00	5,750.00
	Comm.	25.00	38.95	52.43	65.90	77.88	89.05	100.23	111.40	122.58	133.75
5 7/8	Money	587.50	1,175.00	1,762.50	2,350.00	2,937.50	3,525.00	4,112.50	4,700.00	5,287.50	5,875.00
	Comm.	25.00	39.28	52.91	66.55	78.44	89.73	101.01	112.30	123.59	134.88
6	Money	600.00	1,200.00	1,800.00	2,400.00	3,000.00	3,600.00	4,200.00	4,800.00	5,400.00	6,000.00
	Comm.	25.00	39.60	53.40	67.20	79.00	90.40	101.80	113.20	124.60	136.00
6 1/8	Money	612.50	1,225.00	1,837.50	2,450.00	3,062.50	3,675.00	4,287.50	4,900.00	5,512.50	6,125.00
	Comm.	25.00	39.93	53.89	67.85	79.56	91.08	102.59	114.10	125.61	137.13
6 1/4	Money	625.00	1,250.00	1,875.00	2,500.00	3,125.00	3,750.00	4,375.00	5,000.00	5,625.00	6,250.00
	Comm.	25.00	40.25	54.38	68.50	80.13	91.75	103.38	115.00	126.63	138.25
6 3/8	Money	637.50	1,275.00	1,912.50	2,550.00	3,187.50	3,825.00	4,462.50	5,100.00	5,737.50	6,375.00
	Comm.	25.00	40.58	54.86	68.95	80.69	92.43	104.16	115.90	127.64	139.38
6 1/2	Money	650.00	1,300.00	1,950.00	2,600.00	3,250.00	3,900.00	4,550.00	5,200.00	5,850.00	6,500.00
	Comm.	25.00	40.90	55.35	69.40	81.25	93.10	104.95	116.80	128.65	140.50
6 5/8	Money	662.50	1,325.00	1,987.50	2,650.00	3,312.50	3,975.00	4,637.50	5,300.00	5,962.50	6,625.00
	Comm.	25.00	41.23	55.84	69.85	81.81	93.78	105.74	117.70	129.66	141.63
6 3/4	Money	675.00	1,350.00	2,025.00	2,700.00	3,375.00	4,050.00	4,725.00	5,400.00	6,075.00	6,750.00
	Comm.	25.00	41.55	56.33	70.30	82.38	94.45	106.53	118.60	130.68	142.75
6 7/8	Money	687.50	1,375.00	2,062.50	2,750.00	3,437.50	4,125.00	4,812.50	5,500.00	6,187.50	6,875.00
	Comm.	25.00	41.88	56.81	70.75	82.94	95.13	107.31	119.50	131.69	143.88
7	Money	700.00	1,400.00	2,100.00	2,800.00	3,500.00	4,200.00	4,900.00	5,600.00	6,300.00	7,000.00
	Comm.	25.00	42.20	57.30	71.20	83.50	95.80	108.10	120.40	132.70	145.00
7 1/8	Money	712.50	1,425.00	2,137.50	2,850.00	3,562.50	4,275.00	4,987.50	5,700.00	6,412.50	7,125.00
	Comm.	25.00	42.53	57.79	71.65	84.06	96.48	108.89	121.30	133.71	146.13
7 1/4	Money	725.00	1,450.00	2,175.00	2,900.00	3,625.00	4,350.00	5,075.00	5,800.00	6,525.00	7,250.00
	Comm.	25.00	42.85	58.28	72.10	84.63	97.15	109.68	122.20	134.73	147.25
7 3/8	Money	737.50	1,475.00	2,212.50	2,950.00	3,687.50	4,425.00	5,162.50	5,900.00	6,637.50	7,375.00
	Comm.	25.00	43.18	58.76	72.55	85.19	97.83	110.46	123.10	135.74	148.38
7 1/2	Money	750.00	1,500.00	2,250.00	3,000.00	3,750.00	4,500.00	5,250.00	6,000.00	6,750.00	7,500.00
	Comm.	25.00	43.50	59.25	73.00	85.75	98.50	111.25	124.00	136.75	149.50
7 5/8	Money	762.50	1,525.00	2,287.50	3,050.00	3,812.50	4,575.00	5,337.50	6,100.00	6,862.50	7,625.00
	Comm.	25.00	43.83	59.74	73.45	86.31	99.18	112.04	124.90	137.76	150.63

		1	2	3	4	5	6	7	8	9	10
7 3/4	Money	775.00	1,550.00	2,325.00	3,100.00	3,875.00	4,650.00	5,425.00	6,200.00	6,975.00	7,750.00
	Comm.	25.00	44.15	60.23	73.90	86.88	99.85	112.83	125.80	138.78	151.75
7 7/8	Money	787.50	1,575.00	2,362.50	3,150.00	3,937.50	4,725.00	5,512.50	6,300.00	7,087.50	7,875.00
	Comm.	25.00	44.48	60.71	74.35	87.44	100.53	113.61	126.70	139.79	152.88
8	Money	800.00	1,600.00	2,400.00	3,200.00	4,000.00	4,800.00	5,600.00	6,400.00	7,200.00	8,000.00
	Comm.	25.00	44.80	61.20	74.80	88.00	101.20	114.40	127.60	140.80	154.00
8 1/8	Money	812.50	1,625.00	2,437.50	3,250.00	4,062.50	4,875.00	5,687.50	6,500.00	7,312.50	8,125.00
	Comm.	25.00	45.13	61.69	75.25	88.56	101.88	115.19	128.50	141.81	155.13
8 1/4	Money	825.00	1,650.00	2,475.00	3,300.00	4,125.00	4,950.00	5,775.00	6,600.00	7,425.00	8,250.00
	Comm.	25.00	45.45	62.18	75.70	89.13	102.55	115.98	129.40	142.83	156.25
8 3/8	Money	837.50	1,675.00	2,512.50	3,350.00	4,187.50	5,025.00	5,862.50	6,700.00	7,537.50	8,375.00
	Comm.	25.00	45.78	62.61	76.15	89.69	103.23	116.76	130.30	143.84	157.38
8 1/2	Money	850.00	1,700.00	2,550.00	3,400.00	4,250.00	5,100.00	5,950.00	6,800.00	7,650.00	8,500.00
	Comm.	25.00	46.10	62.95	76.60	90.25	103.90	117.55	131.20	144.85	158.50
8 5/8	Money	862.50	1,725.00	2,587.50	3,450.00	4,312.50	5,175.00	6,037.50	6,900.00	7,762.50	8,625.00
	Comm.	25.00	46.43	63.29	77.05	90.81	104.58	118.34	132.10	145.86	159.63
8 3/4	Money	875.00	1,750.00	2,625.00	3,500.00	4,375.00	5,250.00	6,125.00	7,000.00	7,875.00	8,750.00
	Comm.	25.00	46.75	63.63	77.50	91.38	105.25	119.13	133.00	146.88	160.75
8 7/8	Money	887.50	1,775.00	2,662.50	3,550.00	4,437.50	5,325.00	6,212.50	7,100.00	7,987.50	8,875.00
	Comm.	25.00	47.08	63.96	77.95	91.94	105.93	119.91	133.90	147.89	161.88
9	Money	900.00	1,800.00	2,700.00	3,600.00	4,500.00	5,400.00	6,300.00	7,200.00	8,100.00	9,000.00
	Comm.	25.00	47.40	64.30	78.40	92.50	106.60	120.70	134.80	148.90	163.00
9 1/8	Money	912.50	1,825.00	2,737.50	3,650.00	4,562.50	5,475.00	6,387.50	7,300.00	8,212.50	9,125.00
	Comm.	25.00	47.73	64.64	78.85	93.06	107.28	121.49	135.70	149.91	164.13
9 1/4	Money	925.00	1,850.00	2,775.00	3,700.00	4,625.00	5,550.00	6,475.00	7,400.00	8,325.00	9,250.00
	Comm.	25.00	48.05	64.98	79.30	93.63	107.95	122.28	136.60	150.93	165.25
9 3/8	Money	937.50	1,875.00	2,812.50	3,750.00	4,687.50	5,625.00	6,562.50	7,500.00	8,437.50	9,375.00
	Comm.	25.00	48.38	65.31	79.75	94.19	108.63	123.06	137.50	151.94	166.38
9 1/2	Money	950.00	1,900.00	2,850.00	3,800.00	4,750.00	5,700.00	6,650.00	7,600.00	8,550.00	9,500.00
	Comm.	25.00	48.70	65.65	80.20	94.75	109.30	123.85	138.40	152.95	167.50
9 5/8	Money	962.50	1,925.00	2,887.50	3,850.00	4,812.50	5,775.00	6,737.50	7,700.00	8,662.50	9,625.00
	Comm.	25.00	49.03	65.99	80.65	95.31	109.98	124.64	139.30	153.96	168.63
9 3/4	Money	975.00	1,950.00	2,925.00	3,900.00	4,875.00	5,850.00	6,825.00	7,800.00	8,775.00	9,750.00
	Comm.	25.00	49.35	66.33	81.10	95.88	110.65	125.43	140.20	154.98	169.75

		1	2	3	4	5	6	7	8	9	10
9 7/8	Money	987.50	1,975.00	2,962.50	3,950.00	4,937.50	5,925.00	6,912.50	7,900.00	8,887.50	9,875.00
	Comm.	25.00	49.68	66.66	81.55	96.44	111.33	126.21	141.10	155.99	170.88
10	Money	1,000.00	2,000.00	3,00000	4,000.00	5,000.00	6,000.00	7,000.00	8,000.00	9,000.00	10,000.00
	Comm.	25.00	50.00	67.00	82.00	97.00	112.00	127.00	142.00	157.00	172.00
10 1/8	Money	1,012.50	2,025.00	3,037.50	4,050.00	5,062.50	6,075.00	7,087.50	8,100.00	9,112.50	10,125.00
	Comm.	25.16	50.33	67.34	82.45	97.56	112.68	127.79	142.90	158.01	173.13
10 1/4	Money	1,025.00	2,050.00	3,075.00	4,100.00	5,125.00	6,150.00	7,175.00	8,200.00	9,225.00	10,250.00
	Comm.	25.33	50.65	67.68	82.90	98.13	113.35	128.58	143.80	159.03	174.25
10 3/8	Money	1,037.50	2,075.00	3,112.50	4,150.00	5,187.50	6,225.00	7,262.50	8,300.00	9,337.50	10,375.00
	Comm.	25.49	50.98	68.01	83.35	98.69	114.03	129.36	144.70	160.04	175.38
10 1/2	Money	1,050.00	2,100.00	3,150.00	4,200.00	5,250.00	6,300.00	7,350.00	8,400.00	9,450.00	10,500.00
	Comm.	25.65	51.30	68.35	83.80	99.25	114.70	130.15	145.60	161.05	176.50
10 5/8	Money	1,062.50	2,125.00	3,187.50	4,250.00	5,312.50	6,375.00	7,437.50	8,500.00	9,562.50	10,625.00
	Comm.	25.81	51.62	68.69	84.25	99.81	115.38	130.94	146.50	162.06	177.63
10 3/4	Money	1,075.00	2,150.00	3,225.00	4,300.00	5,375.00	6,450.00	7,525.00	8,600.00	9,675.00	10,750.00
	Comm.	25.98	51.95	69.03	84.70	100.38	116.05	131.73	149.40	163.08	178.75
10 7/8	Money	1,087.50	2,175.00	3,262.50	4,350.00	5,437.50	6,525.00	7,612.50	8,700.00	9,787.50	10,875.00
	Comm.	26.14	52.28	69.36	85.15	100.94	116.73	132.51	148.30	164.09	179.88
11	Money	1,100.00	2,200.00	3,300.00	4,400.00	5,500.00	6,600.00	7,700.00	8,800.00	9,900.00	11,000.00
	Comm.	26.30	52.60	69.70	85.60	101.50	117.40	133.30	149.20	165.10	181.00
11 1/8	Money	1,112.50	2,225.00	3,337.50	4,450.00	5,562.50	6,675.00	7,787.50	8,900.00	10,012.50	11,125.00
	Comm.	26.46	52.92	70.04	86.05	102.06	118.08	134.09	150.10	166.11	182.13
11 1/4	Money	1,125.00	2,250.00	3,375.00	4,500.00	5,625.00	6,750.00	7,875.00	9,000.00	10,125.00	11,250.00
	Comm.	26.63	53.25	70.38	86.50	102.63	118.75	134.88	151.00	167.13	183.25
11 3/8	Money	1,137.50	2,275.00	3,412.50	4,550.00	5,687.50	6,825.00	7,962.50	9,100.00	10,237.50	11,375.00
	Comm.	26.79	53.58	70.71	86.95	103.19	119.43	135.66	151.90	168.14	184.38
11 1/2	Money	1,150.00	2,300.00	3,450.00	4,600.00	5,750.00	6,900.00	8,050.00	9,200.00	10,350.00	11,500.00
	Comm.	26.95	53.90	71.05	87.40	103.75	120.10	136.45	152.80	169.15	185.50
11 5/8	Money	1,162.50	2,325.00	3,487.50	4,650.00	5,812.50	6,975.00	8,137.50	9,300.00	10,462.50	11,625.00
	Comm.	27.11	54.22	71.39	87.85	104.31	120.78	137.24	153.70	170.16	186.63
11 3/4	Money	1,175.00	2,350.00	3,525.00	4,700.00	5,875.00	7,050.00	8,225.00	9,400.00	10,575.00	11,750.00
	Comm.	27.28	54.55	71.73	88.30	104.88	121.45	138.03	154.60	171.18	187.75
11 7/8	Money	1,187.50	2,375.00	3,562.50	4,750.00	5,937.50	7,125.00	8,312.50	9,500.00	10,687.50	11,875.00
	Comm.	27.44	54.88	72.06	88.75	105.44	122.13	138.81	155.50	172.19	188.88

		1	2	3	4	5	6	7	8	9	10
12	Money	1,200.00	2,400.00	3,600.00	4,800.00	6,000.00	7,200.00	8,400.00	9,600.00	10,800.00	12,000.00
	Comm.	27.60	55.20	72.40	89.20	106.00	122.80	139.60	156.40	173.20	190.00
12 1/8	Money	1,212.50	2,425.00	3,637.50	4,850.00	6,062.50	7,275.00	8,487.50	9,700.00	10,912.50	12,125.00
	Comm.	27.76	55.52	72.74	89.65	106.56	123.48	140.39	157.30	174.21	191.13
12 1/4	Money	1,225.00	2,450.00	3,675.00	4,900.00	6,125.00	7,350.00	8,575.00	9,800.00	11,025.00	12,250.00
	Comm.	27.93	55.85	73.08	90.10	107.13	124.15	141.18	158.20	175.23	192.25
12 3/8	Money	1,237.50	2,475.00	3,712.50	4,950.00	6,187.50	7,425.00	8,662.50	9,900.00	11,137.50	12,375.00
	Comm.	28.09	56.18	73.41	90.55	107.69	124.83	141.96	159.10	176.24	193.38
12 1/2	Money	1,250.00	2,500.00	3,750.00	5,000.00	6,250.00	7,500.00	8,750.00	10,000.00	11,250.00	12,500.00
	Comm.	28.25	56.50	73.75	91.00	108.25	125.50	142.75	160.00	177.25	194.50
12 5/8	Money	1,262.50	2,525.00	3,787.50	5,050.00	6,312.50	7,575.00	8,837.50	10,100.00	11,362.50	12,625.00
	Comm.	28.41	56.73	74.09	91.45	108.81	126.18	143.54	160.90	178.26	195.63
12 3/4	Money	1,275.00	2,550.00	3,825.00	5,100.00	6,375.00	7,650.00	8,925.00	10,200.00	11,475.00	12,750.00
	Comm.	28.58	56.95	74.43	91.90	109.38	126.85	144.33	161.80	179.28	196.75
12 7/8	Money	1,287.50	2,575.00	3,862.50	5,150.00	6,437.50	7,725.00	9,012.50	10,300.00	11,587.50	12,875.00
	Comm.	28.74	57.18	74.76	92.35	109.94	127.53	145.11	162.70	180.29	197.88
13	Money	1,300.00	2,600.00	3,900.00	5,200.00	6,500.00	7,800.00	9,100.00	10,400.00	11,700.00	13,000.00
	Comm.	28.90	57.40	75.10	92.80	110.50	128.20	145.90	163.60	181.30	199.00
13 1/8	Money	1,312.50	2,625.00	3,937.50	5,250.00	6,562.50	7,875.00	9,187.50	10,500.00	11,812.50	13,125.00
	Comm.	29.06	57.63	75.44	93.25	111.06	128.88	146.69	164.50	182.31	200.13
13 1/4	Money	1,325.00	2,650.00	3,975.00	5,300.00	6,625.00	7,950.00	9,275.00	10,600.00	11,925.00	13,250.00
	Comm.	29.23	57.85	75.78	93.70	116.63	129.55	147.48	165.40	183.33	201.25
13 3/8	Money	1,337.50	2,675.00	4,012.50	5,350.00	6,687.50	8,025.00	9,362.50	10,700.00	12,037.50	13,375.00
	Comm.	29.39	58.08	76.11	94.15	112.19	130.23	148.26	166.30	184.34	202.38
13 1/2	Money	1,350.00	2,700.00	4,050.00	5,400.00	6,750.00	8,100.00	9,450.00	10,800.00	12,150.00	13,500.00
	Comm.	29.55	58.30	76.45	94.60	112.75	130.90	149.05	167.20	185.35	203.50
13 5/8	Money	1,362.50	2,725.00	4,087.50	5,450.00	6,812.50	8,175.00	9,537.50	10,900.00	12,262.50	13,625.00
	Comm.	29.71	58.53	76.79	95.05	113.31	131.58	149.84	168.10	186.36	204.63
13 3/4	Money	1,375.00	2,750.00	4,125.00	5,500.00	6,875.00	8,250.00	9,625.00	11,000.00	12,375.00	13,750.00
	Comm.	29.88	58.75	77.13	95.50	113.88	132.25	150.63	169.00	187.38	205.75
13 7/8	Money	1,387.50	2,775.00	4,162.50	5,550.00	6,937.50	8,325.00	9,712.50	11,100.00	12,487.50	13,875.00
	Comm.	30.04	58.98	77.46	95.95	114.44	132.93	151.41	169.90	188.39	206.88
14	Money	1,400.00	2,800.00	4,200.00	5,600.00	7,000.00	8,400.00	9,800.00	11,200.00	12,600.00	14,000.00
	Comm.	30.20	59.20	77.80	96.40	115.00	133.60	152.20	170.80	189.40	208.00

		1	2	3	4	5	6	7	8	9	10
14 1/8	Money	1,412.50	2,825.00	4,237.50	5,650.00	7,062.50	8,475.00	9,887.50	11,300.00	12,712.50	14,125.00
	Comm.	30.36	59.43	78.14	96.85	115.56	134.28	152.99	171.70	190.41	209.13
14 1/4	Money	1,425.00	2,850.00	4,275.00	5,700.00	7,125.00	8,550.00	9,975.00	11,400.00	12,825.00	14,250.00
	Comm.	30.53	59.65	78.48	97.30	116.13	134.95	153.78	172.60	191.43	210.25
14 3/8	Money	1,437.50	2,875.00	4,312.50	5,750.00	7,187.50	8,625.00	10,062.50	11,500.00	12,937.50	14,375.00
	Comm.	30.69	59.88	78.81	97.75	116.69	135.63	154.56	173.50	192.44	211.38
14 1/2	Money	1,450.00	2,900.00	4,350.00	5,800.00	7,250.00	8,700.00	10,150.00	11,600.00	13,050.00	14,500.00
	Comm.	30.85	60.10	79.15	98.20	117.25	136.30	155.35	174.40	193.45	212.50
14 5/8	Money	1,462.50	2,925.00	4,387.50	5,850.00	7,312.50	8,775.00	10,237.50	11,700.00	13,162.50	14,625.00
	Comm.	31.01	60.33	79.49	98.65	117.81	136.98	156.14	175.30	194.46	213.63
14 3/4	Money	1,475.00	2,950.00	4,425.00	5,900.00	7,375.00	8,850.00	10,325.00	11,800.00	13,275.00	14,750.00
	Comm.	31.18	60.55	79.83	99.10	118.38	137.65	156.93	176.20	195.48	214.75
14 7/8	Money	1,487.50	2,975.00	4,462.50	5,950.00	7,437.50	8,925.00	10,412.50	11,900.00	13,387.50	14,875.00
	Comm.	31.34	60.78	80.16	99.55	118.94	138.33	157.71	177.10	196.49	215.88
15	Money	1,500.00	3,000.00	4,500.00	6,000.00	7,500.00	9,000.00	10,500.00	12,000.00	13,500.00	15,000.00
	Comm.	31.50	61.00	80.50	100.00	119.50	139.00	158.50	178.00	197.50	217.00
15 1/8	Money	1,512.50	3,025.00	4,537.50	6,050.00	7,562.50	9,075.00	10,587.50	12,100.00	13,612.50	15,125.00
	Comm.	31.66	61.23	80.84	100.45	120.06	139.68	159.29	178.90	198.51	218.13
15 1/4	Money	1,525.00	3,050.00	4,575.00	6,100.00	7,625.00	9,150.00	10,675.00	12,200.00	13,725.00	15,250.00
	Comm.	31.83	61.45	81.18	100.90	120.63	140.35	160.08	179.80	199.53	219.25
15 3/8	Money	1,537.50	3,075.00	4,612.50	6,150.00	7,687.50	9,225.00	10,762.50	12,300.00	13,837.50	15,375.00
	Comm.	33.29	61.68	81.51	101.35	121.19	141.03	160.86	180.70	200.54	220.38
15 1/2	Money	1,550.00	3,100.00	4,650.00	6,200.00	7,750.00	9,300.00	10,850.00	12,400.00	13,950.00	15,500.00
	Comm.	33.45	61.90	81.85	101.80	121.75	141.70	161.65	181.60	201.55	221.50
15 5/8	Money	1,562.50	3,125.00	4,687.50	6,250.00	7,812.50	9,375.00	10,937.50	12,500.00	14,062.50	15,625.00
	Comm.	33.61	62.13	82.19	102.25	122.31	142.38	162.44	182.50	202.56	222.63
15 3/4	Money	1,575.00	3,150.00	4,725.00	6,300.00	7,875.00	9,450.00	11,025.00	12,600.00	14,175.00	15,750.00
	Comm.	33.78	62.35	82.53	102.70	122.88	143.05	163.23	183.40	203.58	223.75
15 7/8	Money	1,587.50	3,175.00	4,762.50	6,350.00	7,937.50	9,525.00	11,112.50	12,700.00	14,287.50	15,875.00
	Comm.	33.94	62.58	82.86	103.15	123.44	143.73	164.01	184.30	204.59	224.88
16	Money	1,600.00	3,200.00	4,800.00	6,400.00	8,000.00	9,600.00	11,200.00	12,800.00	14,400.00	16,000.00
	Comm.	32.80	62.80	83.20	103.60	124.00	144.40	164.80	185.20	205.60	226.00
16 1/8	Money	1,612.50	3,225.00	4,837.50	6,450.00	8,062.50	9,675.00	11,287.50	12,900.00	14,512.50	16,125.00
	Comm.	32.96	63.03	83.54	104.05	124.56	145.08	165.59	186.10	206.61	227.13

		1	2	3	4	5	6	7	8	9	10
16 1/4	Money	1,625.00	3,250.00	4,875.00	6,500.00	8,125.00	9,750.00	11,375.00	13,000.00	14,625.00	16,250.00
	Comm.	33.13	63.25	83.88	104.50	125.13	145.75	166.38	187.00	207.63	228.25
16 3/8	Money	1,637.50	3,275.00	4,912.50	6,550.00	8,187.50	9,825.00	11,462.50	13,100.00	14,737.50	16,375.00
	Comm.	33.29	63.48	84.21	104.95	125.69	146.43	167.16	187.90	208.64	229.38
16 1/2	Money	1,650.00	3,300.00	4,950.00	6,600.00	8,250.00	9,900.00	11,550.00	13,200.00	14,850.00	16,500.00
	Comm.	33.45	63.70	84.55	105.40	126.25	147.10	167.95	188.80	209.65	230.50
16 5/8	Money	1,662.50	3,325.00	4,987.50	6,650.00	8,312.50	9,975.00	11,637.50	13,300.00	14,962.50	16,625.00
	Comm.	33.61	63.93	84.89	105.85	126.81	147.78	168.74	189.70	210.66	231.63
16 3/4	Money	1,675.00	3,350.00	5,025.00	6,700.00	8,375.00	10,050.00	11,725.00	13,400.00	15,075.00	16,750.00
	Comm.	33.78	64.15	85.23	106.30	127.38	148.45	169.53	190.60	211.68	232.75
16 7/8	Money	1,687.50	3,375.00	5,062.50	6,750.00	8,437.50	10,125.00	11,812.50	13,500.00	15,187.50	16,875.00
	Comm.	33.94	64.38	85.56	106.75	127.94	149.13	170.31	191.50	212.69	233.88
17	Money	1,700.00	3,400.00	5,100.00	6,800.00	8,500.00	10,200.00	11,900.00	13,600.00	15,300.00	17,000.00
	Comm.	34.10	64.60	85.90	107.20	128.50	149.80	171.10	192.40	213.70	235.00
17 1/8	Money	1,712.50	3,425.00	5,137.50	6,850.00	8,562.50	10,275.00	11,987.50	13,700.00	15,412.50	17,125.00
	Comm.	34.26	64.83	86.24	107.65	129.06	150.48	171.89	193.30	214.71	236.13
17 1/4	Money	1,725.00	3,450.00	5,175.00	6,900.00	8,625.00	10,350.00	12,075.00	13,800.00	15,525.00	17,250.00
	Comm.	34.43	65.05	86.58	108.10	129.63	151.15	172.68	194.20	215.73	237.25
17 3/8	Money	1,737.50	3,475.00	5,212.50	6,950.00	8,687.50	10,425.00	12,162.50	13,900.00	15,637.50	17,375.00
	Comm.	34.59	65.28	86.91	108.55	130.19	151.83	173.46	195.10	216.74	238.38
17 1/2	Money	1,750.00	3,500.00	5,250.00	7,000.00	8,750.00	10,500.00	12,250.00	14,000.00	15,750.00	17,500.00
	Comm.	34.75	65.50	87.25	109.00	130.75	152.50	174.25	196.00	217.75	239.50
17 5/8	Money	1,762.50	3,525.00	5,287.50	7,050.00	8,812.50	10,575.00	12,337.50	14,100.00	15,862.50	17,625.00
	Comm.	34.91	65.73	87.59	109.45	131.31	153.18	175.04	196.90	218.76	240.63
17 3/4	Money	1,775.00	3,550.00	5,325.00	7,100.00	8,875.00	10,650.00	12,425.00	14,200.00	15,975.00	17,750.00
	Comm.	35.08	65.95	87.93	109.90	131.88	153.85	175.83	197.80	219.78	241.75
17 7/8	Money	1,787.50	3,575.00	5,362.50	7,150.00	8,937.50	10,725.00	12,512.50	14,300.00	16,087.50	17,875.00
	Comm.	35.24	66.18	88.26	110.35	132.44	154.53	176.61	198.70	220.79	242.88
18	Money	1,800.00	3,600.00	5,400.00	7,200.00	9,000.00	10,800.00	12,600.00	14,400.00	16,200.00	18,000.00
	Comm.	35.40	66.40	88.60	110.80	133.00	155.20	177.40	199.60	221.80	244.00
18 1/8	Money	1,812.50	3,625.00	5,437.50	7,250.00	9,062.50	10,875.00	12,687.50	14,500.00	16,312.50	18,125.00
	Comm.	35.56	66.63	88.94	111.25	133.56	155.88	178.19	200.50	222.81	245.13
18 1/4	Money	1,825.00	3,650.00	5,475.00	7,300.00	9,125.00	10,950.00	12,775.00	14,600.00	16,425.00	18,250.00
	Comm.	35.73	66.85	89.28	111.70	134.13	156.55	178.98	201.40	223.83	246.25

		1	2	3	4	5	6	7	8	9	10
20	Money	2,000.00	4,000.00	6,000.00	8,000.00	10,000.00	12,000.00	14,000.00	16,000.00	18,000.00	20,000.00
	Comm.	38.00	70.00	94.00	118.00	142.00	166.00	190.00	214.00	238.00	262.00
19 7/8	Money	1,987.50	3,975.00	5,962.50	7,950.00	9,937.50	11,925.00	13,912.50	15,900.00	17,887.50	19,875.00
	Comm.	37.84	69.78	93.66	117.55	141.44	165.33	189.21	213.10	236.99	260.88
19 3/4	Money	1,975.00	3,950.00	5,925.00	7,900.00	9,875.00	11,850.00	13,825.00	15,800.00	17,775.00	19,750.00
	Comm.	37.68	69.55	93.33	117.10	140.88	164.65	188.43	212.20	235.98	259.75
19 5/8	Money	1,962.50	3,925.00	5,887.50	7,850.00	9,812.50	11,775.00	13,737.50	15,700.00	17,662.50	19,625.00
	Comm.	37.51	69.33	92.99	116.65	140.31	163.98	187.64	211.30	234.96	258.63
19 1/2	Money	1,950.00	3,900.00	5,850.00	7,800.00	9,750.00	11,700.00	13,650.00	15,600.00	17,550.00	19,500.00
	Comm.	37.35	69.10	92.65	116.20	139.75	163.30	186.85	210.40	233.95	257.50
19 3/8	Money	1,937.50	3,875.00	5,812.50	7,750.00	9,687.50	11,625.00	13,562.50	15,500.00	17,437.50	19,375.00
	Comm.	37.19	68.88	92.31	115.75	139.19	162.63	186.06	209.50	232.94	256.38
19 1/4	Money	1,925.00	3,850.00	5,775.00	7,700.00	9,625.00	11,550.00	13,475.00	15,400.00	17,325.00	19,250.00
	Comm.	37.03	68.65	91.98	115.30	138.63	161.95	185.28	208.60	231.93	255.25
19 1/8	Money	1,912.50	3,825.00	5,737.50	7,650.00	9,562.50	11,475.00	13,387.50	15,300.00	17,212.50	19,125.00
	Comm.	36.86	68.43	91.64	114.85	138.06	161.28	184.49	207.70	230.91	254.13
19	Money	1,900.00	3,800.00	5,700.00	7,600.00	9,500.00	11,400.00	13,300.00	15,200.00	17,100.00	19,000.00
	Comm.	36.70	68.20	91.30	114.40	137.50	160.60	183.70	206.80	229.90	253.00
18 7/8	Money	1,887.50	3,775.00	5,662.50	7,550.00	9,437.50	11,325.00	13,212.50	15,100.00	16,987.50	18,875.00
	Comm.	36.54	67.98	90.96	113.95	136.94	159.93	182.91	205.90	228.89	251.88
18 3/4	Money	1,875.00	3,750.00	5,625.00	7,500.00	9,375.00	11,250.00	13,125.00	15,000.00	16,875.00	18,750.00
	Comm.	36.38	67.75	90.63	113.50	136.38	159.25	182.13	205.00	227.88	250.75
18 5/8	Money	1,862.50	3,725.00	5,587.50	7,450.00	9,312.50	11,175.00	13,037.50	14,900.00	16,762.50	18,625.00
	Comm.	36.21	67.53	90.29	113.05	135.81	158.58	181.34	204.10	226.86	249.63
18 1/2	Money	1,850.00	3,700.00	5,550.00	7,400.00	9,250.00	11,100.00	12,950.00	14,800.00	16,650.00	18,500.00
	Comm.	36.05	67.30	89.95	112.60	135.25	157.90	180.55	203.20	225.85	248.50
18 3/8	Money	1,837.50	3,675.00	5,512.50	7,350.00	9,187.50	11,025.00	12,862.50	14,700.00	16,537.50	18,375.00
	Comm.	35.89	67.08	89.61	112.15	134.69	157.23	179.76	202.30	224.84	247.38

PART II

SPECULATING

10 · If You Must Play the Market . . .

I HAVE TRIED, perhaps too hard from your point of view, to make a strong case for conservatism. If you can find a strong company that is growing rapidly and that has not yet come to light, you will probably make more money in that company's stock than you will in trading. In fact, commission costs are so high today that even full-time tape watchers and traders have trouble trying to make money on in-and-out trading—or even by trading on a month-to-month basis. Most lose, and many lose heavily.

As an investor you should be seeking gains over time. As a speculator you might as well realize that you are at the track. One major difference is that at the track each horse has four legs and a jockey. You won't have a leg to stand on much of the time when you are speculating. Crooked jockeys are plentiful in Wall Street. Whatever you do, avoid hot tips. Wall Street will love you if you don't. The sharpies can pick you off by sucking you in and hammering you down, and the brokers will pile up commissions to your detriment.

Nevertheless, there are techniques that can be used successfully in rising markets to build capital in your portfolio. You can play market swings. Major swings don't go unheralded—even in their early stages when there is still time to profit from them.

If you had bought Smokestack America*—giant companies like those in the Dow Jones industrial average—you could certainly have benefitted from an institutional swing toward these stocks.

* So-called because in earlier years their stock certificates featured belching smokestacks—the smoke of prosperity.

You know that the major banks have reduced holdings of the so-called Nifty Fifty stocks—some of which lost their grow power, it should be noted. But there is bound to be a renewal of interest in the group, particularly among the companies which prove to have strong growth potential even today. A company need not grow by Nifty Fifty standards of 15 to 20 percent a quarter to have institutional appeal. If quarterly gains reach 12 percent compounded, the company will exceed the earnings growth of all but a relative handful of listed stocks.

Remember that these stocks are still widely held and are thus subject to institutional bombing attacks as before. It might just be your luck to buy shares the day before a Nifty Fifty chairman steps forth to surprise Wall Street with the announcement that growth is dead for now—that earnings will be flat for the current year. That's what James J. Shapiro of Simplicity Pattern did in the first week of June 1976. Within two days, the stock was down 1⅞ points to 12. That cut the market price in half from the 1976 high of 23½.

There are other trends you can play in relative safety—as long as you avoid fads like new issues and franchisers. As this chapter was written, the major drug company stocks were selling at some of their most attractive multiples in many a month. They were by no means cheap, however. Merck, a quality stock, sported a P/E of 22, down a notch from its "norm" of 27. That could be a bargain if the government doesn't make too much noise about the industry's pricing and there isn't too much adverse publicity about drugs produced by any member of the industry that have undesirable side effects. The point is, if you play hunches about forthcoming trends, you'll have to be nimble. You risk institutional disappointment with your favorite vehicle.

Here, then, are several trading techniques that are widely used by speculators for short-term market rewards. I warn you again. No one is going to give you much help in this quest. You'll have to have determination and a sense of timing. I advise you to hold for months rather than weeks, but with a clear-cut knowledge of why you purchased a particular stock. Once the action is over—in your view—don't hang in there waiting for your short-term gains to become long-term. That's an almost surefire way of losing all you've gained and then some. Remember that those who caught the action before you will cash in to lock up their gains before yours mature.

LAPPY'S LAW

If happiness is a stock that doubles in one year, then Happy Lappy will have to change his name. Lappy's done far better than that on more than one occasion recently, and this experienced speculator regards his success as a direct outgrowth of his decision to limit his frame of reference. Any speculator would be wise to follow Lappy's Law—or some similar formula that rules out all but a few choice stocks. What Lappy is looking for is action in a few quality stocks. He explained:

"There is no point in playing stocks on the American Exchange or those trading over the counter. That may be okay for some, but I regard the risks as excessive for the kind of short-term profits I seek. Right away, then, the list is narrowed to fewer than 2,200 stocks. Then you focus on stocks in which options are traded and eliminate the few utilities in the group because they don't move that much. You are down to less than 200 stocks. Next rule out the second-string companies in each group. You choose U. S. Steel and eliminate secondary stock, Bethlehem Steel. You keep Exxon, Mobil, and Standard of Cal and eliminate Gulf and Texaco among the oils. IBM becomes your only computer maker and Texas Instruments your semi-conductor stock. You should wind up with ten to a dozen stocks—leaders in their industries. You will have picked the stocks the institutions go for. They are all big stocks, and there is extra activity because of the option market action. In short, these are the quality stocks that get the most action, and action is what makes money for speculators like me."

TAKE YOUR PROFITS (?)
AND RUN

A broker I know who has customers wishing to speculate urges that they concentrate on low-priced "movers"—stocks that fluctuate more than average.

Suppose, for example, that you find such a stock and that it looks promising on technical grounds. It is trading just below a resistance level—a price, say, at which many holders bought it and got stuck years ago. They are waiting for it to reach their acquisition price so that they can sell at break-even. The company's prospects are improving, a base of support is building, and the stock looks good for a 4-point move from its present price of 12.

A commitment for 100 shares would involve no more than $1,200—$650 on a margin purchase—but would not produce much profit. If you are half right and the stock goes up just 2 points, your profit would be $200 less commissions of $30 (in) and $30 (out) or a $60 chunk of your $200. That's too much to make the prospects interesting.

But if you bought 1,000 shares at a cost of $12,000 and experienced the same 2-point profit, you'd have $2,000 less commissions of $220 (in) and $220 (out) or $440 of your $2,000 profit. The commission per 100 shares is $22 compared with $30 on the 100-share transaction.

If you should follow this speculative approach to investing—and I am not urging that you do so—be sure to sell on the first sign of weakness. Try not to lose more than 15 percent so that you'll "live to invest another day." My broker friend argues that a man with $10,000 to $20,000 to invest can make money on this sort of trading—if he sticks to one stock at a time; one he has convinced himself has good prospects. Try it. You may like it. Most traders lack something—timing, grit, whatever. They regularly lose money.

PLAYING SOCIAL TRENDS

I once lost a stock market argument with an editor on absurd grounds. It was on the eve of the Surgeon General's report on cigarettes many years ago. Everyone knew that the report would be a knock, and the tobacco companies' shares had been pounded down for weeks in anticipation of the publication of the report.

I was writing a daily stock market column and was fascinated to see what happened to the cigarette company stocks in the day's trading before the release of the report. All tobacco shares except those of one company were flat—the news had been fully discounted in advance. Liggett & Myers shares were up more than a point. Reason: An enterprising rival newspaper had sent a reporter to interview a member of the Surgeon General's staff who said that his brand—one produced by Liggett & Myers—was found to have less tar and nicotine and was thus less of a threat to health than the rest.

My argument with the editor was over whether we should report why Liggett & Myers shares were up. The editor took the position that it had been unethical for the panelist to give an interview on the eve of publication and that we should not become a party to his wrong by reporting it. I was flabbergasted. The editor, a decent sincere fellow and a generally thoroughgoing professional, had missed the point.

In dealing with the stock market we try to establish cause and effect—not morality. Ethical questions are irrelevant in stock gains and losses. The stock market is amoral. If you're going to understand it, you must realize that. It's quite another thing to decide not to *invest* in tobacco, liquor, munitions, or drug stocks. That's your privilege. But it's pointless to deny what's happening.

It should also be understood that the stock market is an imperfect reflection of events. It has a life of its own, moving in response to what people *think* is happening—or is going to happen. It didn't matter, up to a certain point, that Equity Funding turned out to be a fraud. As long as investors believed that it was the most phenomenal insurance company ever to come down the pike, the stock went up.

Big fortunes are made on expectations. And, of course, those with inside information can make lots of money by playing a market built on their own puffery—your misplaced hopes.

You too can make lots of money playing stocks that appear to have great futures—even when they don't. Better you play stocks that actually do have great futures, but sometimes you may not be able to distinguish between fact and fancy. If your timing is right, it won't matter. But since your timing will be imperfect, pick with care when you play the trends. Make it your business to find out as much as possible, and be right on the facts so that bad timing won't destroy your investment. Remember: In the short run what America thinks is important. In the long run, it is what corporate America produces that counts.

Investors in Bowmar Industries were playing a trend of sorts, and the Bowmar Brain was as good a hand-held calculator as any—if not *the* best. Trouble was, Bowmar was not a giant company, nor was it a producer of the circuitry that made the Brain possible. Ultimately, it was forced into reorganization by competition from the producers of integrated circuits—including giant Texas Instruments.

But some investors in Bowmar who recognized the risks—that the circuitry producers would probably take over the market—made lots of money in Bowmar and sold out before the collapse.

Bowmar capitalized on a trend it helped create—near universal use of hand-held calculators. The best and most sweeping kind of trend is the social trend backed by long green from Washington.

Happily, this is the kind of trend you can spot by reading your daily newspaper. "Kennedy to Put Man on Moon by 1970." That headline was a clear sign to social-trend watchers that there was to be enormous growth for electronic circuitry that would be required to control and communicate with objects in space. Shares of Texas Instruments soared, and so did the shares of scores of other companies with a piece of the action. Owens Corning developed a ceramic coating for a re-entry vessel, adapted it as a stove-to-table-to-refrigerator serving dish, and the shares took off. There are many examples of stock that whooshed. There are far more examples of promising space-age stocks that aborted.

More recently, the federal government focused on education and began spending money to improve textbook quality, comprehensiveness, and format. Shares of publishing companies enjoyed rare and unaccustomed popularity. Before the trend had run its course, publishing houses became takeover candidates. Several were bought for many times their book value. CBS paid a quarter of a billion dollars for the dilapidated Holt, Rinehart & Winston. Many little guys made it in the publishing stocks—this time at the expense of the big guys.

There are many other trend stocks. Makers of auto pollution-control devices had their day—and there are still big winners, no doubt, that will arise out of environmental concerns. Some "quality of life" stock is just waiting to happen. Some trend stocks are distasteful holdings. The defense stocks sometimes move spectacularly—when the government goes to war. The tobacco stocks benefited from a trend back to cigarettes after people shrugged and said, "The other guy will get cancer; I'm going to enjoy my cigarette."

No question, you can make money if you detect a stock that will benefit from a broad or social trend—especially trends fostered by the government. Where's the action to be found today? Many believe communications is still to be a spectacular growth area. The government is still fostering satellite development and the circuitry that goes with it. There are Wall Streeters who are excited by the fact that the Federal Communications Commission is allowing vast expansion of the Citizens Band radio. CB radios are becoming quite popular. Some believe that this current fad (and it probably is a fad) may last for several years, enjoying explosive growth. Look for a maker of sets—one with more staying power than Bowmar if you can find one; one that makes its own sets and doesn't just import parts or sets from Japan.

It seems quite clear that the nation's major cities have goaded the federal government into spending more money in town. (Many a suburban, federally subsidized sewer program has already been canceled in a rechanneling of funds to the cities.)

The question in every case is, what companies are likely to get the money? Will it be builders of multiple dwellings? Not so as Wall Street will notice it, perhaps. But what about the makers of security equipment; the makers of addict maintenance drugs? Maybe. Maybe not. You'll have to figure these things out if you want to play social trends. But you can be assured that wherever the heavy hand of government falls there will be mucho money to be made. If you "play" this market, your first stop is as near as the newspaper.

SWINGING WITH SAM

Samuel C. Greenfield has made a career out of his Low High Theory of Investment, and he even wrote a book with that title.*

If you want to speculate by the numbers, this Wall Street broker's technique is probably as safe as any.

Sam says you can't argue the point—stocks do fluctuate. And each year they inevitably set a low and a high. Obviously, if you can catch them when they are low and sell them when they are high, you've got to make money—as long as the swing is wide enough to more than pay the brokerage. Even with today's rising commission scales the spread has got to be *that* wide.

Sam says that the best time to catch the average stock near its low is just after the end of the year. December, as you know, is the last month for investors to sell stocks and establish tax losses.

But wait. Some stocks come out of December selling near their highs for the year. You're unlikely to make money with these stocks using Sam's methods. Avoid them. On the other hand, if you can buy the shares of a solid company at or near its low for the prior year just after you welcome the New Year, you've got a good

* Coward McCann, Inc., New York, 1968.

chance for a handsome profit and probably within four or five months, Sam says.

If you want to know just how far a stock is likely to move—and you surely do—do an analysis of prior lows and highs. That will give you an idea as to what could happen this year—though there is no guarantee that the stock won't go down instead of up.

That's why you're going to do a thorough fundamental analysis of the company before you follow through. The company doesn't have to be a stand-out—as long as it is a solid company with a history of substantial earnings. Sam chose Pet, Inc., the food company, to demonstrate his system. Pet is "an unromantic stock with no great institutional or Wall Street following." But despite ups and downs in the earnings column, it's a solid performer with a good earnings record.

Let's look at Pet's history of lows and highs for the past ten years. You can get similar prices for all major corporations from Standard & Poor's *Listed Stock Reports*, or from *Moody's Quarterly*, or from *Value Line Investment Survey*, to name just three of several different sources.

Pet's average rise over the years was 55 percent. Mr. Greenfield assumes, then, a 50 percent spread between the low and high so far this year. If the price rose to 50 percent above the 1976 low, it

PET, INC.

Year	Lowest Price	Highest Price	Percent* Spread	Annual Earnings per Share
1967	25	34	35%	$1.77
1968	25	41	65	2.66
1969	34	46	35	2.95
1970	28	42	50	3.05
1971	36	51	40	3.23
1972	32	56	75	2.83
1973	21	38	80	2.93
1974	16	26	60	3.27
1975	17	28	65	3.59
1976	24	28	17%†	N.A.

* Rounded off to nearest 5 points, except in 1976, which is actual.
† High as of June 10 when price was 25½.

would reach 36. If the stock price dropped 50 percent from its already established high, it would go to 19. Thus Mr. Greenfield figures the downside risk to be a price of 19 and the potential on the upside, 36.

That is, Pet will make a spread—no doubt about it. It is not safe to assume that the move will be up. But a study of the company and the industry has convinced Mr. Greenfield that there are reasonable prospects and he is thus willing to bet on it—invest in the stock. "It's a good food company and all the good food companies are showing good increases in earnings this year. I expect the same for Pet."

The theory can be applied to many situations:

1. A stock moves down. When to buy it? Only if it makes the percentage spread on the downside. Then, in Mr. Greenfield's opinion, it will become a buy.

2. A stock makes a new high. Can it be bought? Only if it has not yet made the anticipated percentage spread. For example, Exxon had made a high with a gain of 18 percent and could move higher since its spread is 35 percent in the Greenfield theory.

3. Split is announced. This is a sell signal according to some Wall Streeters. Not so, says Mr. G—if there is room to travel up in the stock's spread. He found room to grow post-split for both Exxon and Continental Oil in 1976. At the split price (adjusted), both had gains of roughly half their 35 percent spread potentials.

4. Good companies at high prices. Mr. Greenfield believes both Chemitron and Airco to be "fine companies." He was unwilling to buy them in June, however, because they had "already made their spreads. It is dangerous to buy near their tops because the risk factor is too great."

5. Out-of-favor industries. Mr. Greenfield commented on an oversupply of fertilizer which had caused the manufacturers' stocks to decline. "Stay away from them until they have made their percentage spreads on the downside." Williams & Co. was down 50 percent and still vulnerable in Mr. Greenfield's opinion because the fertilizer maker's normal spread was 75 percent.

Summing up, Mr. Greenfield commented that his technique could be likened to a fuse designed to prevent an overload of speculative enthusiasm. In very good markets, people rush in to buy even after stocks have made their normal spreads on the high side.

"If you study the history of stock movements you will discover how many stocks made terrific spreads in bull markets only to fall apart later in the year or in the next year."

Mr. Greenfield warns that his Low High theory is no substitute for good judgment. But it is a workable device for achieving satisfactory results in the stock market. It is important to remember that extraordinary events whether they affect a particular company or the stock market as a whole can result in unusual spreads in given years. Those unusual spreads are as likely to be on the downside as the upside.

Speculators who anticipate a certain spread in a given stock can play the Low High game in the options market. The investment is much less and the rewards are heavily leveraged. More bang for a buck. Investors who try this one should remember that options expire valueless when the underlying shares don't reach the payoff level. If you believe Mr. Greenfield is right when he says the action often comes early in the year, you will want to apply his technique in options with calls that expire by mid-spring.

11 · The Option Play

A GREAT DEAL has been written about the conservative strategies that can be employed in the listed option market—those four exchanges set up to trade options to buy (call) and sell (put) stock.*

But while it is certainly true that options can be used defensively,

* The Chicago Board Options Exchange, the American Stock Exchange, the Philadelphia Exchange, and the Pacific Coast Exchange.

even the defensive techniques are regularly abused—as we shall see. In a book like mine, then, the listed option discussion clearly belongs in the speculative section. Never forget that listed options work primarily because speculators are actively seeking a fast buck. You couldn't use the conservative strategy—writing calls against stock you own—if there wasn't a speculator out there at the betting window to buy that option you wish to sell. If you decide instead to do what he does—buy calls—you're the gambler.

The clearest form of this sort of speculation is to purchase a call which gives you the right to buy 100 shares of a particular stock at a specific price and within a set period of time. You pay a premium for that privilege that will cost you anywhere from $6.25 per 100 shares optioned (quoted as $\frac{1}{16}$) to more than $5,000. You're only doing it because you're hoping to make a killing within a few months' time. With relatively little movement in the underlying shares, the value of your option may appreciate several times over. No movement, no profits. In fact, your investment may be completely wiped out and you will lose the money spent on commissions as well.

The commissions are usually quite substantial. One of my readers who bought 200 Reynolds shares and wrote a call option against them discovered that he had risked $9,001 (the cost of the Reynolds shares) for a potential gross profit of $1,200 (the premium received for the call). But his broker "gobbled up" $400 of that gross profit in commission charges. The reader calls the whole option market a bunko game—grand larceny and the broker take all.

The market where such transactions take place—the listed option market—is still quite new, though options have been bought and sold for many years. Until the Chicago Board Options Exchange came along, an option once given almost inevitably remained the property of the purchaser.

Since there was no central market where options could be traded, the owner of the option either exercised it or, assuming the underlying shares didn't rise enough to provide a profitable call, he simply allowed the option to expire and took his loss.

The listed options exchanges altered that. Brilliantly conceived by the CBOE, the exchange techniques provided needed standardization. Listed options expire on set days in particular months of the year instead of any business day chosen by the parties to an unlisted option. The CBOE decreed set exercise or "striking" prices for particular options, another innovation. The exchange also provided a market where the options could be bought and sold. That was the real advance. This meant there would be an active secondary market where options could now be traded. The holder was no longer locked in.

IN THE BEGINNING, CALLS

There are two basic options—puts and calls. We have explained calls previously.

The purchaser of a put—like the man who sells a stock short—is betting that the price of the stock will drop. If this happens, the value of the put goes up. Puts give the holder the right to sell 100 shares of a particular stock within a specified time period and at a specific price. Here's one strategy: As the owner of shares in which you have a profit at, say, 20, you might be willing to pay a small price or "premium" for the right to have someone else buy those shares at 20 in the event that the market price dropped, reducing or eliminating your profit on the underlying shares. If you can put the shares to someone else at 20 you will have a profit (less commissions) despite the decline in the market. On the other hand, if the market for the shares should rise, and the stock reached 25, the unrealized profit at 20 would be increased by another 5 points. On a listed option exchange, you could sell the put for profit instead of putting the shares to another.

Dennis L. Mirus, a Chicagoan who is an expert on options, believes puts to be clearly superior to short sales, which they roughly parallel. A short-seller sells borrowed shares hoping for a price decline so that he can "cover" (purchase and replace the borrowed shares) for a profit. The short-seller can act only if the present price of the shares is higher than their price before the present level was established. That is, he must do it on an "uptick"—a rule that does not affect the put market. Puts cost less money to establish than short sales, and less is at risk. The put purchaser pays a premium, and that plus commissions represent the limit of his risk. In a short sale, the risk is essentially unlimited, since the shares may double or triple, putting the short-seller farther and farther behind.

There are plenty of option strategies—so many, in fact, that bright people with a market bent are having trouble sleeping nights as they think up new ways to use these potentially profitable trading techniques. Happy Lappy is currently engaged in a delicately orchestrated combination of techniques which he believes could just make him a million dollars. It could also cost him a great deal of money. (Fortunately, perhaps, a discussion of this complex set of transactions is beyond the scope of this book.) Things have to break his way, and he is taking a big gamble in assuming that they might.

Before we go further, though, you'll need a few more definitions.

Break-even point—the point at which the amount of premium received for an option will approximately offset a decline or advance in the market value of a security.

Covered writer—the seller of a call (an option writer) who owns the underlying stock subject to the option. When a put is involved, the covered writer is short the stock.

Equity level—the level above which the writer of an option cannot make any additional gains. The equity level, as a result of writing a call option, is defined as the exercise price plus premium(s) received.

Expiration date—the day on which an option runs out and becomes worthless.

In the money—Once an option is "in the money" it has an intrinsic value because the current market price of the underlying shares is above the striking price of the call, or below the exercise price of a put.

Naked options—call options written (sold) by someone who does not own the underlying shares; put options written by someone who is not short the underlying shares.

Option writer—one who sells options.

Optioned stock—common stock which underlies an option contract.

Out of the money—This refers to an option with no present intrinsic value because the current price of the stock is less than the exercise price of the call or above the exercise price of a put.

Premium—the price paid to the writer of a call or a put. The premium is determined by supply and demand factors: the time left before the expiration date, the volatility of the underlying shares, and general market conditions.

Short sale—the sale of borrowed shares supplied by the customer's broker. At some time in the future, the short-seller hopes to buy the shares at a lower price and return them to his broker.

Spread—the purchase of one option and sale of another in the same stock. The investor hopes to profit from a change in the difference in the prices of the two options.

Straddle—a combination of a put and a call on the same stock. If one exercises one side of the straddle the other side remains intact.

Striking price—the price at which an option is exercisable. It is the price at which the buyer of a call may purchase 100 shares of stock, and the price at which the put buyer may sell 100 shares of stock.

Underlying stock—the stock which the buyer of a call can buy from the writer, and the stock which the buyer of a put can sell to the writer.

THE "SAFE" OPTION PLAY
—AND THE MAN WHO CRACKED IT

During the go-go years of the late 1960s, when even the cats and dogs were having their day in the stock market, I received a telephone call from an investor who said, "Tell me, Mr. Metz, do stocks go down?" It is this kind of ignorance and a related quality—blind trust—that leads to the biggest losses suffered in Wall Street.

If you are going to buy and sell stock options, it is essential that you suffer from neither shortcoming. You must be fully cognizant of the risks involved. Otherwise, a broker who knows just enough to confuse you will probably relieve you of a substantial part of your money.

I regard the point to be of sufficient importance that I am going to relate the story of a veteran investor who, late in life, forgot the basics. He was badly mauled using the most conservative option practice—writing call options against shares he owned.

I have already told you what calls are, but they are such an unfamiliar idea to most of us that I'm going to explain them in terms of something more familiar—houses.

Suppose you have a house in a thriving suburb. You figure it is worth $35,000 because that's what the man down the street paid when he bought a similar property just weeks ago. Nevertheless, there is a man who is convinced that real estate in your attractive, growing town—and your place in particular—will soon be worth considerably more money. Hoping to profit on his convictions, he offers you $1,000 today for the right to buy your house for $40,000—$5,000 more than you believe it is presently worth—at any time within the next three months.

That's a nice bit of extra income for betting that your house won't make you richer in three months than you are today. You say, "Fine, give me the grand." You have just written a call option against your house, fully realizing that if the speculator should prove to be right, that if your house rapidly increases in value to, say, $42,000 before his option runs out, you'll receive a check for $40,000 and have to start looking for a new place to live. That's essentially how call options work, but the important area for trading calls—which can, by the way, be on any type of property—is in stocks.

Let's take the story one step further—into the realm of the markets listing calls. It was some years ago that some clever individuals in Chicago decided to set up a market for people who "write" calls—folks who ordinarily own stocks and who want an extra source of income—and the folks who buy and trade calls.

Understand that calls have been written for years, but once written they had remained in the hands of the original purchaser to be exercised or to expire when the option time span ran out. The Chicagoans felt options ought to be freed to trade independently. Let's go back to that call you wrote on your $35,000 house. An exchange in such seldom-written options would permit the buyer of the call to sell it to someone else.

If he did so when it was possible to get $38,000 for your house, he might receive more than $1,000 for the option—provided there was still some time left and reasonable hope that the house would be worth more than $40,000 before the option ran out. If it was only worth $38,000 on the last day of the option period, the option would be virtually worthless.

If the house was already worth $41,000 when the option holder sold his call, he would get more than $1,000 for it, since the option would be "in the money"—exercisable at more than the so-called striking price, $40,000. Remember, though, that many options expire valueless because the 100 shares of stock usually covered by the option will prove not to have been worth the striking price before the option runs out.

Those who buy options invest relatively little money for a chance to earn very substantial profits in a short time. Let's say that during the life of the option, IBM announces that it will build a major facility nearby, and the value of your house quickly rises to $45,000. The option holder who paid $1,000 for the privilege of buying your house for $40,000 will have a profit of several thousand dollars on his commitment of just $1,000. Try to do that in the stock market in three months. It does happen in options. Far more frequently, however, options expire valueless and the holder loses his entire investment. He's a speculator. You're a conservative investor seeking additional income at a relatively small risk to your holdings. At least that's the theory.

Let's consider, however, what happened to a nice old gentleman with lots of money and somewhat less common sense who got involved in writing options against his holdings a couple of years ago.

The old gentleman believed then and believes now that his broker is one of his very best friends. When the broker got onto our friend, he held shares in such solid companies as Eastman Kodak, Exxon, American Telephone, and IBM. He wasn't necessarily going to get a great deal richer holding shares of such giant companies,* but the holdings were nevertheless in some of the leading and most progressive companies in the nation. In short, at his advanced age of 75, he had an excellent chance of holding his own in the stock market. It should be noted that he probably would have had more peace of mind and contentment had he sold his stocks and purchased corporate bonds. At his age, he certainly didn't need the worry, the uncertainty, and the shock that sometimes comes of holding common stocks, however solid.

The broker the old gentleman was soon to regard as a good friend started serving his client shortly after the options exchange was set up in Chicago on April 26, 1973. The bear market was still devastating share owners. Nevertheless, the gentleman's portfolio was worth $275,000 and holding up pretty well. You'll remember that the major banks and other institutions kept stocks like Kodak, IBM, and Exxon as a haven far into the final reaches of the bear market.

The broker was one of those marvelous con men who, for all we know, may even have conned himself—may have believed himself to be sincere.

With stocks going nowhere, it wasn't difficult for this broker to persuade his new client to write options against his shares. It even made sense. Our old friend could pick up a substantial amount of

* Remember that billion dollar companies have to have their periods of greatest growth behind them as we explained in Chapter 9.

income, the broker said, since the "action" in the ongoing bear market was in options. He explained that many who were unwilling to buy stocks would be more than happy to pay fairly substantial premiums to be able to call shares on the strength of some belated rally in the stock market itself and would give options sudden value.

The broker explained that his customer's stocks—solid holdings though they were—were subject to setbacks, in which case the customer would have offsetting income from the sale of the options on the shares he owned.

It sounded good, and in *that* market it *was* good. Premiums were high and stocks like the old gentleman's were steady. He began writing options, and the income began to roll in. The income grew and became a fairly substantial part of his investment program. It cost him nothing—except for commissions. His stocks didn't go up, so nobody called his shares and he was better off than ever before.

There is a universal human quality called greed, as we all know. Even those who forsake it—ministers and social workers—are tempted from time to time, and the rest of us fight it or attempt to control it throughout life. Greed is clearly no respecter of persons, and it is certainly no respecter of our elders. This old man was receptive, then, when his broker, who it goes without saying was also venal, suggested a few changes in his client's share portfolio.

Why not sell some Kodak for Polaroid; some AT&T for Xerox? Kodak was after all an old and conservative company, and Polaroid, the broker said, represented the wave of the future. And AT&T? Who are we trying to kid? That stock never goes anywhere, the broker argued—give or take 10 points. Xerox, on the other hand, just could invade the duplicator market, and mimeographing was probably ten times as big as copying. Xerox explosions could reverberate in Wall Street once more.

Perhaps the old man felt that owning a piece of the future as the broker outlined things could somehow earn him immortality. He wasn't crackers, but he was enjoying life.

He took the bait. He broke the cardinal rule of option writing. Never tailor your option-writing program around stocks that you do not want to own for their own sake. As we have seen, the old man's stock-buying instincts had been excellent—until he became good friends with his broker. It is arguable that he belonged in bonds, not stocks. But if he was to be in the stock market, he was in stocks in which disasters would be less than earthshaking.

But we all know what happened late in the bear market. The Nifty Fifty plunged. As you might expect, he lost money on his Polaroid shares, which had already begun their slide to one-tenth of their high, and Xerox also took a dive, as did other more obvious cats and dogs in his portfolio.

He also made some money on his options—nobody calls stocks on their way down. The profit for the option holder, as we have seen, arises out of climbing stock prices. It got so bad, in fact, that the once substantial premiums speculators had paid for options on stocks dropped to a fraction of the substantial sums the old gentleman received when he first started writing.

Within little better than a year this is where he stood: He had earned $15,000 in option income, though the income had dwindled to the marginal point. He had lost $75,000 in the underlying values of his shares.

There was more. Remember that what makes options so attractive to brokers is the fact that they run out so quickly. Sell a man a stock and he may keep it for years. The broker may never see the client again. Sell an option, and the customer may be persuaded to repeat the exercise in a few months.

But commission costs on options amount to about as much as they do on stocks themselves. By contrast to the substantial paperwork involved in transferring a stock, which helps to justify some of the charges, the costs of executing an option are scandalously low. A substantial number of option transactions do not even go to the floor of an exchange—they represent mere bookkeeping entries within some large brokerage houses that simply do the transaction in house between two clients.

What dear friend broker did was to write the shortest possible options on each of his customer's stocks, arguing that it was foolish for the customer to wait for his income any longer than necessary.

However, the old gentleman's shares slipped more and more; they became less and less popular with the option buyers as the market went through its final purge. "Premiums," as the income is called, were evaporating, as we have already indicated.

Meanwhile, the rapid turnover of options in the old man's account constituted a broker's dream—an annuity, if you will. While the old man was losing in every market sense and certainly on taxes, he was also writing checks to his broker to the tune of $14,000 in commissions.

An honest broker who heard the old man's tale pointed to his folly as gently as possible and suggested he sell his shares, forget about options, and buy quality corporate bonds. The broker was rebuffed, however, because the gentleman couldn't bring himself to sever ties with his present broker.

"I can't," he said. "He's one of my best friends. It wouldn't be fair to turn my back on him."

Or safe, either. In Wall Street, an old fool and his money are soon parted.

LISTED CALL PREMIUMS*
(very quiet stocks)

Stock & Strike Price	3 Months	6 Months	9 Months
10	$100.00	$125.00	$150.00
15	118.75	143.75	175.00
20	137.50	162.50	200.00
25	150.00	175.00	212.50
30	162.50	200.00	237.50
35	187.50	225.00	262.50
40	212.50	250.00	300.00
45	237.50	287.50	325.00
50	275.00	337.50	387.50
60	387.50	437.50	487.50
70	500.00	600.00	700.00
80	575.00	650.00	750.00
90	675.00	775.00	850.00
100	725.00	862.50	937.50

* Suggested call premiums for new series whose strikes are the same as the market for quiet stocks such as AT&T, Federal National Mortgage, etc.

LISTED CALL PREMIUMS*
(stocks of average volatility)

Stock & Strike Price	3 Months	6 Months	9 Months
10	$ 112.50	$ 150.00	$ 175.00
15	125.00	162.50	187.50
20	162.50	187.50	225.00
25	187.50	212.50	237.50
30	237.50	262.50	287.50
35	287.50	312.50	337.50
40	325.00	350.00	387.50
45	387.50	412.50	450.00
50	425.00	462.50	500.00
60	500.00	550.00	600.00
70	625.00	662.50	700.00
80	675.00	725.00	775.00
90	750.00	800.00	900.00
100	837.50	937.50	1,000.00
120	950.00	1,050.00	1,175.00
140	1,100.00	1,200.00	1,300.00
240	1,250.00	1,775.00	2,000.00

* These are suggested listed option premiums for both buyers and writers for *new* options series issued at the same strike as the stock is trading on the market.

LISTED CALL PREMIUMS*
(volatile stocks)

Stock & Strike Price	3 Months	6 Months	9 Months
20	$ 225.00	$ 300.00	$ 337.50
25	287.50	350.00	400.00
30	300.00	375.00	425.00
35	375.00	412.50	450.00
40	400.00	450.00	500.00
45	425.00	500.00	612.50
50	487.50	637.50	687.50
60	600.00	675.00	775.00
70	687.50	775.00	837.50
80	737.50	850.00	937.50
90	825.00	975.00	1,050.00
100	887.50	1,025.00	1,150.00
120	1,000.00	1,225.00	1,400.00
140	1,200.00	1,425.00	1,587.50
240	1,750.00	2,250.00	2,750.00

* Suggested call premiums for new series whose strikes are the same as the market for volatile stocks (such stocks as Digital, Haliburton, etc.).

If you plan to do what this man thought he was doing—sell options against your stocks for added income—you'll need guidelines telling you what premiums to demand before you sell.

The tables above, prepared by Paul Sarnoff, options director of Conticommodity, reflect "empirically derived" premiums. Writers should not sell their options for less, nor should call buyers pay more. The buyer secures his options at the same premium that the seller receives—with commissions added for the buyer and deducted, of course, from the seller. In addition, there is a one-cent SEC fee charged the writer for every $300 of value involved in the option premium.

10-TO-1 SHOT

Happy Lappy's been concentrating on the listed options market lately, and that's where he has made his biggest scores. He favors options because the "risk to reward ratio" is "tremendous." You invest relatively little—taking a bettor's chance of losing everything —and make long-shot profits if you are right. You seldom are right, he points out, but a few big winners make up for a multitude of losers. His Mobil profits in early 1976 make the point.

On January 2, when Mobil shares were trading on the New York Stock Exchange at 48, he bought 20 Mobil February 50 options. The options cost him $7/16$—43.75 cents each, or $43.75 per 100 shares of optioned Mobil stock. Total cost: $940 including commissions.

His options gave him the right to call—purchase from the option writer—2,000 shares of Mobil at 50 until February 20. More to the point, he could resell the options on the Chicago Board Options Exchange for a profit if the price of the underlying Mobil shares exceeded 50 before February 20. Otherwise the options would expire on that date, worthless. It was a long chance. Almost nobody believed it would happen in the 34 market days remaining before the options were to run out. That's why they cost so little. That's also why they were a good go-for-broke speculation.

Market psychology at the time was dominated by the tax-loss selling that had put a damper on the market in the final days of 1975. January 2 was the first day of trading in the new year. Nobody—and that includes Lappy—thought that January would produce one of the greatest bull rallies in history.

That didn't have to happen for Lappy to make money. All that had to happen was that the market would conclude as Lappy had that Mobil was undervalued at 48. A little more than 2 points of action on the upside—something over 4 percent—would mean pay dirt. The rally came and Mobil was carried along with the rest of the market.

On January 26—less than a month after purchase—Lappy sold 10 of his 20 options for $3,669. He had made $3,200 over the cost of the 10 options and still had half his calls. He sold them a bit at a time, on February 3, 6, 10, and 12, picking up an additional $3,790 on the second batch of 10. His profits—a dollar or two less than $7,000 over and above cost. That's an 800 percent gain in a month and a half.

He commented, however, that if he did the same thing ten times, chances are nine wouldn't work out that well. What you need is a quality stock and perfect timing. He explained that most people who try this time their transactions badly.

On the other hand, anybody who bought options in November and December of 1975 and held them until the January rally got underway would have had to work hard not to make money—the rally was that strong. Since that golden January, though, the market has "wiggled all over the place" and provided few opportunities for big profits. In mid-June, the market, as measured by the Dow Jones industrials, was within 2 percent of where it was in late January.

Lappy had one other big winner in early 1976, but it involved complex option transactions in Pittston, the coal producer. It is not the kind of strategy recommended to the individual both for reasons of complexity and because of commission costs. He made over $30,000.

When the stock market moves sideways, commission costs rule out active trading—unless your broker will grant you substantial discounts on option transactions. Lappy, who trades constantly, gets discounts of 40 percent. He does not pay the $25 minimum transaction fees demanded by some brokers. "If I close out 10 calls at ⅛, I pay $7 and change—not a $25 minimum transaction fee.

"Without my discounts I wouldn't be able to trade the way I do —the discount is usually my profit. If a man cannot get at least 20 percent and avoid minimum transaction fees he's going to have a lot of trouble making money. In my experience, a trader who does $2,000 to $3,000 in gross commissions a month can get 20 to 30 percent in option commission discounts."

The discount incentive is a powerful one for Lappy. "I never thought I would be carrying on like this. Every time they increase my discount, I find I do more trading than before. On some transactions I make money and on others it's a turnaround—no profit, no loss after commissions. But you never know when you'll hit that big winner, so you keep trying."

12 · Option Hedges

BEFORE THERE WAS a listed option market, the small investor rarely got involved in arbitrage—or its close relative, hedging. Arbitrage was a game for professionals. Commissions ordinarily wiped out hopes of reasonable profits for the individual. Now it's a somewhat different story. There are a number of profit possibilities in option arbitrage and hedging, though commissions do pare returns significantly.

Arbitrage? Don't grit your teeth. The concept is not so hard to understand as you might expect. An arbitrageur typically seeks profit through price disparities that exist simultaneously between the same or related securities in the same or different markets.

You might call the drugstore stamp machine an arbitrageur. It "buys" 95 cents worth of "paper"—stamps—and sells that paper to you for a dollar. The stamp machine, in effect, is taking advantage of a "low price" in one market—the post office—and selling to you in a "high price" market—the drugstore.

Or consider this arbitrage—possibly apocryphal. During a period of soaring newsprint, a man reportedly backed his truck up to the New York Times Building, bought thousands of pounds of Sunday papers at retail, and carted them directly to a junk dealer for an arbitrage profit on the "scrap."

You'll soon discover that there are many possibilities for arbitrage and hedging with options, and the only ridiculous aspect will be the commissions. You can make money in some cases nevertheless. The strategies abound. You may buy a stock and sell (write) a call against it, earning a premium. You keep your stock if its price does not advance above the call price, but the position so established is nevertheless a hedge.

That's the standard fully covered option-writing play already covered. You can buy calls and sell stock short. Or you can buy a call and sell a put on the same stock. Or you can buy one call and sell a different one—whether for a different price on the same maturity or the same price on a different maturity.

In any event, the risks in a properly constructed arbitrage are less than the potential rewards. What's more, risks (factor in the commission costs) are measurable in advance. You can take comfort in knowing your maximum exposure—a most attractive feature of the game.

FULLY COVERED OPTIONS

Let's consider the conservative game of writing calls against stock you already own—properly handled this time.

Nicholas R. Bokron, a Hartford, Connecticut, stockbroker, is the author of the excellent elementary book *How to Use Put and Call*

*Options.** He gives an extended example of covered writing, which is reprinted here with permission.

"Writer A has several securities in his portfolio on which he feels Calls can be written. The basic requirement for writing Calls is that the stocks must be such that the writer would not mind selling them if he had to. Obviously any stock position which when sold would give the writer any unnecessary losses or gains for tax purposes, would not be suitable. Finally, stock in which the individual is obligated by agreement not to sell, and securities in which the writing of options may be a violation are also not eligible. . . .

"If the stocks are called, the writer can always replace them with other securities of similar quality. He will look at the premium as a minor compensation for writing a call on a bullish stock. If, however, the stock is not called, he will pocket the premium and be quite content for having received extra income.

"Example 1:

"A $600 premium is offered for a 6-month call on Beta Co., which is currently selling for $50. Writer A holds 100 shares and decides to sell the call with an exercise price of $50. Within the 6-month period, three outcomes are possible. Beta may advance, decline, or stay the same.

"Beta advances. Because of the exercise price it would make no difference if Beta goes up to $75 or $175. Writer A must sell at $50 (assuming he does not want to offset the call). He accepts this risk and is content with an upward movement in Beta. The premium is his profit.

"Beta declines. Whether Beta goes to $45 or $25, he probably would have maintained his position and has an additional $600 income.

"Beta remains unchanged. Psychologically this appears to be the best result. Beta remained flat over the last 6 months, his equity in Beta did not change, but he is ahead $600. Writer A would not be happy, having sold the call, to see Beta advance considerably.

* Published by John Magee, Inc., Springfield, Massachusetts.

Nor would he be happy if Beta declined in value and he had maintained his long position. . . .

"Many writers like to have their portfolios constantly at work. . . . Suppose Writer B buys 100 Omega Company at $40, writes a 6-month call with an exercise price of $40, and receives a $400 premium. There are three possible outcomes during the next 6 months. Omega will either advance, decline, or remain unchanged.

Option is exercised—Omega advances		
Option is exercised @ 40		$4,000
Less commission		64
Net return		$3,936
Plus premium		400
Equity level		$4,336
Minus total cost (100 Omega @ 40 plus commission)		4,064
Profit		$ 262
Return on investment (profit/total cost)		7%
Annualized		14%
Option expires—Omega declines or remains unchanged		
Total cost		$4,064
Minus premium		400
Cost/breakeven point		$3,664

"If Writer B decides to sell Omega, he can add about $58 (commission cost on sale at 36⅝) to his breakeven point and his new breakeven point is $3722.

"If Writer B decides to keep Omega, and writes another call, his cost basis for determining his new breakeven point is $3,664. It is quite important to realize that once an option expires, new options may be written. Let us assume that Omega was $35 when the option expired. At about $164 below the breakeven point, a loss in equity is evident. However, Writer B is able to sell another 6-month Call and receives $350. His exercise price is now $35. By doing this, he will lower his breakeven point to $3314 ($3664 less $350), thus turning an obvious loss into a profit for the present. The following analysis will take the writer through the next 6 months.

"A profit potential of $127 after holding Omega for one year may not seem like much (about a 3% return on the total cost).

Option expires—Omega declines or remains unchanged

Cost of Omega	$4,064
Minus first premium	400
First breakeven point	$3,664
Minus second premium	350
Second breakeven point	$3,314

Option is exercised—Omega advances

Sale of Omega @ 35	$3,500
Minus commission	59
Net return	$3,441
Plus first and second premiums	750
Total return	$4,191
Minus total cost	4,064
Profit	$ 127
Return on investment (profit/total cost)	3%

However, it is Writer B's intent not to hold Omega unless he has sold an option on it. By writing options as Omega declined, Writer B may be hedging his losses while constantly receiving income from owning Omega."

Let's look at a few complex strategies. Ivan F. Boesky, a member of the New York Stock Exchange who does business under his own name in Whitehall Street, is an arbitrage specialist. He has prepared a number of examples of option hedging that illustrate some of the less complex of scores of highly complicated strategies. His examples record results after commissions so that you can determine whether you are actually likely to make a profit in a particular case—or just spin your wheels. Prices in the examples reflect closing levels on January 21, 1976.

SPREADS

A spread, as you will recall, is undertaken through the purchase of one option and the sale of another option on the same stock. The investor does not buy the shares themselves, hoping rather to profit from a change in the initial difference between the prices of the two options. There are spreads for bulls—those who expect the underlying shares to rise—and spreads for bears. The latter expect that the underlying shares will fall.

Suppose you had done a bull spread in mid-January when Sears Roebuck shares were selling at 69¼. For example, you might have bought Sears April 70s—the right to purchase 1,000 Sears shares at a striking price of 70. The cost to you would have been at 3—$300 per 100-share call; a total cost on the 10 calls of $3,000. At the same time, let's say you sold 10 Sears April 80s (exercise price 80) at ¾—$75 per 100-share call. You would have received a total premium of $750.

The most you could lose would be $2,250 plus transaction costs. That is, you can lose all you invested in the options you bought if they expire worthless. But this loss is reduced by the premium you got for the 80s—or $3,000 less $750.

If you are right and Sears advances to 80, the 70s would advance to 10, since they can be exercised at 70 on a stock worth 80. That means proceeds of $10,000 on the ten options, less the cost—$3,000. The gain is $7,000. These are the results at expiration on the assumption of Sears at 80 and in tabular form:

	Before Commission	After Commission	
Proceeds on options at 80:			
Cost of 80s 0 (expire worthless)	$ 750.00	—$ 89.93	$ 660.07
Gains on 80s	$ 750.00		0
Proceeds on options at 70:			$ 660.07
Cost of 70s	$10,000	—$213.62	$9,786.38
Gain on 70s	— 3,000	—$119.90	— 3,119.90
Total invested	7,000		$6,666.48
	$2,250.00		2,459.83
Gains as % of investment	344.4%		297.8%

Remember that many such spreads are closed out as total losses. Now let's look at a bear spread. Mr. Boesky describes the following bear spread. With McDonald's Corporation shares trading at 61½, you buy 10 McDonald's April 60s at 4 and sell 10 McDonald's 50s at 11½.

The most you are likely to lose is $2,500 plus commissions of $360.19. This would happen if McDonald's closed at 60 or at any price above 60.

In that event, your April 60s would expire worthless and they cost you $4,000. The April 50s which you sold for a 11½-point premium—$11,500—would have to be repurchased to avoid the high costs you experience as the result of the inevitable call. The replacement April 50s will cost you 10 points (option price 50—stock at 60) or $10,000. You thus keep only $1,500 of the premium. Thus your total loss would be $2,500—the $4,000 spent on the worthless options less $1,500 net premium—plus the $360.19 repurchase commissions.

If, on the other hand, the McDonald's shares drop, you will make money. If McDonald's declined to 50 or below, you would profit on the options you sold and the options you purchased would expire without value.

Here are the results in tabular form:

Before Commissions		After Commissions	
Proceeds of 60s	0	(expire worthless)	0
Cost of 60s	$ 4,000		$ 4,129.80
Loss on 60s	($4,000)		($ 4,129.80)
Proceeds of 60s	$11,500		$11,269.61
Value on expiration	0		0
Net gain	7,500	+129.80	7,139.81
Total invested	2,500	−230.39	2,860.19
Gain as % of investment	300%		249.6%

BEARISH HEDGE

You buy 10 Eastman Kodak April 110 options at 8½ and sell 1,000 shares of Eastman Kodak short at the current market price of 115.*

* Assuming puts are allowed to trade as is anticipated, the same hedge could be done with the purchase of 10 puts instead of the short sale of 1,000 Kodak shares. The expenses would be less, the risks reduced, and the investment smaller.

The options have an intrinsic value of 5, since the stock is selling at 115 and they thus cost you 3½ points over and above that. The most you can lose in the hedge—no matter how much Eastman Kodak shares advance—is that 3½ points plus transaction charges. The reason your loss is limited to that 3½ points is that you can always exercise those options—call 1,000 Eastman Kodak shares—and use them to cover your short position.

Suppose Eastman Kodak shares decline to 100 at the time the options are about to expire. The results:

	Before Commissions		After Commissions
Cost of options	$ 8,500.00	+196.86	$ 8,696.86
Proceeds of options	0	(worthless at expiration)	0
Loss on options	($8,500.00)		($ 8,696.86)
Proceeds of stocks	$115,000.00	−807.30	$114,192.70
Cost of stock	100,000.00	+807.30	100,807.30
Gain on stock	$15,000		$ 13,385.40
Total gain	$ 6,500		$ 4,688.54
Total invested	8,500		8,696.86
Gain as % of investment	76.5%		53.9%

TIME SPREAD

This popular method of spreading involves the simultaneous purchase and sale of similar options on the same stock at the same striking prices but with different maturities.

With, say, Polaroid at 33¾, you buy 10 Polaroid July 35 call options at 4⅛ and *sell* 10 Polaroid April 35 call options at 2⅞. It should be obvious that the more time there is left for the option holder, the more value his option has. Thus, the April option would never rise in price to a level above the July option since the striking price of the two options is identical.

How much can you lose on this one? The 10 July options you purchased cost $412.50 each (4⅛) or $4,125. You received premiums of $287.50 each (2⅞) or $2,875 for the ten April options sold. The difference ($4,125 minus $2,875) is $1,250. That sum, plus your transaction costs, is the most you can lose.

If Polaroid closed essentially unchanged—at 33 or thereabouts, but specifically below 35—at the April expiration, your July options should sell at the same price the Aprils did in the beginning. This is because the Julys would have the same time to run as the Aprils did previously. You sell the Julys for 27⁄8.

Here are the results in tabular form:

	Before Commissions		After Commissions
Proceeds on Aprils	$2,875	−$118.66	$2,756.34
Cost of Aprils	0	(expire worthless)	0
Gain on Aprils	2,875		2,756.34
Proceeds on Julys	2,875	−$118.66	2,756.34
Cost of Julys	4,125	+ 131.04	4,256.04
Loss on Julys	(1,250)		(1,499.70)
Total gain	$1,625		$1,256.64
Total investment	$1,250		$1,499.70
Gain as % of investment	30%	(loss)	16.2%

It should be clear from these examples that the commission costs in doing option transactions are not nominal by any means. It should also be clear that these techniques are for those willing to devote a considerable amount of time and thought to their investments. Once these and other techniques are learned, they may become as routine as—well, hanging wallpaper in a domed ceiling; possible, but tricky. These examples are called "simple" by Mr. Boesky, and he notes that there are folks out there who are doing all sorts of things that are more complex than these. My suggestion is to do dry runs before you take the plunge on a sink-or-swim basis. If you hedge carefully, your losses can be kept within known limits. Don't kid yourself—you'll need expert counsel, and more study, perhaps, than just this chapter. Mr. Boesky warns: Don't devote five minutes a day to option hedges and expect to wind up rich. The pros are at it five days a week and don't always succeed.

DOWN AND OUT OPTIONS

The limited price option—informally referred to as the down and out option—combines the excitement of a Dutch auction with the perils of the betting window at Belmont. Its most prominent advocate, Michael B. Salke of Gordon & Co., Boston, admits that the down and outer is riskier, but states that it is also cheaper and potentially more profitable. He added, somewhat defensively, that at Gordon & Co. you get your profits when you are right. It is his contention that the listed option exchanges often do not reflect the full gains investors have been led to expect when the underlying shares advance smartly.

His options are certainly different. The down and out option has a series of expiration prices at interim expiration dates. If the stock you have an option on goes down instead of up, you are out.

Here's an example from the prospectus Gordon & Co. filed with the Securities and Exchange Commission. The Gordon firm is currently on the other side of every option written by the firm.

An investor pays $5,100 for a six-month, ten-day limited price call option covering 800 shares of XYZ, at an exercise price of $50 and with an expiration price of $46.25 during the first monthly term of the option; $47 during the second monthly term; $47.75 during the third monthly term; $48.50 during the fourth monthly term; $49.25 during the fifth monthly term; $50 during the last month-and-ten-day term of the option.

If the market for XYZ falls to $46.25 a share any time within 30 days of the investor's purchase—the expiration price during the first monthly term—and he has not sold or exercised the option, he would have lost his entire $5,100. He would have no possibility of recovery, since his option would have expired.

The Gordon prospectus warns that the expiration price provision in Gordon's limited price options "makes them a less desirable and more speculative option than a conventional option—no investor should commit any amount of money to the purchase of limited price options unless he is able to withstand the loss of the entire amount so committed."

The price expiration feature of the limited price option makes it more attractive to writers (sellers). They are content with smaller premiums than writers of standard options. The prospectus says:

"No buyer should purchase a limited price option if he can purchase a conventional option for a comparable premium."

The option seller who also owns the underlying shares likes the limited price option because he need not hold shares that are declining in price—once the option against them expires.

The option buyer pays even less if he exercises or resells within the life of the option. He gets back a portion of his cost. That is, the option's remaining time has resale value.

Gordon & Co. writes limited price options on most issues—stocks, bonds, and warrants—traded on national security exchanges and on many issues traded in the over-the-counter market. Investors can buy direct from Gordon & Co. at no commission charge—or they can buy through their own brokers. Brokers who buy from Gordon receive a 5 percent discount, and the charge to their customers should be identical to charges direct from the Boston firm, Mr. Salke said.

Other leading brokers have in the past dealt in the limited price options—both puts and calls, like Gordon—without registering them with the Securities and Exchange Commission. Most firms, in view of the substantial risks involved, limited the options to their wealthiest and most sophisticated clients.

PART III

SELLING

13 · Big Winners
Are Good Sellers

REMEMBER THE BASIC RULE of success in Wall Street. Buy cheap and sell dear. Remember John Steinbeck's story *The Pearl?* A poor native finds a great pearl, slightly flawed. He takes it to be polished. He is offered a considerable sum of money for it, but much less than the value of a solid pearl that size. He decides to have a layer or two of the pearl removed, thinking to get a fortune for it if it turns out to be pure almost throughout. But layer after layer comes off and the pearl is still imperfect. Finally, the pearl is gone, the work table covered with shell after shell of imperfect pearl.

This happened to thousands of investors who bought Polaroid, Avon Products, and Simplicity Pattern cheap. The only difference is these investors still have kernels of value. They may never hold a giant pearl again. It mustn't happen to you.

Investors are remarkably like the characters in Anton Chekhov's play *The Cherry Orchard.* They hear the woodchoppers cutting away at the priceless grove and are somehow incapable of speaking out—acting to stop the destruction. There are always a dozen rational reasons for keeping a stock. I told myself I was keeping New York Times stock all through the bear market so that I would know how investors felt. Thank goodness I had only 20 shares. Still, I lost half my money.

John Hartwell, of the Hartwell Campbell mutual fund, one of the best bull market money managers, told me frankly that he had broken the cardinal rule of investing—many times. He didn't sell when his investment judgment proved to be faulty. Nobody's perfect, but we needn't be fools.

If we're wrong, we're wrong. Let's admit it. If we were right, but no longer are, take the money and run. It is better to run with half a loaf than with no bread at all.

You know my philosophy. Whenever you can, buy stocks the institutions haven't discovered and wouldn't touch if they knew about them. But you're bound to crawl in bed on stocks with the mutual funds, banks, and insurance companies from time to time. Or, assuming you've bought well and your company is a big winner, they'll crawl in bed with you. In either event, it is essential that you be prepared to act quickly if the big boys start selling. We've seen that they can sweep away the gains of a decade in a few months of concentrated selling. And once the melee begins, it almost never stops short of disaster.

The mutual funds are the worst. They report holdings quarterly. The last thing they want to admit is that they were the last to get out of Four Seasons Nursing. You'll find that comeback performances are generally slow in coming. Memorex, the computer peripheral equipment and magnetic tape maker, clearly illustrates the point. It was several years after the bombing began before the victim began to recover.* Usually, you won't have the time or capital to wait.

The trouble is, it isn't easy to develop a coherent selling philosophy that will protect you against serious loss. Too many methods will send you to your broker in a frenzy far too early. Frequently, stocks will falter temporarily on minor disappointment, then resume their profitable upward course. You want to be able to hang in there when this happens.

* Memorex fell from 173⅞ in late 1969 after IBM pinched off markets. The stock traded at 1½ for years thereafter and as late as early 1975. Booming profits finally brought a partial comeback—to 30 in early 1976. But the company remained a single IBM price cut away from disaster.

THE STOP-LOSS ROUTE TO RUIN

Theoretically, a stop-loss order is a nifty way to handle the selling problem. You call your broker and tell him to enter a good-until-canceled stop order on the floor of the exchange. He calls the specialist there who handles the stock and the order goes into the specialist's book at the price you stipulate.

The specialist refers to this ledger book constantly. If the price of the stock in question drops to the level at which you have placed a stop, it becomes a market order and the specialist executes it.

Ordinarily stop-loss orders go in at a percentage below the price at which the shareholder bought his stock—10 percent, 15 percent, or whatever he is willing to lose. The shareholder reasons that if he is sold out at, say, 15 percent below his purchase price he'll still have most of his capital and can reinvest in a more promising stock.

Many investors use a series of ascending stops to lock up profits in a rising stock. The method became a bit too popular after Nicolas Darvas, an adagio dancer, wrote *How I Made $2,000,000 in the Stock Market.* Darvas made investing sound as easy as ballroom dancing. The book was popular, and he attributed some of his market success to the two-step stop-loss technique. Buy a promising stock—the bulls were winning in 1960 when the book came out—and stop it, say, 10 percent below purchase price. When the stock has moved up several points, withdraw the old stop and put in a new one at the same relative level below the new price. Locks up profits, right? Wrong. The method got so popular that Wall Street began to notice a new effect. Call it Darvas Disease.

A mild market break would set off thousands of stop orders 10 percent below current market, in turn setting off the 15 percenters. Result: Market disaster.

Some folks still use the Darvas technique. But it is risky—and so are all stop orders in times of stress. Better you develop some method in which human intelligence plays a role—or you may wind up with unnecessary losses. Consider what stop-loss orders did to shareholders of Schenley Industries, the liquor distiller.

It had been a pretty exciting day for the company's shareholders. Schenley was a hot takeover candidate and discussions were under-way with P. Lorillard, the tobacco company. Two bad habits under one roof, sniffed the moralists. But Wall Street saw it differently. There would be obvious economies for a company that merchan-dised both product lines, which were frequently sold by the same merchants. Anyway, the merger had caught the imagination of Wall Street, and Schenley stock was acting well. But suddenly, the shares wavered on a spurt in trading volume. The New York Stock Exchange moved quickly to halt trading. Last price before the halt: 58. It was March 15, 1967.

Rumor had it that the merger discussions had been terminated. The suspense lasted for hours. Finally, just before the close of trading on the Big Board and without clarification from anyone, the Schenley shares traded one more time. Since selling pressure had been mounting, the trade was a disaster. In all, over 300,000 shares crossed the tape at a stunning 8-point loss—50. Cynics com-plained that the Big Board had failed to maintain an orderly mar-ket—though it would be too much to expect the specialist to "eat" all that Schenley stock. There were big foreign sellers and some inadvertent sellers among the Little Guys.

After the close, the New York Stock Exchange told the world what it had learned long before that final trade. The Schenley-Lorillard merger discussions were still under way. Did the Schenley specialist, Robert L. Stott, know that when he made the trade? He told the author as this was written that he did not. Mr. Stott, one of the Big Board's most-respected members, was on the stock ex-change's board of governors at the time.

The Schenley trade at 50 knocked off individual stop-loss orders at a number of interim points on the way down, beginning at 58. Anyone with 100 shares stopped at 58 and sold out at 50 lost $800.

It happened to Herman Lang of Flushing, New York. He was incredulous.

Bob Stott bought 80,000 shares at 50 on that final trade. Meshulam Riklis bought the rest. Mr. Riklis, Rapid American's chief, admitted a couple of days later that he had made a killing. And why not? The stock opened the following morning at 60¾, well above where it had started before the rumor made the rounds. Mr. Riklis said he cleared over a million dollars on his overnight speculation.* Mr. Stott said that he too made a bundle. Obviously, those who placed stop-loss orders at any point between 58 and 50 did not. At least they learned a lesson. Stop-loss orders were and are an imperfect tool at best. Now that institutions bomb stocks on the slightest bad news, the stop-loss order becomes an instrument of self-immolation. A better approach to salvation: vigilance.

THE SELLING BEE

Short of losing all your hard-won gains in a stock that has had its day, the worst thing that can happen to you is for you to misinterpret a short, intensive burst of selling as the beginning of a rout for your favorite longtime holding. If the selling represents interim profit-taking and not a fundamental reappraisal of the company's prospects, you won't want to sell. Winners are not that easy to find.

What you need to do is to review the situation as calmly as you can. If you've been doing your homework right along, chances are you'll be able to figure whether the burst of selling reflects a blip on the radar screen of little significance or the beginning of a serious deterioration in the company's prospects.

* Years later, Mr. Riklis' Rapid American Corporation bought out Schenley in two successive tender offers. The takeover proceedings were awash with lawsuits, as yet unresolved. The second offer came in at a price roughly half that of the first.

14 · Uppers and Downers

Suppose you bought Pittston Company, a major producer of the special coal used to produce steel. You paid 12 at the end of September 1974 and were pleasantly surprised at how quickly you made out. Within weeks the stock reached 16. Should you sell out and look like a hero? A speculator would. He's crapshooting and he's just made his number. He'll bail out and look for another speculation. But if you sell, you've got to find a new game. It's time to have another look at Pittston in the light of that 33-percent gain. Presumably you bought the stock as an investment—because you came to the conclusion that the nation and Pittston would be producing more coal in the energy crisis. It's either coal or nuclear power, and there is more of the former than the latter—cheaper, too. Pittston's metallurgical coal has brought the Japanese calling. For this and other reasons, Pittston is thriving and the backlog is rising. You call a friend in the Street and learn that a leading investment banker has raised its earnings estimate for the company by 50 percent since you first decided to buy the stock. Pittston, which normally carries a price/earnings ratio of 11, has been selling at less than 6 times earnings. The new estimate makes the stock seem even cheaper.

You are aware that the Japanese are seeking a lower price from Pittston (they got it, too) and there is labor unrest. (Wildcat strikes plagued the company in mid-1976.) But you bought Pittston for the long term.

Pittston's coal production could rise by 50 percent by the end of the decade, and even at the lower profit margins Wall Street expects, earnings could rise in the same few years by 25 percent. Hmmm. If the earnings do that and the stock begins to approach its normal price/earnings ratio—or even holds its own—the shares will go higher. These seem to be good reasons for holding Pittston for even better gains ahead—though there is no assurance that the stock will actually go higher. There never is. The stock could begin to sell at an even lower price/earnings multiple and the earnings might not materialize.

A word about growth stocks here. Frequently, investors buy "growth" at price/earnings multiples of 40 or more. Lots of brokers will tell a customer that a stock like Johnson & Johnson, for example, will "never be cheap." It's a risky business. Say a growth stock is earning $1 a share and it is priced at $40. That's a price/earnings ratio of 40. Chances are that's well above its average price/earnings ratio established over the years. Nevertheless, a broker comes out with a new research report predicting the company will earn $1.25 a share. In the first place, make sure the broker isn't the investment banker for the company. The report will say so if that's the case. Anyway, the implicit assumption is that the shares are now worth 40 times $1.25 a share—$50. People fall for this all the time, and sometimes they make money. It is not, in my opinion, a way to get rich or even sleep nights.

It's true that the company might then earn $1.50 a share and be worth a theoretical 60. But sooner or later, that remarkable growth is going to stop—or even appear to stop. Sometimes a single weak quarter can bring on the bombers.

You know, of course, that there never is a guarantee that a stock will go higher. But think how much less likely you are to suffer a serious injury in a bombing raid if your stock is selling at a price/earnings ratio of, say, 4—well below the stock's normal P/E range —than if it has a current P/E of 40—well above its normal range. As a matter of fact, Pittston reached 36 in the first quarter of 1976, but due to a quantum jump in earnings was still selling at a low P/E of 7.

We all make mistakes. The saddest spectacle in any market is the man who rides a stock to the basement because he cannot admit that he was wrong. That's an ego trip of the worst sort. It is easy to understand why some investors bought Bunker Ramo shares at 3 at the end of 1974. The company is in the glamour on-line computer terminal business and its stock quotation machines grace many brokerage office desks, a constant reminder that this company is alive and well—maybe even a live one. One reason the stock was so low in December 1974 was that Bunker would clearly report a loss in 1975. But management was moving to reduce employment and to bring costs under control generally. If the company was successful in its efforts to affect a turnaround, the stock could go considerably higher. In fact, the stock did reach 8 in mid-1975 and the shares seemed to be on the comeback trail. But despite effective cost-cutting and the prospect of an early return to profitability, operations continued in the red all through 1975. When the stock market's bull rally of 1975 ran out, Bunker Ramo shares started down again. By year's end, the shares were back at 3 and a fraction. There's still hope for a turnaround. But a reevaluation would show both encouraging and disturbing signs. The company has reduced debt. But the company's balance sheet shrank by $50 million in 1975 as the company pared assets to finance its operating losses and debt repayment. A mistake? Perhaps. On the other hand, if your long-term analysis suggests that patience will be rewarded through an above-average potential for the shares by the end of the decade, perhaps you are justified in concluding that you've not made a mistake. If you aren't prepared to add to your holdings, you are probably kidding yourself—breaking the cardinal rule. Maybe you don't have enough capital to add to your holdings. Try Leon Levy's rule, then. Mr. Levy, a principal of Oppenheimer & Co., says, "I try never to buy shares in a company I wouldn't want to own outright if I had the money." (He adds, with a twinkle, "Of course I cheat a little.")

BAD PRESS—UPPER OR DOWNER?

Once an industry or a company hits the Wall Street skids—loses popularity there—the siege is apt to be long and hard, perhaps as long as a decade. Consider tobacco. After the Surgeon General ruled cigarettes harmful to health, cigarette ads were banned from television. Giving up smoking became a national preoccupation. However, there was to be a comeback for the tobacco stocks—later, much later. The weed proved to be persistent. Those who bought tobacco shares at the "worst" time did well.

Now the Real Estate Investment Trusts are in the same predicament. Once high-flyers as real estate mania prevailed, the shares of the REITs—mutual funds buying interests in real estate—sank to fractions of a point. Bankruptcy was just around the corner for many in the real estate bust of the early 1970s—one of the worst in history. But now, we begin to hear cautious words from Wall Street that the REITs—some of them, anyway—may come back. It's unlikely to be soon. But if you're in the mood for a long-shot speculation, you could hardly find a long shot with greater possible rewards. Look at the facts: Demand for real estate of many types remains at low ebb. Building-material costs are sky-high, making it too expensive for many to build. As for the single-family home— rarely involved except indirectly in REIT commitments—it is almost priced out of existence. Mortgage money is too dear to make most real estate projects practical—whether private home or office building.

Meanwhile, the trusts continue to mark down properties, since there is simply no way the properties will ever approach the values assigned to them on trust books. Recently, the banks, which the trusts owe billions, have begun agreeing to cancel some trust debt in exchange for properties. Since the swap properties are mostly nonearning assets, the trusts benefit through reduced interest expense without a corresponding decrease in revenues. The swaps sometimes allow the trusts to reduce loss reserves. Since the reserves have already been charged against income, the trust experiences extraordinary gains. The result of all this restructuring by the trusts is that values are beginning to emerge which are not reflected in the stock market. Some trusts are beginning to show prospects of recovery—far down the trail. If you can evaluate the prospects for continued cooperation from lender banks, you may well find among the trusts shares with an excellent chance for recovery in from three to five years.

Scared? If you don't do your homework you should be scared. Remember the rule, though: Buy fear, sell greed. Summing up the bad press problem: Bad news is bad for stocks. But once the bad news is out of the way, a depressed stock will seek its natural level. Millions have been made by the intrepid who found value and invested. You'll have to pick carefully and you'll make mistakes. But if the prices are as low as those of the trusts in mid-1976, the exercise could be worth your while.

IT'S DISCOUNTED

Many times after bad news is released by a company, its stock will hold steady. The bad news has already been discounted. If following a stream of bad news items the stock holds steady, we can assume that all the bad news has been discounted and that the stock can be bought for the long pull. The reverse is also true. If a stock doesn't rise following good news—or, worse yet, if it should actually move lower after good news—it is because the high price of the stock has already discounted the good news.

FAILING EARNINGS

Once you sweep away the froth, you can safely remark that stocks go up because earnings go up. Nobody wants to own the shares of a company that loses money chronically or even of a company that is moving backward rather than forward. Even the threat of an earnings setback can be enough to give a stock the blues. You know what happens when the earnings of a Nifty Fifty stock like Simplicity Pattern waver. The institutions dump it fast. Nevertheless, there are stocks that are worth keeping—even when earnings go down. This includes, of course, some of those stocks the institutions are so quick to dump. A down quarter may be just one down quarter. You should make it your business to find out whether the down quarter is likely to be repeated.

Some believe that a company becomes a sell—willy-nilly—on two down quarters. That's probably a good general rule. On the other hand, this can happen because a fine corporation is spending heavily to enter a new marketing area and is following a conservative policy of writing off costs against earnings as costs are incurred. It's spelled P-O-L-A-R-O-I-D. (Polaroid became a sell for other reasons. The analysts grew too enthusiastic about the SX-70 and bid the stock up too fast too soon, another warning signal for those who don't like to overstay their party welcome.)

Carefully evaluate your company's explanation of any earnings setback. If you are convinced the problem is temporary or if it reflects an act of God, you may be justified in holding or even increasing your position on weakness. Keep an eye on the price/earnings multiple. You should be more suspicious of a company with a P/E of 25 or better than you need be of a company with a P/E of, say, 7—particularly if that 7 is below the company's normal price/earnings multiple.

If your company has a record of solid earnings growth, you may perhaps discount a couple of bad quarters with reasonable safety. If you are going to sit out the storm, it is probably a good idea to use John Magee's 13-week protection limit, discussed in the next section, as a guide to selling. It can keep you out of a lot of trouble —like the Polaroid dive from a shade short of 150 to 15; like Simplicity Pattern's rollercoaster ride from 60 down to 6 in two years ending in late 1974, or its level of eight years earlier when it began its spectacular ride to success.

JOHN MAGEE'S LUCKY 13

Every sound holding in your investment portfolio is going to experience sinking spells from time to time. Stocks will dip with the general market, and they will dip as speculators take profits. They will dip on rumors, and they will dip on bad news. Buying stocks is a little like fishing. When the float dips you don't throw your rod into the lake. You wait silently in anticipation that a fish may take the hook—your prize for patience. On the other hand, you don't want to lose your tackle to the Loch Ness monster. You've got to have some way of telling whether you are experiencing a stock market sinking spell or something really heavy.

We've seen that the stop-loss order has serious shortcomings in a market in which the institutions are banging away at stocks. There must be a better way. Many believe that John Magee has found it. His method requires vigilance and discipline.

Mr. Magee is a Springfield, Massachusetts, market observer. With Robert D. Edwards, he is author of *Technical Analysis of Stock Trends*.* It is regarded as a classic in its field.

Mr. Magee uses a moving 13-week parameter of prices as a selling guide. His sell signal is the lowest price the stock sold for during the 13-week period.

In following Mr. Magee's rule, you sell your stock the day after it closes below the lowest price indicated in the 13 weeks.† At the end of the week, you drop the earliest week in your schedule and add the week just past. If you follow this guideline you'll avoid selling on temporary weakness in most cases. You'll also manage to sell near the top before a sudden and persistent downturn.

The method has proved useful in dealing with stocks that experience volatile swings. Often, a good stock that is headed generally higher will sink a number of points time and again along the way.

Mr. Magee recommended Digital Equipment, the small computer maker, at 70 in March of 1975. Using his moving protective limit rule, clients would have kept the stock all the way up to 182½ and back down to 162 without selling. If the stock was sold at

---

* Published by Mr. Magee at 360 Worthington Street, Springfield.
† It is generally a good idea to sell an hour after the opening—after any initial selling pressure has dissipated.

159, the limit when this was written, his clients would have more than doubled their money. So you see, there were dips along the way, but never a big enough dip to lead to the sale of Digital.

Mr. Magee recommended Deere & Co. on Sept. 27, 1975. At the time, Deere was selling at 47½ and the protective limit was 38¼. The limit was moved up with the stock and was low enough in December—45½—that the stock survived a reaction from 52 to 46. Deere reached 70 in February of 1976, then dropped to 60. By that time the protective limit was 54 and the stock remained in client portfolios.

The 13-week-low selling rule is not an infallible way to beat the market, as Mr. Magee is quick to point out. But it beats the stop-loss order. Many an individual who puts in a stop loss has wondered whether the market didn't make a dip so that his stop loss and others could be picked off by some manipulator. As Mr. Magee puts it, "You can't be manipulated [out of your position] because only you know the limits."*

Mr. Magee says that many people are good at buying stocks well, but few can decide when to sell. "Most sell too soon and lose profits or they wait too long—until they have a big loss."

* On June 3, 1976, the New York Stock Exchange fined specialist Warren R. Haas $18,000 for pricing a stock too low on the opening in July 1975. In the past, Mr. Haas has frequently been offered as an exchange spokesman and has been thrust into the breech when a weaker specialist proved unequal to the task of handling a stock under pressure. Mr. Haas' fine arose out of his handling of a stock assigned to his specialist unit, Benton Tompane & Company. Though unidentified by the exchange, the stock was said to be U. S. Steel. The stock had closed the night before at 58⅞. Mr. Haas opened the shares at 10:01 A.M. at 57, the lowest price at which they traded all day. In setting the price at that level, several stop orders were touched off at 57 though they were slated for execution at prices ranging from 58½ down to 57⅞. The stock closed the day at 57⅞. Mr. Haas was found to have bought some of the 5,000 shares in the opening block himself, without obtaining the approval of a floor official as required by exchange rules. Poor judgment at least. His friends say the fine was a bad rap for a good man. It was a rare case of public censure of a specialist but may be an indication of things to come. The exchange's new board chairman, William M. Batton, had gained attention before assuming the post as author of a report calling for a major overhaul of the specialist system.

THE YIELD METHOD OF SELLING

With the advent of the computer age, Wall Street professionals have been devising new ways to gauge performance and new ways to determine when to bail out. Some of the tests can be applied by small investors even without computers.

For some time now, A. Feldesman & Associates, Inc. of Cleveland have been buying quality stocks offering relatively high yields and selling them when their yields have dropped significantly. Mr. Feldesman charges a basic portfolio management fee of about $2,000 a year and is thus priced out of the range of most small investors. But he has passed along a syllabus that should help those who seek the high yields he insists on before making a commitment.

He looks for quality companies that offer a yield of 7 percent or better. There are many utilities that yield 7 percent—most of the time. However, the utilities do not meet one of Mr. Feldesman's standards. He will not buy a stock with a capitalization consisting of more than 40 percent debt.*

Once he finds a company that passes the 7 percent yield and

* In June 1976 Interactive Data Corp. reported that 330 common and preferred issues out of 2,122 stocks on the Big Board offered yields of 9 per cent, 98 issues offered at least 10. Two out of three stocks yielding 10 were electric utilities, and this list was dominated by preferreds. Relatively few of the issues, whether 9 or 10 percent producers, would qualify for the Feldesman portfolios —everything considered.

DIGITAL EQUIPMENT WEEKLY, 1975–1976

Memo: Following a trend. The black line below the weekly high-low-close chart indicates the lowest price at which the stock sold in the previous 13 weeks. If the stock moves up, this line is adjusted upward from time to time as shown here. If it goes down and breaks this "13-week" line, the stock is sold. The method can protect accrued profits in large degree, retain a good position during a profitable move, and get the investor out before a sharp breakdown, and—safely, before he has lost all his gains or sustained a loss.

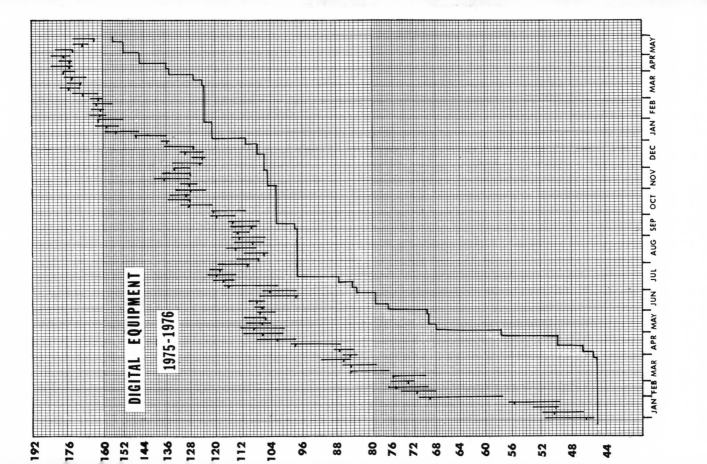

DIGITAL EQUIPMENT

1975-1976

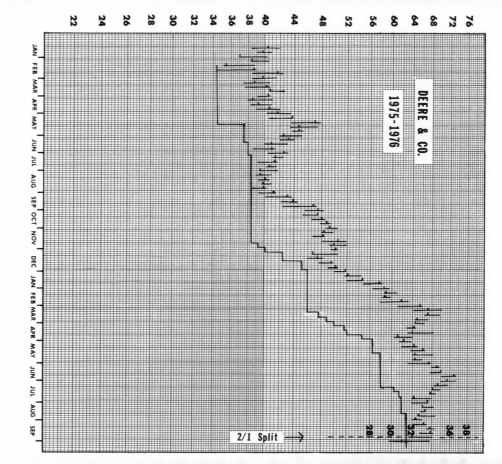

DEERE & CO.
WEEKLY, 1975–1976

Memo: Trend action in DEERE. The solid black line below the high-low-close chart of the stock's price indicates the lowest price during the 13 previous weeks. Eventually it will be broken and the stock will be sold, but the greater part of accrued profits will be retained. In this case the stock actually was sold (by customers of John Magee, Inc., Technical Analysts of Stock Trends), ten days after the September 2-for-1 split, when the adjusted stock broke the "13-week Limit" of 31½.

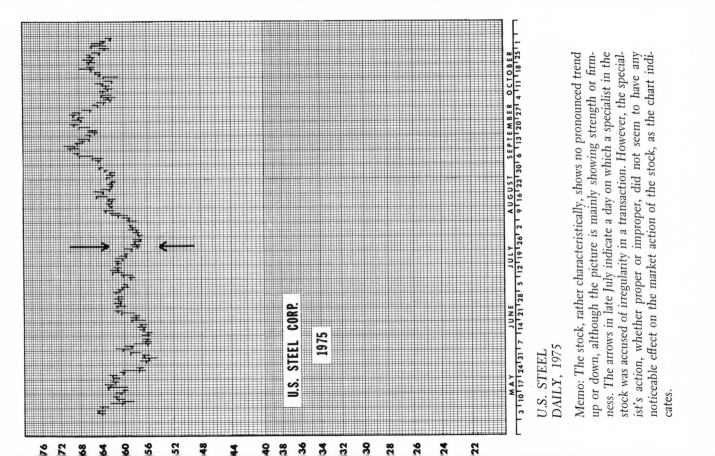

U.S. STEEL
DAILY, 1975

Memo: The stock, rather characteristically, shows no pronounced trend up or down, although the picture is mainly showing strength or firmness. The arrows in late July indicate a day on which a specialist in the stock was accused of irregularity in a transaction. However, the specialist's action, whether proper or improper, did not seem to have any noticeable effect on the market action of the stock, as the chart indicates.

low debt tests, he then looks to see if the company has reduced its dividend during the last ten years. Any company that has reduced its dividend does not qualify. On the other hand, he does not count cuts in extra dividends and cuts in stock dividends.

Mr. Feldesman suggests that any individual who follows his method does not invest more than 30 percent of his capital in one industry and that he limit his investment to 10 percent of his capital in one stock.

The individual will have to invest about $30,000—and in low-priced stocks—in order to diversify sufficiently. It is important that individuals find companies with strong balance sheets and substantial cash flow, two factors that also weigh in Mr. Feldesman's decisions.

Selling is the key to success in the Feldesman system. A cut in the dividend or a deterioration in the balance sheet or cash flow should lead the investor to sell his stock. Also, if the yield of a particular holding drops to 4 percent as the stock goes up, the stock should be sold.

When ther are other 7-percent-yield stocks that meet the Feldesman criteria, he sells shares as soon as yield drops to 5.5 percent.

He commented:

"There are two advantages to this. The investor has increased his initial investment and locked in a capital gain. Most of our year-old portfolios that began with 7 percent yields now yield about 9 percent."

But the system is not perfect, as Mr. Feldesman admits.

"The Achilles heel of my system is the dividend cut. . . . We held Ford Motor Company when it cut its dividend after more than 15 years of rising distributions. We lost money when we got out, but that's a hazard of the game."

Mr. Feldesman also noted that there are times when he moves into cash because yields do not meet his standards for investing. The individual interested in preserving his capital ought to consider doing the same.

GOING FOR BROKE

Speculating in the securities of a shaky manufacturing company? Use this bankruptcy model developed in 1968 by Professor Edward Altman of New York University and avoid investments in companies about to go under.

Divide by total assets each of the four following factors in turn and then assign the indicated weighting factor: working capital, weighted 1.2; retained earnings, weighted 1.4; earnings before interest and taxes, weighted 3.3; and sales, weighted 1.0. Next, divide market value of the equity and preferred shares by total liabilities and weight 0.6. Add the five results, noting pluses and minuses. If the company scores below 1.81, consider it to be bankruptcy bound. For example, a major electronics company bailed out by its principal lender in 1972 would have scored 0.85 then. It is still being propped up by the lender and still scores below 1.81. The equation is not linear, however. That is, the 0.85 score does not necessarily suggest that the company was half as good as needed for investor acceptance. Example 2: Potter Instruments, which failed in 1974, gave ample warning by Altman's test. It scored 0.61 on his scale more than two years before that. One more thing: a result barely above 1.81 is, of course, a distinct warning!

15 · Dollar Cost Averaging

WHEN PURCHASING a vacation homesite, we learned that the developer was offering a 10 percent discount to those willing to buy two adjacent lots, and an additional 5 percent discount for cash.

We jumped at both options. Thus, instead of paying the raw price of $5,200 per lot, each lot came to $4,420.*

It was certainly all we could afford. But we were able to build shortly thereafter because the equity in the two lots served as a down payment on a house.

Later as I sat in the living room, looking at the adjacent lot we didn't own, I became concerned. Our house was in a natural trough, the lots were just 100 feet wide, and it became clear that whoever built on the adjacent lot we didn't own would loom over us. If the new neighbor chose to build a two-story house it would be disastrous for our view and for our privacy.

I determined to try to buy him out. One day I noticed a man pacing the lot next door. I went up the grade to meet him and it turned out that he was the owner. A schoolteacher from New York City, this was his second lot in the 4,000-acre development. He planned to build on the lot as soon as he could sell his other lot, which was on the main drag. He regarded the other lot as an undesirable building site.

I didn't tell him about my plans. I knew, however, that the developer would allow him to exchange any lot he owned for one more to his liking—another sales gimmick extended to all. It was my guess, then, that he would sell the lot I wanted and exchange the main-drag lot for one more to his liking. There were many lots as nice as the one next door.

Anxious to keep the asking price within reasonable limits—I knew I was greedy and was justifiably suspicious of anyone else in the catbird seat—I got my mother-in-law to express an interest. The owner asked $6,200. I thought the price high. I had my mother-in-law bid $5,500. Finally he sold the property to her (me) for $5,700. He had a nice profit and I had the property that meant more to me than to anyone else in the world. The $5,700 I paid was more than the going price for lots in the development, which

* 10 percent off on $5,200 leaves $4,680 and another 5 percent reduces the price to $4,420.

had appreciated to about $5,500. But my cost on the three lots averaged out to $4,860.*

What I did in real estate is a country cousin of dollar cost averaging in the stock market. This method of purchasing calls for steady accumulation of a particular stock at regular intervals. That way some shares cost relatively little and some more—depending on market fluctuations. If the general trend of the stock's price is up, you make money. If the stock is a persistent downer, you lose.

For best results in establishing an average price, the investor commits fixed dollar sums at regular intervals—whether monthly, quarterly, semi-annually, or even annually. Clearly, the more frequently one purchases, the more average the price.

A variation which works less well is to buy a fixed number of shares regardless of price. If you bought ten shares of X at the end of each month and the price went 20-15-10-5-10-15-20, you'd pick up 80 shares for $1,000 and your average price would be $12.50. But if you invested $120 at the end of every quarter on the same moves, you'd get 100 shares for $960 at an average price of $9.60.

Some believe dollar cost averaging is a diehard investor's way of throwing good money after bad. Others believe it is a way to take advantage of price dips to accumulate shares at any reasonable price over time. It can certainly help one avoid buying a chunk of stock at an excessively high price.

Imagine having purchased Winnebago, the recreational vehicle maker, on a one-shot purchase at 48¼, its 1972 go-go high. By the end of 1973—a year and a half later—the fuel shortage struck. The stock crashed and quickly wiped out the diehard Winnebago millionaires. The stock fell to 3.

Is Winnebago a good candidate for dollar averaging? It depends on one's objective. Anyone who began buying Winnebago at 3—

* $4,420 plus $4,420 plus $5,700 is $14,500 divided by 3 is $4,860. As this was written, six years later, the lots were worth $8,000 each.

and almost no one did because nobody buys stock at their lows—would have dollar-averaged small profits. The stock reached 9 in the spring of 1976 but then drifted back to 7.

Obviously, the dollar cost averager would make a killing if Winnebago began to approach its peak level. It could take a while. The best guess is that it will never happen. Winnebago needs high volume to break even and though sales are booming again, many believe the recreation-vehicle adherents are living in a fool's paradise. The gasoline shortage just won't go away, and the big rec vehicles slurp a gallon of octane cocktail every six to eight miles. Waiting for the good old days of cheap, plentiful fuel and possible sharply rising profits for Winnebago could be a drag.

Far stronger companies haven't reached peak levels over longer periods than most investors would care to wait. Witness American Telephone. In 1929, Ma Bell shares reached a peak still unsurpassed a generation later.

It should be quite clear, then, that dollar cost averaging works as long as stocks are on rising trends. When they are sliding long-term, all dollar averaging will do is trim the magnitude of your losses. As the late Burton Crane put it:

"The beauty of the dollar-cost-averaging approach is that a salesman can make a prospect believe that a falling market is a positive boon from heaven."

PART IV

BONDS

16 · Bonds and Related Speculations

A Note for the Hard Core Speculator—For the sophisticated investor who likes to win big and isn't afraid to gamble, discount bonds may be the best speculation in town—the quickest route to the jackpot. Here's the situation. As this was written, quality long-term bonds were yielding as much as 8 percent. Yields have been so generous for so long now—8 percent yields have been available since 1969—that investors have forgotten that such returns are unique in our generation.

To put things in perspective, reflect on this: high yields on bonds were so unusual as late as 1959 that when the United States government offered a yield of 5 percent on long-term bonds, Wall Street became ecstatic. To old timers, who remembered a generation of 3 and 4 percent yields on quality corporate and government bonds, the 5 percent yield seemed almost too good to be true. The bonds were dubbed "The Magic 5s" as they magically disappeared into every portfolio in sight.

But few wise men today believe that 8 percent yields will persist for long. Some believe 3 and 4 percent yields will again become the norm. Others believe that, at the very least, 6 percent yields will prevail—and within a few years. Imagine what would happen to a fat folder of quality corporate and utility bonds now yielding 8 percent if yields dropped to 6 percent. For example: In mid-November American Telephone 4⅜ percent debentures due October 1, 1996, were priced to yield 7.8 percent at 65.67 ($656.70 per $1,000 debenture). If quality bond yields should drop to 6 percent by, say, mid-November 1979, the price of those debentures would rise to about 83 ($830) to reflect the new general level of interest rates. The speculator would have a gain of $170 or so—26 percent. If he bought the debentures at today's prices on 30 percent margin, he would have put up about $200 and have nearly doubled his money.

The Telephone debenture issue is one of scores of quality bond issues selling at heavy discounts. Utilities offer discounts too. For example, Southern California Edison 4⅜s of May 15, 1988,* now yielding 8 percent at a price of 73 ($730), would almost match the Telephone debentures in appreciation were yields to drop generally to 6 percent.

Just keep in mind that this sort of market commitment is a speculation. If the market surprised the experts and yields rose, the holder would be hurt, and if he were on margin he could be wiped out. As Harry Truman said, "If you can't stand the heat, stay out of the kitchen." This is for the sophisticated and not the naive.

THE NEOPHYTE and the dilettante share basic misconceptions about bonds. Most individuals with a reasonable grasp of finance are aware that bonds are issued to raise money for a business or for a governmental unit. But it is important that you know a great deal more than this if you should sip the alphabet soup of debt securities. They are sometimes fraught with risk.

Consider for a moment the corporate bond. Corporate bond holders occupy a very different position from that of the shareholders. The bond holder is a creditor of a corporation and is paid a fixed rate of interest, unlike the part owner of the business—the shareholder—whose fortunes are tied directly to the business's successes and setbacks. If the business should fail, both the bond holder and the shareholder suffer. But the bond holder will get something—as much as 100 cents on the dollar if the bonds were a mortgage on specific assets as they sometimes are. Often, how-

---

* Both the Telephones and the SoCals are callable in 1976, but rates would have to drop generally to below 4½ to make it worthwhile for the company to call the issue.

ever, there is nothing left for the shareholder after all debts are paid.

What is not widely understood is that bonds are not safe from substantial market losses, or that bonds can, under certain circumstances, appreciate. In periods of sharply falling interest rates, for example, some bonds appreciate so rapidly that their gains rival those of growth stocks. This can happen with corporate bonds and it can happen with bonds issued by governmental units as well.

Bond purchases can be made on margin with as little as 25 percent cash, and they thus give the owner twice the leverage potential that can be achieved in buying common stocks, since the latter call for 50 percent "margin."*

Thus, $10,000 worth of bonds that quickly rose in price to $11,000 could produce substantial profits for an individual on minimum margin. That is, his $2,500 cash investment would be worth $3,500 after such a rise—a 40 percent gain.

But mark this. A slide of $1,000 in market value—10 percent, as before—would produce a margin call from the individual's broker. If the investor did not answer immediately with a check for the deficit in his margin account, he would be sold out for a substantial loss.

How big a margin call can he expect in this instance? Figure it thus: After a decline of $1,000 in the market value, his bonds would be worth $9,000. He must maintain his margin at 25 percent of the current market value. Divide $9,000 by 25 percent and we see that his new equity requirement—margin—is $2,250.

Here's what has happened to his margin account in the market decline: The $1,000 decline in price is applied against the $2,500 he originally had in the margin account directly, leaving him with just $1,500. He'll therefore have to raise the difference between $2,250 and $1,500, or $750.

If he doesn't come up with the money quickly—perhaps the same

* Convertible bonds—those that can be exchanged for common stock in the same company at present rates—are subject to 50 percent margin requirements, since for margin purposes they are likened to stocks, not bonds.

day as the market decline—he will be sold out at the best price that can be obtained for the bonds.

This should give you a rough idea of some of the complexities that exist in the markets for government and corporate bonds. There is much more to it than this, as we shall soon see.

In an uncertain age, no investor can afford to ignore the bond market, where those who know what they are about can find a substantial degree of safety.

You don't have to buy bonds on margin, and you don't have to expose yourself to serious market risks. Remember that a strong bond held to maturity will pay off at face amount regardless of interim fluctuations. By choosing bonds that mature on dates that serve your personal investment objectives, you will be able to buy with confidence.

If you wish to speculate, you can do that too. But it's tricky and may call for more sleepless nights than you are prepared for.

In the sections ahead we will discuss corporate bonds, tax exempt municipal bonds, and what are potentially the safest investment of all, bonds issued by the United States Government.

17 · Quality Corporate Bonds

In 1973—the midst of the worst bear market in modern history—some brokers were assuring customers that stocks were not only cheap, but indeed the only place to stash cash. It was an extraordinary argument in view of the crushing losses everybody had experienced. But stocks *had* to come back someday, to be sure—it wasn't the end of the world. The brokers argued for sooner not later, and argued that the unconvinced were about to miss the biggest bull rally in history.

During that drear period, a fellow New York Times writer approached me to say that she had heard this siren call but had thus far resisted it. She said that it was hard for her to give up the 8 percent yield she had earned for over three years on General Motors Acceptance Corporation debentures.* Still, she was bothered by the possibility that she might miss out on the much-talked-about rally.

I told her to sit tight, and marveled at her good judgment in having chosen the top-rated debentures in the first place. But later, thinking over the incident, I realized that there is a vast reservoir of common sense among the investors of this nation. (I tend to forget this because I generally get calls from folks in trouble—not winners.)

There were undoubtedly thousands of investors who listened to some small voice within themselves, turned their backs on stocks during the bear market, and bought top-rated corporate bonds and debentures—clearly among the safest investments in those danger-ous times.

If more individuals would learn to think for themselves—as my *Times* colleague had—there'd be fewer affluent brokers and more affluent customers. Never forget that a broker makes his living on commissions. If you wonder why brokers seldom recommend bonds, remember that stock commissions are substantially higher than bond commissions. Brokers are bound to spread their bread with butter, not margarine, if given a choice.

Before you succumb to a broker's appeal to chase stocks, be sure your instincts aren't telling you to shun the market for the greater safety of quality bonds.

What Grace did was simple. She looked for a higher yield in a quality bond, reasoning that if General Motors' financing subsidiary went down the drain the whole nation would be bankrupt. (Wall Street often quips: As General Motors goes, so goes the nation.)

You may be surprised to learn that there is much more to corporate bonds and debentures than meets the eye. There are short- and long-term strategies. And there are bull and bear market

* Nonconvertible but similar to and as safe as bonds.

strategies. Since the bond market's bull and bear markets don't always parallel those of the stock market, it is sometimes possible to find extraordinary values in bonds at times when the stock market is both down and dangerous. I might add that there are many in Wall Street who believe that high interest rates are here to stay. That's probably an overstatement of the future prospects for corporate bonds, but it does seem likely, in view of the anticipated demands for capital on the part of corporations in the years ahead, that bonds will offer high returns for some time. If you are seeking safety and either fear municipal bonds or are not in a sufficiently high income tax bracket to find them appealing, this discussion will interest you.

Any individual in a federal income tax bracket of less than 40 percent is a prospect for corporate bonds. Many retirees might wish to buy corporate bonds issued by the American Telephone and Telegraph Company and its subsidiaries at yields of 8¼ to 8½ percent current as this book was written. They have probably never determined just how to approach the situation. Bonds of other leading utilities are equally attractive, as are the bonds of General Motors, GMAC, and scores if not hundreds of other leading industrial corporations—assuming they are double-A-rated by Standard & Poor's or Moody's or both.

There are several ways for relatively unsophisticated individuals to protect themselves in the bond market. Frank Henjes, who does business under his own name at 100 Wall Street, believes the individual should buy new bonds of a company the individual knows. The bonds should be a part of a $50 million issue—at least—and should be scheduled for listing on the New York Stock Exchange.

Mr. Henjes said that by limiting purchases to such issues the individual would be able to find peace of mind. A resident of North Carolina, for example, would probably be more comfortable with bonds of that state's Duke Power Company, while a resident of Richmond would probably be more at ease with bonds of Virginia Electric and Power.

Why new bonds? In making such purchases the individual can buy "net"—without paying a commission. Underwriters of new bond issues are paid directly by the company for distributing the bonds. "Why pay a commission when you don't have to?" Mr. Henjes asks, noting that new quality bonds were being sold all the time. You need not wait, therefore, for more than a week or so to participate in a new issue to your liking. Individuals will soon find that local brokers concentrate on the corporate bonds of local companies. That takes care of the regional question.

If a bond is part of an issue of at least $50 million—some experts suggest limiting purchases to $100 million issues—the individual can count on a reasonably brisk after-market, particularly so when the bonds are listed on the New York Stock Exchange.

Avoid those issues that will not be listed on the Big Board. Unlisted issues are traded between professionals, and the normal trade involves hundreds of thousands of dollars worth of bonds. The individual who offers ten bonds in that market will find that they will sell well below current prices—if they sell at all. The individual will have little idea of what he should be getting for his ten bonds, either. They are not regularly quoted to individuals.

By contrast, the individual who owns bonds traded on the Big Board will be able to consult the newspaper for quotations. Issues of $50 million and up, rated AA or better, will trade every week. Some will trade every day. The individual will be able to tell what he can expect on resale.

In any case, the broker handling a small trade for an individual—whether the individual is buying or selling—will charge from $5 to $10 per bond commission. Minimum commission: commonly, $25. The bonds are generally issued in $1,000 denominations.

Maturity can be an important consideration. Those who feel they may have to sell their bonds in the near future should limit purchases to bonds having from seven to ten years to run, Mr. Henjes feels.

Those who buy corporate bonds know that there are market risks entailed—particularly for those who do not keep bonds to maturity.

Bonds rise and fall in price to reflect changes in general interest levels. A bond purchased for high yield will drop in price if interest rates generally rise to an even higher level. The owner of such a bond will continue to receive the same yield as before as long as he continues to hold the bond. If he sells under such circumstances, he will get less for his bond than he paid for it.

If the bond market moves the other way, with interest rates going lower, the price of the bond will rise. The individual will continue to get the yield he was getting, but on sale of the bond will receive a profit represented by the difference between the higher current price and the price he paid for the bond.

On the other hand, Mr. Henjes believes too many bond purchasers hesitate when they are asked to purchase a bond with a maturity beyond their anticipated life span. Normally, however, the individual will receive a greater yield on longer bonds of the same quality and company than on shorter bonds.

For those who comment, "I'll be dust before this bond matures," the 45-year-old Mr. Henjes sometimes replies, "So will I." Mr. Henjes added:

"The individual's estate can always sell a good, marketable bond. The only person who can buy a bond to mature at his death is the individual who plans to commit suicide."

Mr. Henjes has prepared portfolios for typical bond purchasers in three different sets of circumstances. Contemplated investments: $50,000 to $60,000.

PORTFOLIO A

This investor is a 35-to-40-year-old executive with children aged six, eight, and ten years. He makes a good salary, but is concerned about future college expenses and his own retirement. He picks three or four good-grade—A-rated or better—corporate bonds that are traded on the New York Stock Exchange. When he has accumulated $3,000 to $4,000 he calls his broker and buys $5,000 (face amount) of these "discount" bonds—all of which are selling at considerably below par so that it doesn't take $5,000 to buy $5,000 face amount. The bonds he has picked are of financially sound companies. They sell at discounts from par because they were issued some time ago when the general level of interest rates was lower. The other feature that has appealed to the investor is that he has picked bonds that mature either at the time of his children's college years or at his retirement. By choosing bonds to mature when he expects to use the money, he reduces (nearly eliminates) market risk. He will not have to risk selling the bonds in the market before maturity at a possible loss of face amount. He has minimized additional taxes because the chosen bonds bear low coupons—3, 3½, and 4 percent coupons—and some of his return will be in the form of capital gains, which are taxed at lower rates than is ordinary income.

PORTFOLIO B

This investor is a widow in her 60s who has been left well off financially. She needs additional income to keep pace with inflation. She buys new bonds at or near par, so the coupon rate represents her actual rate of income. She will stress quality, buying A, AA, and AAA bonds—nothing less. She would no doubt favor telephone issues of AT&T and subsidiaries since they are well known—even to her—and AAA-rated. She does not worry about maturity, as her estate will sell the bonds at her death. These high-grade NYSE bonds are readily marketable at any time—even in the relatively small amounts she will own. She gets maximum income today— when she needs it—and the income is sent to her twice a year, by check, since they are registered bonds. (She is listed as owner on the corporate books.) Chances are she will choose five or six issues with different interest-payment dates so that she will receive checks practically every month. She can add to her holdings or subtract from them by calling her broker to buy or sell five bonds at any time. By selling five bonds she would avoid the penalty of a minimum transaction charge.

PORTFOLIO A

Rating	Amount	Description	Coupon	Maturity	Price	Yield
AAA	10M	ATT	3¼	9-15-84	73½	7.64
	10M	ATT	4⅜	4-1-85	77⅝	7.96
AAA	10M	GMAC	8⅛	6-15-86	98⅞	8.29
	10M	Chase Manh.	8¾	5-15-86	100¾	8.63
AAA	10M	South. Bell Tel	8¼	4-15-96	96¾	8.59
AAA	10M	Pacific Tel	4⅜	8-15-88	70⅝	8.25

PORTFOLIO B

Rating	Amount	Description	Coupon	Maturity	Price	Yield
AAA	10M	Mich. Bell Tel	9.60	10-1-08	105	9.12
AAA	10M	Bell Tel. of Pa.	8¾	7-15-15	101	8.67
AAA	10M	Ford Motor Co.	9¼	7-15-94	102¾	8.98
AA	10M	Indianapolis Power & Light	9.30	6-1-06	101¼	9.18
AA	10M	Weyerhaeuser Co.	8⅝	10-1-2000	100¼	8.60

PORTFOLIO C

Rating	Amount	Description	Coupon	Maturity	Price	Yield	
AA	10M	Ford Motor Cred.	8⅝	6-1-86	100⅞	8.50	
AAA	10M	GMAC	8⅛	6-15-86	98⅞	8.29	
AAA	10M	South. Bell Tel	8¼	4-15-96	96¾	8.59	
AA	10M	Indianapolis Power & Light	9.30	6-1-06	101¼	9.18	
A	10M	Stand. Oil of Ohio	8½	1-1-00	95⅝	8.95	
NR	7.5M	Guardian Mort.	7½	12-1-79	35	21.4 %	(Current Yield)

PORTFOLIO C

This investor is a doctor with high current income and the usual tax shelters designed to bring his tax bracket down to middle-bracket levels. He has become disenchanted with the stock market. He has sold his disappointing stocks and has accumulated a lot of cash, which he has put into safe investments—United States Government notes, bank certificates of deposit, and savings accounts. He now sees the need for future planning. He combines his gambling instinct with the need for future income. He buys deep-discount bonds, special-situation bonds such as the better Real Estate Investment Trusts, and good, high-quality A-rated or better medium to high coupon bonds. Since all are listed, he can watch them in the newspapers to see if his long shots—his riskier holdings —are working out. He can, of course, add to his holdings at any time. He staggers the maturities in the high-grade sector of his portfolio, with some five-to-seven-year, some 12-to-15-year, and some 30-to-40 year bonds. This gives him some short maturities that will be less subject to market fluctuations since they fall due soon. They can thus be used as backup to the liquid assets he carries in his savings accounts.

Investors will find that different approaches are recommended in bear markets than in bull markets. Alan H. McAlpin of First Regional Securities, Inc., 63 Wall Street, says that in bear markets investors ought to soft-pedal efforts to obtain maximum yields and become more concerned about preserving principal and minimizing risks. It may also be necessary that the individual trade to improve position. Thus, the techniques Mr. McAlpin describes call for a greater level of sophistication than is needed by an individual who buys new bonds with the intention of keeping them indefinitely.

A glance at the Moody's reverse (upside down) chart below clearly indicates that AAA-rated bonds decline less in bear markets than do lower-rated issues. The yield "spread" between top-rated bonds and the lowest-rated bonds in the chart—BAA—is naturally the most dramatic.

It can be shown that in poor bond markets relatively short bonds —those maturing in three to five years—trade closer to par than do bonds maturing many years out. (In bond quotations, "par" equals 100. Face or principal amount is usually $1,000.) When a bond drops away from par, the owner, if forced to sell, will suffer a loss of principal. Thus, conservative investors sometimes trade their long bonds at the onset of a bad market and reinvest in bonds falling due within a few years.

Mr. McAlpin gives examples of this difference in performance for long and short bonds in the bear market for bonds of 1974. On March 20, 1974, Household Finance Corporation made a dual offering of 8 percent debentures due 1984 and 8½ percent debentures due 2001. During the following nine months, the AA-rated issues traded at lows of 87½ for the 1984 maturities and 83½ for the 2001 maturities.

Here are further examples of the different fortunes of long- and short-term bonds during the full year 1974. Note that the Pennzoil issues are BAA/BBB rated. The BAA rating is by Moody's, the BBB by Standard & Poor's. Experts urge safety-conscious individuals to seek bonds with higher ratings than this.

EXAMPLE		HIGH	LOW
BAA/BBB Pennzoil 8⅜% 3/1/76		102½	92
BAA/BBB Pennzoil 8⅜% 3/1/1996		101½	72
AAA/AAA Southwestern Bell 7% 9/1/78		100	90
AAA/AAA Southwestern Bell 6⅞% 2/1/11		89½	70
A/A Florida Power & Light 8⅛% 7/1/75		102½	93⅜
A/A Florida Power & Light 8⅛% 8/1/80		103¾	90

Mr. McAlpin echoes Mr. Henjes in stressing liquidity and marketability for individuals, urging them to buy large issues with Big Board listings.

He comments:

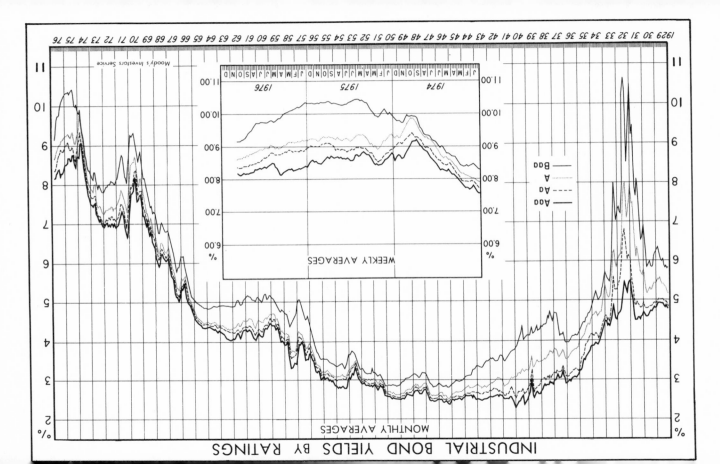

"The greater the liquidity your bonds enjoy, the easier it will be to change your investment to fit a new objective."

CUSHION BONDS

It should be clear by now that when the general level of interest rates falls, bond prices rise. For example, a bond sold at 100 in 1974 to yield 9 percent would trade at a "premium"—above 100 or $1,000 per bond—if interest levels dropped generally. The price of the bond would rise enough to reduce its interest yield to a level comparable to that available on new bonds of similar quality and maturity. Cushion bonds, are, however, a special case.

Cushion bonds are callable or refundable bonds that are selling at a premium. Such bonds are subject to call or redemption by the issuer before compulsory maturity. Corporations often issue bonds in anticipation of a decline in money rates that would permit refunding—the issuance of a new bond issue to replace the old one—at a significantly lower interest cost. Premium prices are paid upon early redemption to compensate the investor for the inconvenience—and loss of potential income—involved in replacing his investment.

But suppose interest rates decline so that bonds generally begin to trade at premiums. A callable bond will resist trading at a premium above its redemption price because potential purchasers fear that the issuing corporation may call the bond and that they will suffer a loss. Prices of call bonds thus tend to lag behind the market once they begin to trade near call price. But in a subsequent falling market, these bonds provide a "cushion" against the early effects of bond market price declines.

Here's Mr. McAlpin's example of how a cushion bond works in a declining bond market.

The AA-rated Public Service Electric & Gas 12 percent first and refunding bonds maturing October 1, 2004, were selling on May 27, 1976, at 112 for a current yield to purchasers of 10.71

percent. The bonds are subject to call at 111.59 at the option of the issuer.

Meanwhile, a sister issue, the AA-rated Public Service Electric & Gas 9⅛ percent first and refunding bonds due March 1, 2000, were selling on May 27 at 99 for a current yield of 9.22 percent. Obviously, these bonds were issued at a period during which interest rates were lower. The call price is close to that of the sister issue.

Were it not for the fact that the 12 percent issue can be called at 111.59—something that may not happen for years, by the way —they could be expected to rise in price and thus offer lower yields —about the same as the 9⅛ percent issue, a bond of comparable quality and maturity.

It is the potential call of the 12 percent issue that provides the "cushion" in a bond market decline. If bond prices generally continued to fall, the yield on the 9⅛ percent issue would rise to about what the 12 percent issue yielded on May 27—10.71 percent. The 12 percent issue—nicknamed Peggy in the trade—would remain virtually unchanged in price and yield. Any further decline, however, would carry the 12s down with the rest of the market. The cushion is effective for braking the early effects of a bond market decline.

FLOATING RATE BONDS

So far the bond market discussion has been limited to fixed-interest corporate bonds. In periods of uncertainty, some investors protect themselves to a degree in down markets through the purchase of bonds offering "floating rates"—that is, bonds which have coupons that "float" or move at intervals in relation to other rates. Coupons are certificates attached to bonds which represent sums of interest due at stated intervals. The "coupon clipper" (or his bank, broker, or other agent) delivers the coupon to the issuer and receives his interest.

Certain floating rate issuers adjust their rates in relation to the prime lending rates of leading banks—the interest rates exacted on loans to the banks' most credit-worthy customers. Others use different "floating" standards. Some rates float in a specified relation to the interest yield offered by three-month United States Treasury bills. Often the issuer will pay a premium of 100 basis points—one percentage point—above another market rate. Thus, in such a case, the floating rate might rise to 8 percent from 7, if the Treasury bill rate rose to 7 percent from 6. Remember that the object is to provide the buyer with a bond that is exposed to limited market risk. Issuers of this vehicle tend to be financial organizations such as banks and credit companies, because their revenues often move with commercial interest rates. The issuers want to tie costs to revenues. The bonds are not necessarily safe. Their riskiness depends on the quality of the issuer. Real Estate Investment Trusts issued many such floating rate bonds, and many purchasers are faced with the prospect of default and repayment at a fraction of face amount. Ratings are especially important for the purchaser of bonds—whether they are fixed-interest obligations or floating rate bonds. Keep this in mind; limit purchases to AA-rated bonds or better and you'll probably stay out of trouble.

BULL MARKETS FOR BONDS

In bull markets for bonds, prices of bonds rise, while their interest yields decline. Bull markets are not difficult to spot. You'll notice stories in the financial press about falling rates for Federal Funds and a decline in the discount rate. You don't have to know too much about those key indicators of the trend of interest rates to recognize the beginning of a bull market. The prime lending rate of major banks is a more spectacular indicator if only because it is so widely reported. If a bull market does begin to develop, any indication of a decline in the rate of inflation—an easing in the rate of climb of the cost-of-living index—will be further evidence of a developing bull.

When a bull market is underway, investors can afford to be more aggressive. They can buy somewhat riskier bonds and seek the greater total returns available in bull markets. You won't be looking for maximum interest return so much as you will seek to maximize the total of interest plus capital gains. Surprisingly, the total returns available in a brisk bull market for bonds can sometimes exceed reasonable expectations in the stock market.

You will remember that in bear markets the short maturities offer better protection than the long. But in bull markets, the best opportunities for capital gains are to be found in long maturities. In bull markets, then, the volatility of the longer issues can be made to work for you.

The most recent bull market for bonds occurred between the end of September 1975 and the end of February 1976. Let's look at what happened to a top-quality issue of short New York Telephone Company bonds and contrast that with what happened to a long issue of New York Bell.

Let's look at the short bond first. At the end of September 1975, an investor could have purchased AAA-rated New York Telephone 8 percent notes due March 15, 1983, at 96⅝ (the offering price—later expressed in this example as 96.625 for purposes of a decimal calculation). At that price, the purchaser had a current return of 8.28 percent and a yield to maturity of 8.62 percent. Yield to maturity is current yield plus capital gain or loss, annualized, to the investor. It is the yield to be experienced if the bond is held to maturity, when it will be worth par—100.

By the end of February, the robust bull market had carried the price of the NYT 8 percent notes to 101. Remember that the current return at purchase was 8.28 percent. The current return provides the basis for figuring total return—interest plus capital gain. The price has appreciated to 101 from 96.625 or by 4.375 points. Divide 4.375 by original cost (again 96.625) and you get 4.53 percent—the capital gain experienced over the five-month holding period. Add the current yield, 8.28 percent, and the capital gain, 4.53 percent, and your total annualized return is 12.81 percent.

Remember that this is a one-shot gain, which could be locked up by a sale at the current price.

That's a nice gain, to be sure. But let's look at what happened to the AAA-rated New York Bell 8 percent general and refunding bond due July 15, 2008, over the same five-month period.

At the end of September 1975, the bonds could have been purchased at the offering price of 85¾ for a current return of 9.33 percent and a yield to maturity of 9.41 percent. Five months later, the same issue was offered at 93¾ for a current return of 8.53 percent and a yield to maturity of 8.57 percent.

The price appreciation in the long bond has been 93¾ minus 85¾ or 8 points. Divide 8 by the purchase price of 85¾ (85.75) and you come up with an appreciation of 9.33 percent, annualized basis. Add that to the current return at purchase of 9.33 percent and you have an 18.66 percent total return. Clearly, if the Bell issues are representative, there is a wonderful opportunity for substantial profits in bull markets—particularly in the long bonds.

Here are further examples of the phenomenon from an earlier bull market for bonds—January 1 through February 26, 1975.

Long bonds: A/A Potomac Electric Power 9½% 8/15/05s improved in price over that period from 94 to 100 (6 points). AA/AA Pacific Gas & Electric 9⅛% 6/1/06s improved from 97½ to 102 (4½ points).

Short bonds: BAA/AA San Diego Gas & Electric 9.30% bonds maturing 12/15/79 improved from 98¾ to 101½ or 2¾ points. AA/AA Baltimore Gas & Electric 10% bonds maturing 6/1/82 improved from 105 to 106½ or 1½ points. A/A Florida Power & Light 8⅛% bonds maturing 8/1/80 improved from 96½ to 98 or 1½ points.

Frequently, as we have noted, bonds are subject to call before maturity—whether through the operation of a sinking fund or through a regular call feature. Before you buy a bond, you should check into the redemption features to be sure that the issue will not be called or refunded at a price lower than it will cost you. Most new issues will not be subject to call or refunding for a stipulated period of time—usually five or ten years. Sinking fund calls are usually at par. But some price protection—usually of from 4 to 10 points—is offered in case of a refunding call.

FACTORS IN BOND PRICES

Investors should be aware that there are a number of factors that can affect bond prices. If, for example, an unusually large number of corporations whose bonds carry A ratings marketed bonds over a 30-day period, the price of outstanding A-rated bonds would be unlikely to keep pace with prices of AA-rated and AAA-rated bonds.

The actions of large institutions can have an effect on the prices of bonds as well. For example, during periods in which savings banks are experiencing substantial outflows of funds, they may sell substantial quantities of bonds. If the money is rolling in, the savings banks might be expected to add to bond holdings and thus affect prices favorably.

When casualty insurance companies have extraordinarily large damage claims from hurricanes and tornados, they may buy fewer bonds than usual and even become heavy sellers. Years of light damage claims can mean heavy bond purchases.

The Pension Reform Act of 1974 probably had a favorable impact on the bond market and may have helped fuel the bull markets of early 1975 and late 1975. The act holds institutional investors to standards of prudence in their investment policies which were implied but unstated previously. Warnings in the act led many institutions to reduce their holdings of stocks and to turn to the safer corporate bond market. This promises to lend a degree of support to bonds that was previously lacking, and the effect is likely to be long-term, but difficult to measure.

ALTERNATIVES TO CORPORATE BONDS

There are a number of investment media that compete for attention with bonds. You should be aware of them. Sometimes savings bank interest rates rise to high enough levels that individuals are led to shift funds out of corporates and into the banks. Government bonds, with their impeccable safety credentials, sometimes appeal to corporate bondholders—particularly so in times of uncertainty.

Obviously, a bull market for stocks can sometimes drain funds from corporate bonds. Relatively few may have switched directly from stocks into corporation bonds during the early 1970s, but the superior yields in that period were clearly to be found in the bond market.

Inflation is a downer for corporate bonds. During periods of high inflation, the value of any future stream of fixed interest payments is seriously eroded. The danger to yields is substantial, for the inflation rate must be viewed as a compounding factor, while interest on bonds is usually viewed as a simple interest rate.

What investors want to know is whether corporate bonds are likely to be a worthwhile alternative to stocks in the years ahead. Ashby Bladen, senior vice-president, investments, of the Guardian Life Insurance Company of America, made a speech in early 1976 which was entitled: "Is There Any Hope for Long-Term Bonds?" His answer was, "If there isn't, then there isn't much hope for the other popular investment media either."

He went on to say that the yields on long-term bonds are not likely to fall back toward their historically normal range of around 3 to 6 percent unless the accelerating inflation and the growing economic and financial instability that have plagued the United States during the last decade begin to subside.

In any event, let's look at a table indicating the rate of inflation and the rates obtainable in treasury bills, high-quality corporate bonds, and common stocks over the past 50 years.

The table offers a clear indication that, over the last ten years at least, investors did at least as well in corporate bonds as they did in stocks. Over longer periods, stocks were clearly the winners—and they may be again.

1926–1975
MARKET INDICES AND INFLATION

	COMPOUND ANNUAL RATES OF RETURN			
	5 years 1971–75	10 years 1966–75	15 years 1961–75	50 years 1926–75
Inflation (Consumer Price Index)	6.8%	5.7%	4.2%	2.3%
Treasury bills	5.7	5.6	4.7	2.3
Quality corporate bonds	6.0	3.6	3.7	3.8
Common stocks	3.2	3.3	6.5	9.0

Data from *Stocks, Bonds, Bills and Inflation: Year-by-Year Historical Returns*, by Roger G. Ibbotson and Rex A. Sinquefield.

FOREIGN BONDS

A number of AAA-rated foreign bonds are listed on the New York Stock Exchange and thus may be considered as a possible alternative to bonds issued by American concerns. Now that the interest equalization tax is extinct—it used to penalize United States citizens on their foreign holdings, stocks, and bonds—the foreign AAA bonds can help individuals upgrade their holdings, usually with a cut in maturity and without loss in yield. Mr. McAlpin believes that world capital markets are becoming international and views the dropping of the interest equalization tax as a step in that direction. He expects foreign bonds to gain acceptance gradually and to become popular as they become more familiar.

A WORD TO THE WISE

Anyone with an interest in a corporation wants to know what is going on. Shareholder needs are routinely served through annual and interim financial reports. Research reports from brokerage houses are published periodically to supplement information from official sources.

Bond holders are not so well served—but they can take steps to assure themselves of adequate information so that they can stay abreast. Most corporations are willing to mail annual reports to anyone who writes for them, and this includes all corporations important enough to warrant an investment by the individual. When you buy bonds, then, write the issuing corporation and ask to be put on the mailing list.

If you buy new bonds, to avoid brokerage costs, you should ask for the offering circular—the prospectus. It must meet disclosure requirements of the Securities and Exchange Commission. The circular offers a wealth of detailed information concerning the assets of the company and its general creditworthiness.

The contract terms under which the bonds are issued—that is, the indenture—will be set forth, as will the circumstances under which modifications can be made to this contract between issuer and bond holder. You will also be apprised of the conditions under which a default will be considered to have occurred. If you shop carefully, you shouldn't face this prospect.

If you are buying an outstanding issue of bonds, try to get the prospectus anyway. The information, though somewhat out of date, will still be useful. If no issuing circular is available, ask for a circular covering similar bonds issued by the same company. A substantial amount of information in the current circular will prove useful.

18 · Preferred Stocks

Some years ago, an inexperienced market observer was reviewing the Wall Street events of the day on a daily television show. In reporting on the ten stocks recording the biggest changes for the day, she first mentioned a stock that was down 5 points to 70. "Oh, oh," she commented. "Something going on there!"*

Not so. What had happened, however, was that the stock was a preferred. Like many such issues, the shares of that preferred rarely traded. This, the first trade in several days, had to reflect the generally negative change in investor thinking since the last trade. Preferreds were a mystery to the commentator—just as they are to most people. They are worth studying.

For once you have mastered the bull and bear market strategies involved in trading corporate bonds, you will find that preferred stocks offer similar avenues to profit. In bull markets for these securities, it is sometimes possible to reap substantial total returns over short periods of time—rivaling the short-term rewards to be found in common stocks. And in bear markets, there are cushion preferred stocks, the prices of which resist down markets—just as do the prices of cushion bonds.

But first a definition. Preferred stocks are senior equity securities with a fixed dividend or dividend rate. The preferred dividend must be paid before any dividend may be paid to owners of the corporation's common stock. In a liquidation, they have a claim senior to that of the owners of common stock.

On the other hand, holders of preferred shares generally do not have voting rights. Since the dividend is stated and is not altered if corporate earnings rise, the price of preferred stock is influenced more by interest rate levels than by the earnings of the company. That is, preferreds act more like bonds than stocks and thus react to bull and bear markets for fixed-interest securities.

Here's an example of a typical preferred issue followed by an indication of the meaning of the various terms used to describe it.

* That observer, Roberta Hammond, on WOR-TV's *Stock Market Observer*, quickly became an expert and thereafter rarely made a mistake—even on the fine points. She is a non-financial television personality in Texas today.

Rating	Size of Issue	Issuer	Div. Rate % or Div. Amt	Type	Par	Price
A/A	1,000,000 shrs NYSE listing	N.Y. State Elec & Gas	8.48% or $2.12	Cum	$25	22½

The rating by Moody's/Standard & Poor's indicates the quality of the stock. Just as in bond issues, the highest rating is AAA, the next highest AA, and upper-medium grade is designated A—like this issue. Ratings of BAA/BBB or below indicate that there are elements of speculation in the stock.

Coverage is another term of importance (not indicated in the example) because it tells the number of times the dividend is covered by the earnings. It is an indication as well of the degree of safety enjoyed by the dividend.

The size—1,000,000 shares here—will give you an idea of how marketable or liquid is the market for the shares. Some preferreds do trade every day, and ordinarily this is the sort of issue most individuals should seek. Normally, the greater the size of the issue, the greater ease a buyer or seller will have in trading. A New York Stock Exchange listing is an excellent attribute from the small investor's point of view.

The issuer in the example is New York State Electric & Gas Company. That is the company responsible for the payment of the quarterly dividend payments on the preferred stock.

The dividend rate is expressed as a percent of par (8.48 percent). The amount of the dividend, $2.12, is expressed in dollars and cents. Unless the issuer is in arrears, the dividend would be payable on a quarterly basis.

Preferreds, like income-producing common stocks, go ex-dividend after the payout is declared. Thus the price will be higher just before the dividend than just after. Dividend dates and ex-dividend dates thus play an important role in a preferred stock's price level.

Cumulative preferreds, like the N.Y. State Electric & Gas preferred, provide that if the dividend is not paid, the obligation to pay it continues. Thus, no common stock dividend can be paid until the preferred arrearage is eliminated.

The offering price is the market price for the preferred stock. The par value of this preferred stock is $25. Once the offering price goes above par—$25—the yield to the subsequent buyer will be below the stated dividend rate. If the price is below par, he gets a yield above the stated dividend rate.

Like their distant relatives, corporate bonds, preferred stocks are generally protected against refunding (refinancing) by the corporation for a period of from five to ten years. If the general level of interest rates declines, then, making the preferred issue relatively attractive in terms of the current market, the investor will not lose his high interest return at least until the end of the restricted period.

Similar protection is offered against "call." The preferred shares cannot be retired out of earnings—except at a stated premium above the original offering price.

Here's an example: Duke Power $2.69 cumulative preferred shares cannot be refunded before March 16, 1980, by a debt or equally ranked preferred issue at an interest cost to Duke of less than that of the $2.69 preferred. That interest cost is 10.76 percent. (Applied to the $25 original offering price, the 10.76 percent return yields the $2.69 that gives the preferred its designation.) What this means is that the holders of the preferred would have the option of purchasing any more attractively priced security—one offering a higher return—if the company were to refund the Duke preferred with equally ranked or senior securities before March 16, 1980. The company is unlikely to issue such securities.

The Duke preferred is currently callable, but at a premium—$27.69. The issue remains callable at that price until March 16, 1980, when it will thereafter be callable at $26.50. Ultimately, the issue is callable at $25.35.

A sinking fund works differently, since it allows for the retirement of a stated number of shares over time—usually by lot or market purchase and always at no premium in price. The sinking fund may begin before the expiration of the refunding protection. The sinking fund gives support to the issue in the market and is separate from refunding provisions.

Preferred issues, like corporate bonds, can be used defensively or aggressively—depending upon the conditions of the market, bull or bear. In rising markets, speculators* concentrate on discount preferreds. In bear markets, cushion preferreds offer resistance to declines.

Here's an example from Mr. McAlpin:

On June 1, 1976, the A/A-rated Baltimore Gas & Electric 9.35 percent preferred shares were trading at 85 to yield 11 percent. The issue was subject to call at 110 until 1984. There was no sinking fund. If interest yields were to drop in a rising market, prices of the preferred shares would rise. If the yield dropped 3.5 percentage points—350 basis points, in Street parlance—the Baltimore preferred's price could appreciate 25 points—from 85 to 110—without a call. Thus the possible reward could be 25/85 or 29.41 percent, plus the current return of 9.35 percent, or a total of 38.76 percent.

In bear markets, cushion preferreds offer some protection, as the following example will suggest:

On June 1, 1976, A/A-rated Cleveland Electric Illuminating $12 cumulative preferred stock was trading at 110 for a yield of 10.91 percent. The issue could be called at 112 until 1984. If rates were to fall by 100 to 350 basis points, causing preferred prices generally to rise, the issue would not trade much higher than 112— an appreciation of only 2 points. Investors would be afraid to pay more than 112 because of the possibility of a call at 112. The total return possible in this case would be just 13.81 percent.

Thus on December 31, 1975, the Cleveland Electric preferred traded at 112 (up 2) while the Baltimore Gas & Electric had im-

* Don't forget that word—speculators. As a trafficker in such securities you are speculating, not investing.

proved to about 92 (up 7). The Baltimore issue's original discount purchase price of 85, then, had resulted in a 17.85 percent return. The Clevelands languished at 13.81 percent.

On the other hand, if the market had headed lower, the Cleveland Electric $12s would hold up well—with an interest yield superior to issues like the Baltimores—and the latter would decline.

Therefore, it can be seen that cushion preferred stocks, like cushion bonds, brake the early effects of a price decline.

Individuals who choose to play the preferred market will find that given the obvious trade-off of some reduction in marketability for higher yields, the cumulative feature, and the senior status of preferred stock, they can often fulfill the conservative objectives pursued by investors seeking current income better than can investors in low-grade common stocks.

Generally, preferred stock should be purchased instead of otherwise similar bonds when the preferred yield is greater, when the marketability at $25 par is greater, and when there is more frequent payment of income.

19 · In Unistates There Is Strength

THE GOVERNMENTS of leading democracies—England, to mention a sterling example, and Italy, to add spice—are in serious financial straits. Rampant inflation and rising labor costs have priced British and Italian goods so high relative to those of neighbors that both have had to devalue their currencies. Still, things haven't improved markedly, and this has raised fears that the economic disease infecting the two countries will spread and perhaps someday cause a world depression. It could happen. After all, we can't afford a war.

Here at home we see an all-too-bright reflection of the English-Italian disease in this nation's aging central cities—New York, Philadelphia, others in the Northeast corridor and Detroit. It seems quite clear that we've got to learn to live with the threat of disaster for some years now, regardless of steps taken by President Carter. Most investors seem to realize this, and thus it is no wonder that many are seeking safer havens than the stock market. It is only natural that United States Government bonds are drawing new adherents—especially in view of current high yields and the availability of a daily market on the American Stock Exchange and on the Philadelphia Exchange.

As this chapter was written, interest rates had taken a surprising upturn both generally and in terms of United States Government debt securities. In the month ending in mid-May, Government one-year notes due May 1977 rose from about 6 percent to 6.35 percent. Yields on two-year notes climbed from 6.5 percent to 7 percent.

Governments maturing in May 1982 were priced to yield 7.7 percent—well above normal savings bank rates—and the debt securities of government agencies were yielding a bit more than that. For example, Federal Land Bank 1982s offered a yield of 7.75 percent at mid-May prices.

Until 1975, the small investor told of such yields in the safest investment around could but yearn for a chance to participate. The market was almost entirely institutional. Banks and brokers seldom welcomed investors seeking less than $100,000 worth of Government securities. In short, then, only the rich could hope to participate.

But the two exchanges, the American Stock Exchange and the Philadelphia Exchange, have changed all that. Both offer daily markets in each Government issue. Since the securities are listed, the investor is assured of periodic newspaper quotations. Trades of as little as a single $1,000 Government note or bond are not uncommon under the system, and the market is truly one in which the individual can participate with confidence.

Perhaps the most important innovation to come with listing was the setting up of central agents to record transactions. Amex members set up the Depository Trust Company, and the Philadelphia Exchange has a similar agency.

Both keep track of individual accounts for brokers and make sure individuals get their periodic interest payments. Under the two systems, the individual never takes possession of the Government certificates. This is a welcome relief, since most Governments are "bearer" instruments—they do not carry the name of a registered owner.

Payable to the bearer, they are easily stolen and thus offer the equivalent of cash to the thief. Growing sophistication on the part of professional criminals has led to a number of daring safe-deposit-box thefts, another solid reason for buying and selling Governments through a depository.

Since no physical transfer is necessary, the cost of buying and selling Governments is a lot cheaper than it would be otherwise. It cost about 78 cents to process a DTC transaction, compared with an estimated $20 in bank processing expense, since the bank actually handles certificates and usually sends them to the customer. (There are bank members of the DTC, however.)

The DTC makes bookkeeping entries on the broker's customer account and leaves the certificate on deposit with the Federal Reserve Bank of New York.

One major brokerage house makes a flat charge of $25 to individuals for each trade in Governments, whether 10 bonds or 50 bonds are involved. Another firm charges $5 a bond on orders of up to 10 bonds, but has a minimum charge of $30. Under Securities and Exchange Commission rules in effect for some time now, commissions are subject to negotiation. An individual investor would do well to shop for the best price. Try the discount brokers, too.

Government notes, bonds,* and other securities are directly guaranteed by the federal government. Bonds of its agencies, though not directly guaranteed, are regarded to be of almost equal safety.

Individuals should recognize that Government securities carry market risk as opposed to risks of default. For example, each time that the general interest level changes, the market prices of all debt securities—including Governments—rise or fall to reflect the change.

Thus if yields were to rise above current levels, the market prices of outstanding issues could be expected to ease and thus reflect the new higher yields. That means that if for some reason you found it necessary to sell your bonds after such a move, you would lose a bit of your principal—plus commission charges. Over months, the change could be enough to wipe out accumulated interest earnings, though this is a somewhat unlikely possibility.

The primary considerations in choosing Governments and agency bonds are yield and maturity, with the highest yields generally to be found in bonds of the longest maturities.

Many investors choose bonds that serve specific investment objectives. Some buy bonds that mature at their retirement and periodically thereafter.

Consider this possibility: You have a child who will be ready for college in ten years. Under the so-called Clifford Trust† you can arrange for the child to receive the interest on the bond at his low tax rate. If he isn't working summers, part-time, or otherwise, he will be in the lowest bracket and certain exclusions will pertain. As a result, he will be able to receive substantial income—as much as $750—free of any tax at all. The trust can be set up in such a manner that the bond will revert to the parent at maturity. Thus, the parent can control the proceeds, using them to pay the child's tuition and other college expenses.

If you assume that the child received income on Governments

* Notes and bonds are identical for all practical investor purposes.
† Must be for at least ten years.

amounting to $2,250, his annual tax would work out to 10 percent of that—$225. If his father received the income and was in the 50 percent bracket—federal, state, and local taxes combined—only $1,125 of the income would remain after taxes.

FLOWER BONDS

This may sound morbid, but the federal government offers a discount on estate taxes due if paid with so-called flower bonds. There are still billions of dollars worth of these curious bonds outstanding, and they owe their popularity to the fact that they can be cashed in at face value prior to maturity—upon the death of the owner when they are used to pay estate taxes.

One broker has said that his firm runs flower bonds under the time clock when they are sold, "all the time." What happens is that a fairly wealthy individual is on his deathbed. Estate taxes are payable to the federal government on assets in the estate in excess of $120,000 for a married man or woman, $60,000 for a single person. A representative of the dying individual will call a broker and arrange to buy a flower bond just before the end. In one case a trade was completed at 3:30 P.M. in behalf of a woman who died at 5:15 P.M. that same day.

Most of the bonds, which generally carry low coupons, sold as this chapter was written at about 80—$800 per $1,000 bond. Anyone dying with flower bonds carrying that discount gets 20 percent off when the estate taxes are paid. (Bury retail. But you might as well pay taxes at wholesale prices.) No taxes are due on the capital gain involved.

Flower bonds need not be purchased in contemplation of immediate death. Many are held for years, producing interest income in the meantime—until they are turned in at face value to pay those federal estate taxes.

20 · Municipal Bonds and Municipal Madness: The Big Mac Grind

YOUR AUNT MARY, perhaps, and thousands of other good citizens, certainly, bought $1.6 billion worth of New York City notes in early 1975, assured by the wizards of Wall Street who rate tax-exempt securities that the Big Apple was entitled to a big A. Later, Lebenthal & Co., a dealer specializing in municipal securities, kissed off accumulating evidence that, financially speaking, the apple was rotten to the core. The firm's opinion, widely advertised, was that the quality of the city's securities was just one notch below those of Uncle Sam, to wit: "The Second Safest Investment in the United States."

No one appears to have built a scaffold yet, but a number of devastated note holders would like to string up the lot. Within weeks of the day the city was to pay, it in effect defaulted when it said it didn't have the money and offered instead to exchange Municipal Assistance Corporation—"Big Mac"—bonds for the notes, thus making hamburger of the city's promise to repay the lenders after one year. It was a frantic rescue scheme and it came largely at the expense of those least able to bear it—small investors. They were asked to accept another city promise—this one of ten years' duration, and for substantially less income in the meantime. Even when issued, the new bonds were worth only $6,500 or so—two-thirds the $10,000 the noteholders had lent the city. And while presumably the bonds would rise to be paid off at the $10,000 shown on their face, ten years seemed an unconscionable post-ponement for those individuals who bought one-year paper because one year met personal financial goals and was long enough in any event.

Those who felt strongly enough about the matter to reject the bonds have been informed by chief rescue worker Felix Rohatyn that they'll have to "live a long time" to collect on the notes.

Financially speaking, the plight of the note and Big Mac holders may be somewhat analogous to that of the man condemned to die at dawn who is given a reprieve—until after lunch.*

The lesson in this our financially troubled time is that it is up to you to winnow out the chaff from the few hard kernels of truth in Wall Street. For in tax-exempt bonds, as in common stocks, brokers and dealers are cockeyed optimists with your money. Tax-exempts—once a reasonably safe bet—have become a chance investment that must be weighed carefully, like any other risk.

Don't let this deter you from investing in one of the most rewarding markets anywhere. And don't assume tax-exempts are for the very rich—and not for you. You may well find that a carefully chosen portfolio of tax-exempts will form the foundation of your financial program and will provide a better return on your money than most competing investments.

It is surprising how little you need earn to benefit from the tax-exempt feature. Many of the buyers of those deplorable New York City notes probably earned less income than you do, and the notes made sense for them in terms of yield, though obviously not in terms of safety. This is true because taxes rise even when rates are left alone.

Many individuals are totally unaware of this phenomenon, a direct result of inflation. The dollar is worth about half what it was 20 years ago, when the tax brackets up to the high levels were identical to what they are today for married taxpayers filing joint returns.

* The holdouts are to have the last laugh. New York State has ruled the moratorium unconstitutional, and the scramble is on to find $1 billion to repay the notes.

Thus, those of us who have managed to keep pace with inflation through raises and additional income of other sorts will find that we have been thrust into higher tax brackets. Under our progressive tax system, Uncle Sam takes an ever larger bite out of our additional income dollar—whether we get them through sweat or the watering-down of values.

Obviously, then, one's tax bracket is not as some imagine it to be—the quotient obtained by dividing last year's total income tax into last year's total income.

What you actually want to know is the rate of tax assessed against your final incremental dollar of income. That is, if you had an adjusted gross income—bureaucratese for the sum upon which tax is imposed—of $28,000, you will be in the 36 percent bracket. Any additional income would be taxed at that rate, unless, of course, the additional income boosted you into the next higher bracket, in this case 39 percent (married taxpayers, joint returns).

If you pay state or local income taxes too, don't forget to include these levies in determining the worthiness of tax-exempts for your portfolio. Residents of New York City, among the most heavily taxed citizens in the nation, pay both city and state income taxes, and those taxes certainly run into money. A married New York City resident with two children and taxable income of $28,000 would pay at a combined rate of about 32 percent.

With or without state and local income taxes, it is fair to say that most people are in higher tax brackets than they think. It's worth a little checking on your part to determine your bracket. If you've checked and aren't sure you have the right answer, call an accountant and ask him to redo your calculation. The instruction sheet that comes with your tax packet will tell you what you need to know about your bracket.

Once you know what bracket you are in, you can easily determine what tax-exempt income is worth to you. Use this formula:

$$\frac{100\% \text{ times } \% \text{ tax-free yield}}{100\% \text{ minus } \% \text{ tax bracket}} = \% \text{ taxable equivalent yield}$$

For example, assume that you are in the 40 percent tax bracket and you want to know what a 6 percent tax-free return is worth to you. Applying the formula:

$$\frac{100\% \times 6\%}{100\% - 40\%} = \frac{600}{60} = 10\%$$

WHERE TO BUY 'EM

Municipal bonds can be purchased from a stockbroker, from a bank, or from a specialist in municipal bonds. The latter are "dealers," not brokers. Remember this distinction: A dealer has an inventory of bonds and a broker does not. A broker will go to a dealer to get the bonds he sells you, and since he can check several dealers he may get you a broader selection than a dealer. But a good dealer makes his money on mark-up—not commission. Deal directly with him and you may pay less than you do if you go to a broker.*

In any case, look around. Don't buy from a stockbroker just because you have an established relationship with him unless he's prepared to do a good job for you. You want to be sure that no matter whom you deal with—broker, banker, or dealer—you will be getting specialized knowledge on the subject. If you do have an established relationship with a banker or stockbroker, see how well he understands municipal bonds. Don't stop at this. Clip a couple of ads of municipal bond services from the newspaper and see what these concerns can do for you.

They'll send brochures. Read them. If they are well done, they will stress the variety available in the municipal bond market and will help you determine which types and selections are most suitable for you. You'll soon discover that there are hundreds of possible selections.

Each concern will include a list of current offerings. Examine

* Major brokers are also *dealers* in municipals, and the customer does just as well buying from this shop as from a pure dealer.

these lists with care. Is the list well diversified, or are there large concentrations of certain bonds—month after month? If the list is concentrated, note what types of bonds are represented. These lists offer a fairly accurate reflection of what the firm's customer portfolios will contain. Are they your kinds of bonds?

Second-guess the municipal bond house. Look at the bonds each house has sold in years past. Ask for the brochures of the past several years. There are, as you know, a few municipalities with uncertain futures at present. Were there a high percentage of such bonds in municipal house A's lists? On B's list? If so, consider this in the context of the hundreds of sound alternatives the firm had to choose from. Even more important: Make sure the bond dealer was—and is—willing to buy back any bond sold at whatever market price is current.

At this point in your investigation you will be ready to select two or three bond dealers offering a combination of the most educational brochure, the most diversified list of offerings, and the most satisfactory past history.

WHAT TO BUY

The critical decision, of course, concerns what to buy. As I have indicated, many a municipal bond buyer has been conned by a salesman. You'll need to have some knowledge on this point so that you don't wind up with the wrong types of municipal bonds.

Would you believe that many retired individuals who pay little or no income tax have been shunted into municipal bonds even though the tax-exempt feature has no meaning for them? Obviously, the man who pays little tax gets a bigger net return from taxable corporation bonds with their invariably higher yields—quality for quality.

Assuming that municipal bonds are for you, here's how to proceed. Learn the distinction between premium bonds and discount bonds. Premium bonds sell in the market at prices above par—100 in the bond tables of the newspaper. That is to say, a $10,000 bond selling at 110 will cost you $11,000. It sells at a premium because its when-issued interest yield was high relative to yields of similar bonds issued currently.

Discount bonds sell at prices below par—a $10,000 bond selling at 90 will cost you $9,000. It sells at a discount because current yields on similar new bonds are higher than the discount bond yielded upon issue.

Discount and premium bonds emphasize different types of return. Discount bonds give a higher deferred return, but a lower present return. Premium bonds give high present returns.

If you can wait for part of your return, the discount bond is probably your best buy. You will receive a relatively low interest payment periodically, but will be able to redeem the bond at maturity at par value and thus pick up the balance of your return. You will have to pay capital gains tax on the appreciation of your principal—the sum you receive at maturity less the sum you paid when you purchased the bond—when the bond comes due at par.

Don't let this discourage you from buying discount bonds. They are priced to give higher annual yields than other bonds, even after you subtract the maximum individual capital gains tax. The lower price of discount bonds more than compensates for the capital gains tax and for the fact that part of your return is deferred. And they can appreciate—a key advantage.

Now for premium bonds. If you want the highest possible current return, look to these bonds. Don't be reluctant to pay above par for a bond. It's not like paying boutique prices for a suit you can buy for less off a plain pipe rack. Remember that the yield of the premium bond has been set in a competitive and current market, and when you buy a bond you are buying a yield, not dollar price. Although you're paying over par, you are also receiving a higher coupon rate than the yield you bought, so the premium is returned to you in coupon form.

On long-term bonds which won't mature in your lifetime but will eventually be left in your estate, you should look for very high current yields.

As I have already indicated, people who do not take the time to educate themselves on the subject of municipal bonds, to establish investment goals, and to learn how to match municipal bonds to their goals, usually buy bonds that are not right for them. Most people satisfy themselves that the bond is of high enough quality and then reach for the highest yields they can find.

Almost without exception those who follow that course end up with very long-term bonds or they buy into a municipal bond fund which will consist of long-term bonds. Let's call this misplaced greed. (If you're going to be greedy you should at least be right.)

Long-term bonds and/or bond funds fluctuate much more widely in the market as interest rates go up or down. If you may have to sell your municipal holdings in five or ten years for some presently unforeseen reason, you will be taking a dangerous gamble with the market when you buy long-term bonds and/or municipal bond funds.

Stoever Glass & Co., a Wall Street municipal bond house, says that this is the most common and most costly mistake municipal bond buyers make—particularly those who have never bought such bonds before.

Do not misunderstand. Long-term bonds and bond funds are right for some people. But there is a good chance that you are not one of those people. Remember that municipal bond maturities range from six months to 40 years. Longer bonds have higher returns than shorter bonds, but they fluctuate more in the market. Shorter-term bonds give you lower returns, but more protection against market fluctuations.

The best way to explain what bonds one should buy is to give a series of portraits of individuals with different investment objectives and indicate the kinds of bonds—maturities, etc.—they should buy. The bonds in each example are quality bonds, but by no means unusual. They are picked primarily because they carry relative safety and because they make good illustrative holdings.

There are references in the profiles to the Bond Buyer's Index of Weekly Averages. This independent service, discussed later in this chapter, publishes a composite average for A-rated bonds of various maturities on new issues sold during the preceding week. For the week these portfolios were constructed the averages were as follows:

UNWEIGHTED AVERAGE (NEW ISSUE)
GENERAL OBLIGATION YIELDS*

5-year	10-year	15-year	20-year	25-year
4.83%	5.58%	6.21%	6.56%	7.65%

* From *The Bond Buyer*, week ending March 12, 1976, Moody's A-rated.

The three examples that follow, which were constructed by Stoever Glass & Co., illustrate the various considerations every municipal bond buyer should take into account before he settles on a purchase or a portfolio of municipal bonds. As you can see, municipals offer considerable flexibility and surprisingly high yields—even to individuals in relatively low tax brackets. All prices are as of March 12, 1976.

MODEL PORTFOLIO NO. 1

A 52-year-old New Jersey doctor would like to retire in ten years. He has managed to shelter a limited amount of his current income through a Keogh plan (see Part VI). He owns stock but wants additional forms of savings. No one can say what his stock will be worth at retirement, and he needs assured income from his capital. He is presently in the 50 percent tax bracket and probably will be in this bracket as long as he is working. He is a prime candidate for a portfolio of municipal bonds. Here is a sample of the type of bonds that would be appropriate for him.

You will notice that the suggested bonds come due shortly after the doctor's planned retirement at 62. New Jersey bonds were chosen because of the likelihood that there will soon be a New Jersey income tax. The bonds, which are of course exempt from federal income taxes, would also be exempt from any New Jersey

Par Amount	Security	Coupon Rate	Maturity	Yield to Maturity	Total Cost
10,000	Sayreville	3.20%	5/1/86	6.75%	$ 7,426.70
10,000	Clifton	3.15%	4/1/86	6.75%	7,405.80
10,000	Tenafly	3.00%	3/1/86	6.75%	7,313.50
10,000	Verona S/D	3.20%	6/1/86	6.75%	7,411.60
10,000	Ewing S/D	3.30%	11/1/87	6.80%	7,219.00
10,000	Chatham	3.70%	3/1/88	6.85%	7,457.00
10,000	Wayne S/D	3.45%	5/1/88	6.85%	7,230.20
70,000					$51,463.80

(S/D = School District)

income tax.

The portfolio sacrifices some current income in order that the doctor will be able to obtain a much higher ultimate yield at maturity. At the time the portfolio was constructed, the Bond Buyer's Index average new issue yield for ten-year bonds was 5.58 percent.

That is to say that the available alternative—assuming tax-exempt bonds of the same maturities—would be a portfolio of par or premium bonds yielding about 5.25 percent. If the doctor had purchased 50 5.58 percent bonds at par, his total income at the end of ten years would have been $27,900.

Now look at how much better off he is in buying the discount bonds in the model portfolio. By using such bonds he will end up with a net appreciation of principal of $13,902 ($18,536.20 less a 25 percent capital gains tax), plus total tax-free coupon income of $24,673. With this discount portfolio, then, his total gain would be $38,575 or an additional $10,675 of tax-free income.

MODEL PORTFOLIO NO. 2

The vice-president of a publishing company plans to retire next month when he reaches age 62. An annual pension of $18,000 and income from other investments will keep him and his wife in the 35 percent tax bracket for life. They have decided to invest $75,000 received from the sale of company stock in tax-exempt municipal bonds therefore even though he will be retired.

The objective of the portfolio, then, is to supplement the couple's other income as much as possible. The chief consideration is to provide them with maximum current income.

Here is the proposed portfolio:

Par Amount	Security	Coupon Rate	Maturity	Yield to Maturity	Total Cost	Current Yield
10,000	Huntsville, Ala.	8.00%	11/1/98	6.65%	$11,600	6.92%
10,000	Salt River, Ariz.	7.80%	1/1/97	6.75%	11,200	6.99%
10,000	Monroe Co., Mich.	7.60%	10/1/93	6.60%	11,000	6.89%
10,000	Cranford, N.J.	7.30%	10/1/96	6.60%	10,800	6.78%
10,000	Pennsylvania	7.25%	4/1/96	6.55%	10,800	6.73%
10,000	Lucas Co., Ohio	7.625%	11/1/94	6.50%	11,200	6.81%
10,000	Tacoma L & P, Wash.	7.30%	1/1/98	6.65%	10,700	6.80%
70,000					$77,300	

Premium bonds are appropriate in this case because they give the highest current return. At the time this portfolio was constructed, the average new-issue yield on 20-year bonds was 6.57 percent. The average yield to maturity on this portfolio is 6.61 percent. The average current yield is 6.85 percent. The bonds were chosen from those of a variety of states, because this retired couple plans to move to a state where there is no state income tax and where none is contemplated.

MODEL PORTFOLIO NO. 3

An active New York businessman who must move in and out of investment obligations from time to time to free capital for his various enterprises is taxed at a 60 percent rate by the federal government and 15 percent by the state. He is interested in a good tax-exempt return, but needs maximum protection against fluctuating municipal bond prices.

He doesn't really know that he will need his principal, but as a businessman he will want easy access to it if a business opportunity presents itself. Here is a suggested portfolio:

Par Amount	Security	Coupon Rate	Maturity	Yield to Maturity	Yield After 30% Gains tax
50,000	Endicott	3.10%	10/1/76	6.35%	5.39%
50,000	Harrison	3.50%	12/1/76	6.30%	5.48%
50,000	Dunkirk	3.70%	3/1/77	6.50%	5.69%
20,000	Clay	3.00%	5/1/78	6.75%	5.72%
30,000	Greece	3.50%	6/1/78	6.60%	5.75%

Average Net Yield on Portfolio—5.58%.

At the time this portfolio was constructed the average new-issue yield for one-year New York municipals was about 5 percent. Discount bonds were used in this portfolio for their higher net return to maturity. Also with such soon-to-mature (short) bonds, this is to the investor's advantage. If you compare his net return to the average yield of one-year bonds—5 percent—it becomes obvious why these bonds make sense.

Generally speaking, short buyers (buyers of short bonds, that is) should buy discount bonds. There isn't such a long wait to collect on the appreciation, and the investor earns more on the discount bond than he would on a par bond.

Had the investor known exactly when he would need his money, he could have purchased bonds which matured on that date. Since he did not know for sure but had to consider resale as a strong possibility, the maturities were varied. If it turns out that the businessman does not need the money for other purposes, he can just roll the money back into the same kind of bonds coming due a year later. If he does need the money he can sell any or all of the five different issues, quickly and with minimum vulnerability to market fluctuations.

THE BLUE PINK CHIP: PRE-REFUND MUNICIPALS

New York City's default on $1.5 billion worth of one-year notes in late 1975 sent a shock wave through the municipal bond market as investors from coast to coast worried that they might suffer the same fate as tens of thousands of schoolteachers, accountants, and clerks in the Big Apple.

Losses of 40 percent or more resulted, and note holders who refused to swap for Municipal Assisstance Corporation ten-year bonds—which quickly dropped to deep discounts—are still trying to get satisfaction. Small wonder the entire municipal bond market hit the skids, and there are still tens of thousands of investors who wouldn't touch a tax-exempt with a beanpole.

But there is a safe alternative in the tax-exempt market for individuals content to own tax-exempts with relatively few years to run. It is the pre-refund bond. These are bonds that were originally ordinary municipals but that now have AAA ratings because they have acquired the backing of the United States government—or effectively so.

They are bonds subject to call for refunding in five or ten years. They have been issued during a period of relatively high interest rates and the issuing community wants to take advantage of current lower rates. It cannot call the bonds until the five- or ten-year period elapses, but it can reduce its costs. It sells new municipal bonds and uses enough of the proceeds from the new municipals to buy United States Government or agency bonds to pay the interest on and ultimately retire the old issue.

This works for the municipality because it receives interest on its United States Government bonds tax-free. Even in a period of relatively low interest yields, there will be enough income from a comparable amount of U.S. Governments to pay the interest on the pre-refunded issue. Servicing of the old municipal issue is handled by a trustee. Since the municipal bond holder's lien is now secured by U.S. Governments,* the rating rises from whatever—BAA, for example—to AAA.

In short, a new, top-quality instrument has been created. Interest

* Some pre-refunds are guaranteed by bank certificates of deposit. Ordinarily they will not carry ratings as high as pre-refunds backed by United States Government and agency bonds. Make the distinction if safety is your game.

yields on pre-refund bonds are in line with but slightly higher than those provided by equal-term high-grade municipal bonds. The reason the pre-refunds earn a little more—15 to 20 basis points more (100 points is 1 percent)—is that they are little understood. Investors will not pay quite so much as they might if they did understand them.

You can buy pre-refunds from any dealer. They generally trade at premiums—yielding less than they did before their pre-refunding. Remember that you pay no commission in a municipal bond transaction in buying from a dealer. Like any merchant dealing from inventory, he has paid a price and hopes to get a resale price high enough to earn a reasonable profit.

If interest rates begin to slide—as many anticipate—there will be lots of pre-refunds cropping up. Be sure your dealer knows the field and can speak knowledgeably about pre-refunds. If he cannot, find one who does know and can help.

THE BOND BUYER'S INDEX

As a buyer of municipal bonds, you should be aware of the trend of tax-exempt interest rates. You'll quickly discover that the index compiled by a publication called *The Bond Buyer* is the Dow Jones industrial average of the municipal market.

But unlike the DJI, which represents an actual average of prices for 30 industrials, the Bond Buyer's Index represents expert opinion. Each Thursday at midday, *The Bond Buyer* calls ten to 15 tax-exempt dealers to see how each would value a new 20-year municipal bond if each name in the 20-bond index had actually issued a new bond. The index is clearly hypothetical, since bonds are not issued weekly—by any tax-exempt authority. Ratings for the nine states and 11 cities represented in the index range from AAA down to BAA, with the average falling between AA & A. Dealer values for each issuer are averaged, then the 20 results are added together and averaged again. The resulting figure becomes the index for the week—stated as a yield. The index truly reflects the movement in 20-year municipals—but not that of the rest of the maturities in municipal bonds.

There is also an 11-bond index which is compiled in exactly the same way as, and using the same figures that appear in, the 20-bond index. The difference is that the 11-bond index extracts a group with an average rating somewhat higher than the 20-bond index—specifically AA as rated by Moody's.

The component "bonds" in the index are changed from time to time. For example, New York City was in the index in 1973, as were Nassau County and Oklahoma City. These and others have been dropped, others added.

Asterisks in front of the names in the current list indicate that the name is also used in the 11-bond index.

20 Bonds in the Bond Buyer Index (April 1976)
(20 year maturity)

	Moody's Rating		Moody's Rating
*California	AAA	*New Jersey	AA
*Georgia	AAA	Baltimore, Md.	A
*Illinois	AAA	Cleveland, Ohio	A
*North Carolina	AAA	*Massachusetts	A-1
Chicago, Ill.	AA	*New Orleans, La	A-1
Columbus, Ohio	AA	New York State	A-1
*Denver, Colo.	AA	*Pittsburgh, Pa.	A-1
*Florida	AA	St. Louis, Mo.	A
*Hawaii	AA	Boston, Mass.	BAA
Memphis, Tenn.	AA	Philadelphia, Pa.	BAA

As the table below indicates, yields decreased slightly through the early 1960s, then rose rapidly, peaking in 1970 after the sharp rise in 1969. Yields declined sharply from mid-1970 through March 1971, then climbed quickly until midyear before dropping sharply by year-end 1971. They were fairly stable during 1972–73 before skyrocketing to a then-record 7.15 percent in mid-December 1974. During 1975, yields stayed at high levels and set an all-time record of 7.67 percent during October 1975.

The index has dropped over 100 basis points from the high to 6.55 percent on April 22 and April 27, 1976. Somewhat lower yields may be in store, and this could be expected to cause a rash of pre-refunding by municipalities—and AAA quality bonds for investors.

Below is the yearly range of the Bond Buyer's Index—1960–1976.

	High Yield %		Low Yield %	
1976	7.13	(1/8)	5.83	(12/29)
1975	7.67	(10/2)	6.27	(2/13)
1974	7.15	(12/12)	5.16	(2/7)
1973	5.59	(8/2)	4.99	(10/11)
1972	5.54	(4/13)	4.96	(11/22)
1971	6.23	(6/24)	4.97	(10/21)
1970	7.12	(5/28)	5.33	(12/10)
1969	6.90	(12/18)	4.82	(1/23)
1968	4.85	(12/26)	4.07	(8/8)
1967	4.45	(12/7)	3.40	(1/19)
1966	4.24	(8/25)	3.51	(1/20)
1965	3.56	(12/9)	3.04	(1/18)
1964	3.32	(3/19)	3.12	(12/17)
1963	3.31	(11/14)	3.01	(3/21)
1962	3.37	(1/4)	2.98	(10/18)
1961	3.35	(9/7)	3.26	(2/23)
1960	3.78	(1/7)	3.27	(8/18)

MUNICIPAL BOND FUNDS

Investors interested in municipal bonds who fear the selection process will be their undoing can buy shares in municipal bond funds organized and selected by professionals. These funds are enormously popular; industry-wide sales of them reached $2.2 billion in 1975, and were expected to total nearly $3 billion in 1976.

The portfolios, consisting mainly of municipal bonds with maturities of 25 years or longer, are completely assembled before the shares are sold to investors. The funds are essentially unmanaged thereafter, and the funds liquidate as the bonds mature. Minimum units range from $1,000 to $5,000. There can be no improvement in yield through adroit sale and purchase, but 1976's tax-exempt returns on new funds ranged to a satisfying 7.57 percent. There are no coupons to clip, no safe-keeping concerns, and no redemption fee. Investors love those monthly interest checks.

Meanwhile, the Kemper Corporation, an insurance holding company, has begun offering the first municipal bond fund organized along mutual fund lines. The company organized its fund as a limited partnership—carefully skirting IRS prohibitions against the tax-free distribution of tax-exempt income by mutual funds—and offers minimum investments of $100 followed by increments of as little as $25. The portfolio is managed—that is, bonds are bought and sold to improve position—and the vehicle grows with net new purchases by shareholders. Shares can be redeemed at net asset values, just like the shares of ordinary mutual funds.

The fund's progress is being closely watched by the industry, since the "open end" feature—the right to add new shares as they are sold—is regarded as highly attractive to the industry.

PART V
MUTUAL FUNDS

21 · Mutual Disaster— Why Most Mutual Funds Are Not for You

CRADLED IN A PLUSH LEATHER contour chair high above the mean streets of Manhattan, the author spoke some time ago with one of the financial community's best-known money managers. Through the window of that elegant corner office was Central Park—vivid and immediate.

Outside the master suite, in heavily carpeted halls lined with modern art, fashion-conscious secretaries sat languorously occupied. The acoustically deadened offices caused this stranger to start at the sound of his own voice.

In the executive's inner office (deskless, a sublime conceit), the conversation turned to the stock market—a stock market, I might note, that had stripped many of those who trusted this expert of a third of their capital.

My companion was above all that, though. He was eager to talk of the conquest of future markets. For he was—and is—still a king. Unlike scores of other stricken money managers who were destroyed by the difficult markets of the 1970s, he was attached to a rich organization impervious to market collapse.

It is the shareholders of this mutual fund organization who took it on the nose, not the carefully tailored market expert who answered my questions.

This is not to say that our cultured friend is a bad man. The point, rather, is that you and I cannot afford to keep him. His fees and his mistakes have rendered his services prohibitively expensive.

But you can bet that you'll be hearing from this man's agents—and if not from his agents, then from those of other fat-cat mutual fund managers who wish to sell you shares in such losing propositions.

Until recently, anyway, mutual funds were an appealing product for the broker-salesman. The sellers did and do receive up to 8½ percent of what you put into a $5,000 purchase, and that $425 compares with 1½ percent—$80—on a stock purchase of similar size. It should be noted that selling the stock would cost you another 1½ or $80. The mutual fund charge is a one-time item.

Even so, the funds aren't selling new shares at a rate as great as shareholders are turning them in. Chalk up "net redemptions" to shareholder disgust and broker apathy. Mutual fund shares were never purchased voluntarily. They had to be sold. Where once the 8½ percent commission was sufficient incentive, it no longer is. The mutual funds have stiff competition from the newcomer listed options exchanges. Look at it this way. If a salesman gets you to buy $5,000 worth of mutual fund shares, that money is presumably locked up indefinitely. If the salesman persuades you to participate in stock options instead, he'll be back in as few as three months to sell you again.

The funds have grown so alarmed at their inability to compete that they are talking about bringing back the front-end load. The Securities and Exchange Commission regards the front-end load as something of an evil—as indeed it is. Under these contractual plans, the customer buys shares on a long-term purchase basis. Up to 50 percent of the first year's payment goes to the sellers. If one stays with the plan, the individual's commission costs eventually average down to 8½ percent. But most dropped out and took a bath, and there is little reason to believe that wouldn't happen again if the front-end load came back strongly.

As we shall see mutual funds have been a dubious investment at best—and may very well be marginal in future, unless you are lucky enough to climb aboard a rare winner. We'll talk about the question of no-load funds that hire no salesmen and charge no commissions later.

Before we look at the record, let's adopt a premise. I think it is fair to say that at the very least, a mutual fund should help the investor overcome the ravages of inflation. But as we shall see, this has been difficult to accomplish over the last two full market cycles.

A market cycle is the span of time over which the stock market, as measured by a representative market average, moves from a peak to a trough and back to a peak again. When this process continues through another trough to a second peak, a double market cycle has occurred.

Believe it or not, by the inflation test of performance, only three mutual funds out of a universe of hundreds were successful over the last double market cycle.

The three winners were a motley lot, including a tiny Canadian only recently available in the United States, and a second fund that invests in gold shares, which may well be out of favor in the years ahead. (I'm not a gold bug though it is obvious something fans these shares to fever pitch from time to time. I call it hysteria. When hysteria cools, so do the gold stocks.) The third fund that succeeded barely edged out inflation. It and several others in the top ten bought bonds and preferred shares.

By any measure, the result was unusual for so long a period—specifically, seven and a half years. During most such periods the average fund would do much better.

The critical question is whether we'll have conditions in future like those of the past several years, when the combined forces of recession, high unemployment, unusually rapid inflation, and record high interest rates conspired to produce disaster for investors.

Perhaps the next seven and a half years will be kinder to mutual funds. That possibility is what led me to include a lengthy section on mutual funds in this book.

Look at the table below for the results of the double market cycle beginning at the market peak of November 30, 1968, and ending March 31, 1976:

Assets (millions) 12/31/75	Fund	Objective	Gain 11/30/68– 3/31/76
$ 19.8	Templeton Growth	growth	195.5%
80.0	International Investors	gold	97.9
159.1	Investors Selective	bonds & pref	58.6
16.5	Founders Special	venture capital special situations	53.7
27.9	Keystone B-2	bonds & pref	53.3
5.1	Mutual Shares	growth & income	48.6
293.3	Pioneer Fund	growth & income	48.5
28.8	Contrafund	aggressive growth	47.9
6.2	Paramount Mutual	growth & income	47.4
323.8	Keystone B-4	bonds & pref	46.0
	Standard & Poor 500 stock index (income included)		23.0
	Consumer Price Index advance (approximate)		58.0

Source: Computer Directions Advisors, Silver Spring, Maryland. Dividends assumed reinvested.

It naturally follows that most mutual fund shareholders are invested in the very largest vehicles in the industry. They have been sold by the most successful fund salesmen—and that's why they are so big.

Assets (millions) 12/31/75	Fund	Objective	Gain or loss 11/30/68– 3/31/76
$1,438.2	Affiliated	growth & income	+39.8%
1,463.4	Dreyfus	growth & income	— 3.9
1,234.1	Investment Co. of America	growth & income	+30.4
2,113.4	Investor's Mutual	balanced	+17.3
2,039.1	Investors Stock	growth & income	+ 6.9
1,373.8	Massachusetts Investors Trust	growth & income	+12.7
1,112.9	Price Growth Stocks	growth	+ 6.4

Source: Computer Directions Advisors, Silver Spring, Maryland. Dividends assumed reinvested.

After you look at the table charting the results achieved by the largest funds—those with $1 billion plus under management—it will be surprising if you are not convinced that, in mutual funds, anyway, bigness can be bad. The funds represented in the performance race over the double market cycle are listed in alphabetical order.

Brokerage firms rarely talk to their customers about the investor who acts as his own salesman—the individual who clips the notice of a no-sales-charge—"no load"—mutual fund out of the newspaper and sends for a contract. The no-load funds, which do not belong to the commission-oriented trade group, the Investment Company Institute, have grown in importance in recent years as more and more investors have realized their attributes.

The key fact for the investor is this: Given equal performance, the no-load fund is superior to the load fund. The question is: Load or no-load, is any mutual fund worth its salt? You mustn't forget that both types of mutual fund trade and pass the costs of trading onto shareholders. Some critics say that the average mutual fund spends so much money adjusting portfolio holdings it's no wonder the shareholders haven't made money.

22 · The Case for Mutual Funds

IN FAIRNESS to the mutual funds, it should be pointed out that the devastating stock market losses of the first half of the decade of the 1970s were the worst since the Great Depression. Further, most observers look for better times and believe that a disaster of that magnitude is unlikely in the foreseeable future—if in the next generation.

Many look for an extended period of generally rising stock prices for at least five to ten years, a period that would favor individual investors of perspicacity and some well-run mutual funds as well. I believe that or I wouldn't be writing this book.

On the other hand, I must caution that stocks have never reached a level so low that anyone could guarantee that they wouldn't go lower still, given sufficient stock market pessimism. I was interviewed along with two ebullient Wall Streeters on a television show in 1973 and listened aghast as my two fellow panelists assured the folks watching the tube that stock prices were so low they couldn't possibly go lower. Their theory, unstated, appeared to be that lower prices would violate some natural law. When my turn came I said I wasn't at all convinced by their argument, though I would be tickled pink if they were right. They weren't. The 1974 bear was more vicious even than the bear of 1973.

But let's assume that the troubled cities of this nation will find the courage and political clout to restructure dramatically and that England and Italy among the troubled nations of Europe will recover short of bankruptcy. In short, let's assume that the world will be safe for free enterprise for at least five years.

In that event, the best-run mutual funds ought to be able to dull—or even break—the cutting edge of inflation, providing reasonable profits for shareholders.

I frankly don't recommend the mutual fund route—even if you find those big winners among mutual fund shares. Their Johnson & Johnson holdings get watered down by their Equity Fundings. But assuming you haven't time to shift for yourself and have decided to travel the automatic route to market, let's consider the positive attributes of the funds.

Since there will be those who believe in the stock market but cannot devote the necessary time and effort to invest on their own, I am going to state the argument in favor of the funds—and their performance during the bear market—in the strongest possible terms. That is, I am going to quote from a rebuttal to these pages from an official in a mutual fund organization:

"The conventional practice of comparing mutual fund performance against the popular averages greatly distorts the true picture of superior relative performance of mutual funds during the turbulent markets of the past ten years.

"The widely followed Standard & Poor's 500 stock index or the narrower Dow Jones 30 stock industrials index is not representative of broad movements in the stock market nor of the investment experience of individual investors.

"The S & P 500 contains the biggest companies listed on the Big Board. By definition, the biggest companies are the most successful companies and naturally these are the very companies that predominate in institutional portfolios.

"Thus, the S & P 500 is an index of average institutional performance, not the market as a whole. Obviously, the average is always going to reflect the average performance of professional money managers and that is what has happened.

"The average investor doesn't own the big stocks contained in the S & P 500 because they are too high priced (e.g., IBM at 265 a share would require $26,500 to purchase in a round lot). Typically, the average investor who buys his own stocks buys low-priced stocks selling at around $10 a share.

"Overall mutual funds have done better than other money managers as shown in the latest A. S. Hansen tabulation:

COMMON STOCK INVESTMENT RETURNS

	Compound Annual Rates of Return 1966–75 (all dividends reinvested)
Bank Regular Equity Accounts	1.9%
Insurance Company Equity	1.4
Mutual Funds: Growth	3.2
Mutual Funds: Growth & Income	3.8
Standard & Poor's 500 stock index	3.3
Dow Jones Industrial Index (30 stocks)	2.7

"In addition, in the past quarter century, the Johnson Mutual Fund Average of 20 growth funds has outpaced the S & P 500 (e.g., the 'institutional managers' index') and the rate of inflation during 12 out of the 14 ten-year periods in that time span.

"In conclusion, one of the greatly misunderstood concepts in the financial world today is how well the mutual funds have done in protecting shareholder capital against the ravages of the turbulent and volatile markets of the past ten years. Granted inflation and interest rates increased more rapidly than equity values in the past ten years, but with hyper-inflation subsiding and with the revival of securities markets, the traditional role of mutual funds as a means of preserving and enhancing capital should reappear over the next few years.

"In many respects, the double market cycle deflation that occurred in the seven-year period from 1968 through 1974 is comparable to the double market cycle deflation of 1929–1937. In both periods, stocks were drastically defeated following the rampant speculation of the previous periods. After the 'eye of the storm' had passed in the late 1930s, great investment opportunities were created and the base of the great postwar bull market was established. Similarly today, stocks are greatly undervalued and with corporate earnings improving, the base of a major bull market appears to have been laid."

Perhaps the strongest argument for the funds is that in any ten-year period in the past, two out of every three NYSE-listed stocks have gone down in value. This suggests that you will have to be pretty shrewd to find long-term winners on the New York Stock Exchange, or that you will have to find success on the Amex and among unlisted stocks.

As I have already pointed out, Amex and unlisted stocks are generally shunned by the institutions. They offer bigger risks to shareholders generally. But when you pick well, the rewards are bigger as well.

The mutual funds generally buy only Big Board stocks or stocks on the Amex or in the over-the-counter market that could easily qualify for a Big Board listing. Syntex, the chemical concern that makes the raw materials for birth-control pills, is a good example of a Big Board qualifier on the Amex, and American Express trades over the counter. Both are large enough to have a Big Board listing if they chose, and both are favored by the institutions.

But let's assume success. Even if the individual succeeds through direct market investments he may experience costs in excess of those he would encounter if he purchased mutual fund shares.

The successful Chemical Fund—successful over the past ten years by every measure except inflation—offered to show how the individual investor might "fare better" by owning mutual fund shares than by purchasing stocks directly. The figures were, not surprisingly, tailored to the costs of owning Chemical Fund shares, though they would be relevant in general for many funds.

What may not be valid is the assumed compound annual rate of growth—10.6 percent,* all dividends assumed reinvested, a growth rate used for both the Chemical Fund and for the ten stocks "selected" by the individual directly.

In such glorious circumstances—which wouldn't have been realized over the past ten years or even the last fifty—the aggregate market value of the mutual fund shares and those picked by the individual would reach $125,000 over 25 years—net of all expenses direct and indirect.

Chemical Fund points out that the annual cost of maintaining such an account, including the indirect costs which are paid by the fund, was less than one-half of the do-it-yourselfer investment after the first year.

Chemical Fund goes on to note that the initial charge of $1,500 for acquiring Chemical was greater than the $410 in brokerage to acquire the individual portfolio of stocks. This differential "was more than made up within a few years by the lower annual costs of maintaining the investment in Chemical Fund. Moreover, the investor who bought Chemical Fund would be freed from the time-

* The record for Chemical Fund over the past 25 years.

	Chemical Fund	Do-It-Yourselfer
I *Initial Costs:*		
Sales charge (equal to 6 percent on a $25,000 Chemical fund order—no redemption fee)	$1,500	$410[1]
II *Annual Costs:*		
(a) Cost of buying and selling stocks	30[2]	225[3]
(b) Dividend reinvestment	–0–	15
(c) Bookkeeping, custody, and investment management fees	330[4]	420[5]
(d) Withdrawal plan (assuming investor wished to receive a set figure monthly equal to 6 percent of his original investment)	–0–	145[6]
Total annual costs	$ 360	$805

1. Brokerage costs of buying initially ten issues for a total outlay of $25,000 (10 × 50 shares × $50 per share equals $25,000) using discount broker commission schedules.

2. Based on a 10 percent annual portfolio turnover and the actual cost of executing portfolio transactions which averaged 43/100 of 1 percent in commission costs on the actual dollar amount transacted in 1975 for Chemical Fund.

3. Based on annual portfolio turnover of 10 percent and discount broker commissions.

4. Using Chemical Fund's actual expense ratio for such services in 1975 of 53/100 of 1 percent on assets managed.

5. Assuming investor would use an investment advisory service costing ½ of 1 percent on assets managed, plus transaction charges by the custodian bank.

6. Includes bank fees of $10 per transaction plus additional discount brokerage fees on transactions to produce additional money to make a 6 percent annual withdrawal.

consuming and difficult task of selecting securities for investment."

But what about actual results in actual markets? Let's look at the record of the best-performing major mutual funds—those with over $200 million invested—for seven recent ten-year periods.

Chemical Fund, as seen in the table that follows, offers an outstanding example of limited success—and failure to meet the challenge of inflation. During the most recent ten years portrayed in

MAJOR MUTUAL FUNDS WHICH HAVE CONSISTENTLY OUTPERFORMED THE MARKET SINCE 1960
REVISED 7/15/76

Ten-year periods. All dividends and distributions reinvested after deducting maximum sales charges. Includes all mutual funds with assets in excess of $100 million on 12/31/75 which outperformed the Standard & Poor's 500 Stock Index in the most recent ten-year period ending 12/31/75 and at least six of the seven ten-year periods since 1960.

	Fund Assets 12/31/75	Fund Ob-jective	1966–75	1965–74	1964–73	1963–72	1962–71	1961–70	1960–69
Standard & Poor's 500 Index	(millions)		+ 37.6%	+ 12.7%	+ 78.1%	+156.3%	+ 96.7%	+118.3%	+111.0%
Babson Investment Fund*	$ 196	G	+ 56.9	+ 51.9	+126.6	+207.2	+113.2	+111.3†	+126.7(a)
Chemical Fund	883	G	+ 52.0	+ 60.8	+141.7	+273.3	+141.1	+139.5	+153.3
Decatur Income	231	I	+ 70.9	+ 52.4	+110.1	+181.2	+158.1	+164.5	+147.1
Enterprise	198	MCG	+ 57.6	+ 69.4	+206.8	+393.8	+276.8	+275.9	+398.7
Fidelity Fund	597	GI	+ 48.0	+ 34.5	+ 89.0	+181.9	+111.6	+132.8	+128.5
Harbor Fund	126	I	+ 84.2	+ 74.2	+117.3	+160.7	+151.3	+123.5	+115.9
Investment Co. of America	1,234	GI	+ 60.0	+ 49.9	+112.6	+214.0	+135.1	+147.4	+152.0
Istel	115	GI	+116.7	+109.0	+167.4	+216.6	+188.1	+195.1	+213.5
Johnston Mutual*	275	G	+ 58.8	+ 48.8	+144.5	+268.3	+147.1	+140.7	+191.4
Pioneer	293	GI	+ 82.4	+ 64.7	+133.5	+177.0	+123.5	+146.5	+149.3
Price New Horizons*	329	MCG	+108.4	+114.6	+256.7	+573.3	+292.9	+193.8	+233.6(b)
Provident Fund for Income	120	I	+ 62.8	+ 60.8	+105.1	+176.7	+151.9	+129.0	+118.4(c)
Puritan	693	I	+ 58.3	+ 48.5	+ 97.4	+156.9	+124.5	+140.5	+124.6
State Street Investment Co.*	300	GI	+ 47.8	+ 32.6	+ 94.3	+183.2	+117.9	+133.6	+158.1
Washington Mutual	296	GI	+ 64.2	+ 33.6	+ 89.9	+143.3†	+110.0	+136.7	+115.2
Windsor	438	G	+ 64.9	+ 37.9	+ 90.5	+186.0	+ 94.6†	+134.6	+145.4

Source: Fundscope Magazine and Johnson's 1976 Investment Company Charts.
* No-load fund.
(a) from first public offering date April 30, 1960.
(b) from first public offering on January 13, 1961.
(c) from first public offering date August 3, 1960.
† indicates a 10 year period when fund underperformed the S&P 500 Index.
G—Long-term growth, income secondary.
GI—Growth and income.
I—Income.
MCG—Maximum capital gains.

the chart—from January 1, 1966, through December 31, 1975—Chemical Fund gained 52.0 percent. During that same period of time, rampant inflation raised the cost of living 73.4 percent. Thus, in those parlous times, which included the second-worst bear market in modern market history, only Istel, Price New Horizons, Harbor Fund, and Pioneer managed to meet the acid test—capital preservation.

Look at the impact on New Horizons of the 1973–74 bears. New Horizons, with gains of 573.3 in the ten-year period ended December 31, 1972, dropped to a gain of less than half that in the ten-year period ended December 31, 1973—to 256.7 percent. In the ten-year period ended December 31, 1974, the gain had been halved again to 114.6 percent. New Horizons buys growth stocks that are expected to do better than the economy and by a long shot. These stocks—not unlike the ones you are looking for—did especially poorly in the bear market. Let me add that the New Horizons managers proved slow to admit their mistakes.

Considering that the bull market of early 1976 was one of the most phenomenal on record—and that mutual funds generally seem to have shared in the action—there is every reason to believe that several of the funds in the "winner's" list will have gained the upper hand over inflation once again. Yet the record, at present, is unsettling, at best.

23 · Which Mutual Fund?

YOU MUST BE PREPARED to exercise as much care and restraint in picking an investment company as you would in picking an individual stock. The essential difficulty is that you must pick a fund on the basis of past performance, and the past is a woefully inadequate guide to the future. We have seen the best records mutual funds have been able to compile in the chart above. Chances are that the funds in the chart will continue to perform reasonably well. Most of them have been around for many years, have strong managements, and continue to do better than average.

But the record also indicates that none of the top funds would have made you affluent over the past ten years. Assuming you are going to follow your fund shares the way you would follow individual stocks, you may want to consider investments in small mutual funds, since the best of these usually perform much better in bull markets than do the giants.

Most of the small funds represent one man's inspiration—they are not run by committees. Let's see what happened to three of the most successful small funds in the major bull market of the late 1960s. Enterprise Fund was the most spectacular success and is representative of what bigness does to a fund designed to do well through investments in emerging growth stocks. Under Fred Carr, a shy Californian, Enterprise managed to put two years of near 100 percent market gains back to back in 1967 and 1968.

This success caused investors to flock to Enterprise like blackbirds to an elm grove. Suddenly this fund, which had succeeded so spectacularly with a manageable $25 million or so, blossomed into a $250 million, then a $1 billion fund.

Carr, caught up in the enthusiasm, began telling people there were enough companies like the mushrooming Tonka Corporation —a toy-truck maker—to support an Enterprise Fund with $10 billion or more in assets. However, by 1969, the bear market had killed the growth concept and Enterprise collapsed—dropping to 343rd in the mutual fund standings in 1969.

A fraction of the Enterprise early birds made money, and an even smaller fraction may have sold Enterprise in time to hold onto gains. The early birds who stayed too long lost money—along with the hapless late arrivals.

The small mutual funds that stayed small were even worse off. Enterprise at least survived. Neuwirth Fund did not. Neuwirth had the same kind of record as Enterprise before the bear market struck.

The fund's high-living chief, Henry Neuwirth, then watched fund assets dwindle from $80 million to $40 million. He promptly doubled his fees, saying that he needed the money to pay for research. Some uncharitable critics thought Henry needed the money in part to pay for the Rolls-Royce that carried him to the helicopter pad, and for the four-seat chopper in which he shuttled to Manhattan from his Middletown, New Jersey, headquarters.

One-man bands are colorful—but the assets are tied up in a single instrument. One fine day Henry Neuwirth, who was good in bull markets, flew his helicopter into the East River and died.

Fred Mates, who exchanged directorships with the equally successful Neuwirth, played much the same game and with equal successes—for a while. But he bought a substantial piece of Ecological Industries in unregistered shares. When the storm came he was unable to sell the restricted Eco stock and other "letter stock." His fund went south. This brainy analyst, who got out of his depth in the bear market, turned to nightclubbery. Mates Place, like his fund, soon foundered.

FUND MANAGEMENT

Nothing is more important or harder to evaluate than mutual fund management. In the first place, the manager or managers of a major mutual fund may be unknown outside the company. The best single clue to management, then, is a mutual fund's long-term record. You shouldn't be looking for the mutual fund that places first in the annual mutual fund derby. Funds that lead the derby usually work best in extraordinary market environments. A gold shares fund, for example, is unlikely to lead the pack in a year of falling gold prices, though concern over the international monetary situation has helped the leading gold fund head the list more than once. The fund specializes in gold-mining shares of South African companies. That fact hardly inspires confidence. One of the best-managed funds has never placed first, but invariably lands in the top ten funds over succeeding ten-year periods. The point to remember is that consistency will carry you through—not spectacular gains in one market and equally spectacular losses in another. If you have a fund that can chalk up 8 to 9 percent gains on the average—doing reasonably well in down markets—you've probably latched onto a good management.

FUND SIZE

A mutual fund that has been operating for an extended period—of say ten years or so—and has remained smaller than $10 million is probably not a good risk, regardless of how well it may do from time to time. Performance of such small funds tends to be erratic and research analysis sketchy. They can't afford to do the thorough job the best big funds do.

You are probably better off in a fund of $100 million or more. While I used to believe that a fund becomes unmanageable when it attains $250 million size, ten of the 16 funds in the chart on page 223 have assets in excess of $250 million. On the other hand, remember that the record of most of the billion-dollar funds has been uninspiring (see chart page 216).

CHURNING

The best-run mutual funds do relatively little trading. You should beware of a mutual fund that has a turnover of more than 50 percent in a given year. A fund with $100 million in assets that sold $35 million in stocks in a particular year would have a turnover rate of 35 percent. That's low and probably would be indicative of good management—assuming, of course, that the record is good. A turnover of 75 percent or more is bad for two reasons. It suggests indecision and may reflect a tendency on the part of the fund management to "window-dress"—sell shares of stocks that have been bombed before the end of the quarter. The mutual fund does not have to say what it did in mid-quarter—it can go in and out without your knowledge—and it doesn't have to report what it doesn't own at the end of a quarter. The fund with a 75 percent turnover may be speculating or may be paying off brokers with commission business, a reward for the broker's help in selling the fund's shares.*

INVESTMENT MIX

It is probably best to avoid mutual funds that specialize in a narrow area of the stock market. Imagine what would have happened to you had you bought a mutual fund specializing in airline stocks before the energy crisis. Electronic stocks, while hot from time to time, probably show more bankruptcies than most groups. An electronics stock fund would be risky at best.

Anyone who lived through the bear market knows that some mutual funds simply do not work well in certain kinds of markets. The growth funds lost most of their gains, and the income funds—those invested in companies producing income but little in the way of capital gains—became more successful. In 1973 the income funds produced an average dividend yield of 6 percent. They were the top performers in 1973. But this should be qualified. They simply lost less money than the growth-oriented mutual funds. A few did make gains.

SWITCHING HORSES

Operating on the premise that you will keep an eye on your investments, I am going to suggest that you limit your mutual fund purchases to management companies with a full product line—growth funds, growth-and-income and income funds, money market funds, and so forth. These organizations, recognizing the fact that many investors would like to have some say over their assets, allow switching from fund to fund. The fee for this service is nominal—usually a flat $5. Thus by owning shares in a big organization you can maintain some flexibility, shun the stock market for money market instruments when they are doing well and vice versa. I urge

* Turnover rates are readily available to fund salesmen. Ask for them.

you to buy initially into a mutual fund organization with an outstanding record of managing at least one fund. The table on page 223 clearly indicates that growth-and-income funds (six) and income funds (four) can rival long-term results of growth funds (six, of which two are high-risk funds stressing maximum capital gains). It is far better to find a mutual fund management company that has a top record in at least one area than a loser organization with a more complete product line.

SWITCHING BREEDS

Unfortunately, it is seldom possible to switch from one mutual fund group to another without paying for the privilege. Nevertheless, you will certainly want to consider a switch if your fund drops into the bottom quarter of all funds or begins to act erratically. Oddly enough, many fund owners never think to switch. I've had calls from dozens of fund shareholders who have experienced little growth in 20 years. Some even have losses after two decades in a fund. In such cases, a switch is clearly recommended. Since the billion dollar mutual funds have the most money and have, by and large, performed the worst, it is reasonable to assume there are many thousands of shareholders who have done poorly—who might have been better off with their money in a savings bank.

They should consider switching, to be sure. You should consider switching if your fund drops into the bottom quarter of all funds in the performance race or if your fund begins to act erratically. You may also wish to switch if your objectives change. The most common factor motivating a switch may be your retirement. Retirees are ordinarily better served by income or growth-and-income funds than by aggressive growth funds.

Shareholders who have considered switching are often surprised at the costs. Those who own no-load shares find that they sometimes pay a fee for "redemption." About 35 of the no-load mutual funds charge redemption fees, usually 1 percent, though a few funds charge 2 percent. Some funds will not charge redemption fees if the shares have been held for a specified period of time—six months or a year are the terms commonly specified. You can't blame the no-loads for redemption fees—they didn't charge admission and it costs money to move you in and out.

Whether you are coming from a load or a no-load fund, you'll pay plenty to switch into a load fund. You probably paid an 8½ percent load or sales fee to buy your shares, and you'll pay a similar fee to the new load fund. But if you have accumulated a substantial sum in your fund, your reinvestment will cost less than the 8½ percent maximum fee. Remember that those with $100,000 in a fund pay as little as 3 percent to add to holdings. A new commitment of $100,000 in a switch will generally cost no more than 3 percent.

PLAYING FAST AND LOOSE

If you are going to switch from fund to fund, frequently you are on your own. You will be better off once you decide to go the mutual fund route to hold for the long term, shifting only when it becomes clear that something serious is happening to your fund.

Those who switch frequently soon discover that it is difficult to improve positions—to pick upcoming funds and time purchases profitably. First Multifund of America was designed to do just that. The fund invests in other mutual funds, picking and choosing new mutual funds and dropping old ones to catch the latest winners. The fund's record is not inspiring.

But at least they are working at it full time. You'll be devoting part time to the quest, and you may succeed. But chances are you'll do no better and will probably do a great deal worse. Let me stress that switching should be undertaken with caution and even reluctance. The costs you experience in switching will probably handicap your performance for years.

RISK-REWARD RATIOS

Each year, Wiesenberger Services, Inc., puts out a thick book called *Investment Company Services*. Available about midyear at local libraries and some brokerage houses, the manual gives you a record of each leading mutual fund's performance—short- and long-term.

Wiesenberger not only rates the "rewards" of owning fund shares, it rates the risks and the rewards in the context of the risk assumed by shareholders in owning the fund.

Fascinating mathematical concepts are involved, and values are assigned "beta" and "alpha" numbers. Don't be alarmed; it isn't *that* difficult.

The beta coefficient is a mathematical attempt to measure on a systematic basis the risk of owning particular mutual funds vis-à-vis the risks of owning a hypothetical portfolio of all the stock in Standard & Poor's index of 500 stocks. (That index, by the way, includes the bulk of the values of all listed stocks.) The S&P is assigned a beta coefficient of 1.00 at all times. What this means is that the risks of owning a particular mutual fund are rated against the actual performance of the S&P. Thus, if a mutual fund has risen higher in good markets and fallen more heavily in bad ones than the S&P, its beta coefficient will be larger than 1.00. Conversely, if the fund has done less well in good markets and dropped less than the market generally in bear markets, its beta will be less than 1.00. Clearly, then, a mutual fund with a beta of 1.25 would be more risky than one with a beta of 0.75.

Wiesenberger goes a step further with its alpha coefficient. The alpha coefficient is a measure of the relative reward of owning a particular mutual fund in terms of that fund's historic beta factor.

That is to say, if a mutual fund did unusually well over a particular period, it would have registered a bigger gain—or would have experienced a smaller loss—than you would expect given the fund's historically derived risk factor.

Here's an example from Wiesenberger:

The S&P index gains 8.44 percent. Fund A, with a beta factor of 1.50, gains 15.55 percent.

Multiply 1.50 by 8.44 to get a +12.66 anticipated return on the basis of measured beta.

Subtract the 12.66 from 15.55 to get an alpha coefficient of plus 2.89.

On the other hand, Fund B has a beta factor of 2 and also gains 15.55 percent.

2 times 8.44 equals +16.88, anticipated fund return.

15.55 less 16.88 equals minus 1.33 alpha coefficient.

Weisenberger would conclude that Fund A is better than Fund B. The reason for this conclusions is that Fund B entails two times the risk of the general market (S&P equals 1.00, remember) and hasn't come up with the rewards indicated in terms of its objectives and its historical beta coefficient.

24 · Money Market Funds

COMMERCIAL BANK CHECKING ACCOUNTS have long been one of the curiosities of finance. The banks not only keep your money hostage paying no interest, they have actually charged you for the privilege of writing checks against your balance.

In New York State, at least, the situation is changing in favor of a somewhat better deal for the checking account customer. The reason: competition. The New York savings banks have obtained a change in state law permitting them to offer their customers checking accounts. Most have indicated their checking accounts will be charge-free services.

The commercial banks, which fought the proposal tooth and nail, have now done an about-face—or should we say a left-face. Fearful that billions of dollars of free money will walk out of their doors and enter the savings banks for one-stop banking, they are developing gimmicks to hold the loyalty of their customers.

One bank offers a "Grand Reward"—keep $1,000 on deposit separately and you can write all the checks you want without charge. Another bank gives free checking on a $500 balance. Neither the commercial banks nor the savings banks offer interest on deposits in checking accounts. This is something that is presently offered almost exclusively by the money market funds.

It is not a perfect system from the standpoint of the individual who would like to write unlimited checks against an interest-bearing savings account—checks are limited to sums of $500 and up. But it is the next best thing.

The money market funds arose out of the inspiration of Harry B. R. Brown and Bruce Bent, chairman and president respectively of Reserve Fund, the pioneer. The two men used to dream of a place to buy with ease United States Government securities and bank certificates of deposit and other money market instruments.

They were money managers who had a relatively small amount of money to put to work for short periods of time, but it was inconvenient and inefficient to call each bank to buy the debt securities they needed.

Since no one else thought of it, the two men left their jobs to set up Reserve Fund. The fund buys all kinds of money market instruments—bankers' acceptances and letters of credit in addition to bank "CDs" and U.S. Government securities. The idea was to appeal to institutions primarily, and secondarily to individuals. Individuals liked the idea because it gave them a chance to buy a piece of an instrument they couldn't afford to buy in full. Most of the instruments the fund buys come in $100,000 denominations. Reserve Fund's shares cost $1,000 with a minimum purchase of one.

The Reserve Fund was actually marketed four years ago. It was an instant success and has been much copied. In fact it was a competitor, Fidelity Daily Income Fund, launched by a Boston mutual fund organization, which first offered checking account privileges. A number of other major mutual fund organizations are in the business—Dreyfus and Anchor to name two—and there are a number of independents like Reserve Fund as well. Several dozen of the money funds now have some $3.5 billion under management.

As this was written, the money funds were offering about 5 percent in interest—close to their low ebb.* While it is true that this has led to mass redemptions on the part of some shareholders, the industry is not threatened with extinction. There are more attributes than just interest yield that contribute to their popularity.

Individual investors have found the money market funds attractive as a place to "park" funds temporarily withdrawn from the stock market and as a place to put funds that might otherwise lie fallow in a checking account.

As might be expected, the greatest growth for the money funds came at a time when interest rates were setting new records, a period that peaked in the third quarter of 1974. At that point, shareholders in money market funds earned as much as 13 percent interest on their shares. Not just coincidentally, those interest peaks came at a time of devastating declines in stock prices.

But even in times like the present when it is possible to obtain higher interest yields in savings banks, the money funds retain their appeal. For one thing, to obtain the top dollar return of 7 percent or so at the savings banks, the individual must tie up his money for years. He suffers a penalty if he disturbs his funds, and his interest return in that event is reduced to roughly the same level as is currently available in the money market funds.

Service has a lot to do with the success of the money market funds. Reserve Fund, for example, will send a redemption check in the afternoon mail to any shareholder who telephones in the morning asking to withdraw funds.

The fund has its own in-house computers and prides itself on quick service. Other funds rival Reserve for service, though many believe Reserve is the fastest.

The checking privilege is one drawing card that is hard to equal

* In the beginning Reserve Fund offered yields of about 5½ percent, yet the fund had no trouble getting started.

elsewhere. Actually, the customer draws a "draft" on his account with the money fund. A draft is almost identical to a check. It can be drawn to any designated payee. But it cannot be drawn for cash.

Some wealthy individual shareholders draw several drafts a month—to pay the mortgage, perhaps, and other bills that range in size from $500 on up. Drafts are not debited against the shareholder's account until the moment they are honored, and thus interest is paid for as long as one could reasonably expect.

Many individual shareholders withdraw a single monthly check large enough to cover current bills. Such an individual makes his commercial or savings bank checking account the payee and uses the money to cover the small and large checks he writes every month—mortgage or rent, telephone and utility bill, stationery bill, or whatever. Thus the checking account becomes far more versatile than first appears.

In addition to parking funds for redeployment in the stock market, individuals have found other uses for the money market funds. Not long ago, a man opened an account for $45,000 after selling his house. It would be two months before he closed on his new house. At 5 percent, he earned $375 in the interim—which went a long way toward paying closing fees. Storekeepers park funds during the Christmas season until they are needed to buy inventory after year-end. Executors of estates use the money market funds to hold insurance proceeds.

The various money market funds follow different investment policies. Capital Preservation Fund of California invests only in securities of the United States government. This fund has proved to be somewhat popular with investors who fear serious financial distress in one or more sectors of the national economy.

Some funds have made a virtue of holding relatively long paper. Reserve, which stays short and reports interest yields on a daily basis, says that some other funds occasionally report negative interest because of their holdings of long bonds.

Harry Brown explains that a money market fund would lose 10 percent on a 20-year bond if interest rates went up as much as 1 percent. He granted, however, that if such a bond were held during a period when interest rates went down 1 percent, the fund would have a 10 percent profit on the same bond. Most of the funds are invested in relatively short-term obligations, and an average maturity of as much as a year would be considered extraordinary.

A telephone call to any of the major money market funds ought to elicit a comparison of rates among funds, and a trade publication reports to the industry concerning relative returns each week. Follow your instincts. If you find that the money fund is evasive, shop some more. If you are confused by the methods and the representative you talk to cannot clarify to your satisfaction, again, shop some more.

PART VI

TAXES

25 · Tax—
the Long and Short of It

INVESTORS have probably lost as much money waiting for their capital gains to "ripen" as they have through any other single factor—barring a purer form of stupidity. Everybody knows that if you sell stocks after nine months* have elapsed any profits you have earned are "long-term" and ordinarily will be taxed at half one's normal rate. But this is a poor rationale for holding a stock after the reason you bought it no longer obtains.

Suppose, for example, you have calculated that company A will earn substantially more money than had been expected because of a little-noticed increase in prices for its most widely sold product. You bought the shares at 40, and sure enough, within eight and a half months, the shares are selling at 48.

Now the word is out that a militant national trucker's union is mulling a strike. You just happen to know that members of that union are to begin carting the company's Christmas merchandise to market. You face an excruciating decision. Your gains will mature to long-term status within weeks. You'd like to pay taxes on the $800 (8 points on 100 shares) at half your normal rate. You're in the 30 percent tax bracket, so your long-term capital gains tax would be 15 percent of $800 or $120. If you sell now, your tax will be twice as much—$240.

Do you dare wait? The answer is no, and it almost always is. A strike or any other clear setback for a company whose shares have

* Twelve months from 1978 onward.

been rising will have an immediate and perhaps dramatic stock market impact. While you wait for your gains to mature, others will be smarter. There may be some who learned of the price increase before you did, and they may be able to sell now for long-term gains. Others will abandon ship, content with short-term gains.

Just remember that a 1-point retreat will take away most of the extra profit you are trying to preserve at long-term capital gains rates. Never hold a stock once the reason for buying it vanishes. If you do, your gains—all of them, perhaps—will vanish as well.

26 · Tax Shelter
for the Little Guy

THE TAX DEDUCTION for the ordinary man is the interest deduction homeowners claim each year—if you don't count the deduction to which millions are entitled as self-employed proprietors, partners, and free lances and the similar deduction for individuals who work for companies that do not have pension plans.

Keogh (self-employed) and Individual Retirement Account (no pension at work) plans not only offer substantial tax deductions, they also offer opportunities for those who choose to do so to run their own pension-account money. Either plan, then, can become an important plank in your investment platform.

Let's look at the two plans first to determine their possible usefulness to you. Keogh plans are for professional men and women and for partners in businesses—as long as they as owners of the business include all full-time employees in their plans at the same percentage contribution rate as themselves. A full-timer is one who works for the employer for more than 1,000 hours a year. Keoghs are also available to individuals who are covered by corporate *pension plans* if those individuals have free-lance activities that result in additional non-job income. Full-time journalists who write books on the side offer a good example. I have a Keogh plan. Since I have no employees, I am able to qualify for the larger benefits available to Keogh plan owners vis-à-vis those found in IRAs without added cost. I would not qualify for an IRA in any event, since my employer has a pension plan.

The deductible limitation for Keogh plan contributions is the lesser of $7,500 or 15 percent of earned income. There is a minimum allowance contribution of $750 of particular interest to free lances. If you earn any sum up to $750 you can contribute the entire sum to the plan. Presumably, a free lance with a job paying $30,000 a year who earned just $750 as a free lance would want to make a full $750 Keogh contribution.

Anyone who has rejected Keogh plans in the past as of limited interest may be surprised to see how generous they are under present law. Until 1974, the contribution limit was the lesser of $2,500 or 10 percent of earned income.

On page 242 is a table indicating how the Keogh plan would work for a man with an earned income of $50,000 and a full-time secretary who earned $6,000 a year. Contributions for all employees included in Keogh plans are fully vested—the employer can't take them back no matter what.

A Keogh plan can mean a lot to a man with $50,000 of qualified income. All interest, dividends, and capital appreciation on Keogh assets accumulate tax-free—until retirement, anyway.

The chart on the bottom of page 242 will give you an idea why Keogh plans are so popular with those who earn enough—$50,000— to set aside the maximum $7,500. The comparison is of the effect of $7,500 invested annually at an assumed rate of 7 percent under a Keogh plan by an individual in the 50 percent tax bracket to the same individual's after-tax annual investment of $3,750 at an after-tax return of 3½ percent.

The owner-employee who has at least one full-time employee in the plan can make voluntary additions to his Keogh plan over and

FOR AN EMPLOYER WITH A $6,000 EMPLOYEE PAYROLL

Net Earned Income	Approx. Tax Bracket	Deductible Personal Contribution (Total $)	Tax Savings on Personal Contribution (% of Earned Income)		Employee Contributions (Before Tax)	(After Tax)	Net Tax Saving
$75,000*	50%	$7,500	10%	3,750	$600	$300	$3,450
50,000	50	7,500	15	3,750	900	450	3,300
40,000	48	6,000	15	2,880	900	468	2,412
30,000	39	4,500	15	1,755	900	549	1,206
20,000	32	3,000	15	960	900	612	348

* The individual has made the current maximum personal contribution of $7,500, which represents 10 percent of his net earned income of $75,000. Since he is in the 50 percent tax bracket his tax savings on his contribution is $3,750. However, he must also contribute 10 percent of his eligible employees' payroll of $6,000 or $600. Since this contribution is also deductible he has an after-tax cost of $300. The individual employer has a net tax savings of $3,750, less $300, or $3,450. There will of course be a tax payable on the $7,500 contribution when it is distributed at retirement, but it may be based upon a favorable income-averaging rule.

The example was prepared by First Trust Corporation of Denver, a trustee or agent for individual Keogh plans with Dean Witter & Co., the brokerage firm.

Number of Years	Under Keogh Plan	Without Keogh Plan
10	$ 110,873	$ 45,529
15	201,660	74,891
20	328,988	109,759
25	507,570	151,174
30	758,048	200,359
35	1,109,348	258,776

above the qualified sum. These voluntary contributions will come out of after-tax income. However, all income, interest, dividends, and capital appreciation on those after-tax dollars accumulate tax-free until withdrawal. The voluntary contribution limits are 10 percent of earned income, or $2,500, whichever is less. There is no penalty for the withdrawal of voluntary contributions prior to retirement.

The benefits may not be distributed to owner-employees before age 59½ unless he or she is disabled or dies. There is a penalty tax for early distribution, and the owner-employee may not participate in a plan thereafter for the next five years.

Retirement benefits taken in a lump sum would ordinarily be taxed as ordinary income. On the other hand, they would be eligible for a special "averaging" rule if the owner-employee was a participant in the plan for at least five years prior to retirement. This tax is computed as though the individual had no other income, and he will be treated as an unmarried taxpayer who is not the head of a household—regardless of the facts.

Most Keogh plan beneficiaries would consider periodic payments from the plan upon retirement. The benefits are taxed at ordinary income rates, but in retirement the individual ordinarily is in a significantly lower bracket.

A principal in a leading money market fund surprised me recently when he spoke of his IRA plan. I would have expected him to have a Keogh plan, but it turned out that there were too many employees in his organization to make a Keogh plan worthwhile. He thus chose the lesser benefits of the Individual Retirement Account.

The IRA plan, you will recall, is for those who do not have a pension plan at work. Though similar in many ways to Keogh plans, the IRAs have stricter limits. As much as 15 percent of annual earned income, or $1,500, whichever is less, may be set aside on a tax-sheltered basis. The income earned in an IRA plan is not subject to tax until retirement.

The question in either case—whether you have an IRA or a Keogh plan—is what to do with the money. Let's look at your options.

TERM SAVINGS

The obvious solution—the savings bank—is far from the worst. In 1976, for example, New York savings banks offered four-year term accounts for Keogh and IRA money that paid 7.50 percent a year on deposits of $1,000 and up. To accommodate those who start with less money, the banks offer two-in-one accounts providing for the automatic transfer of pension funds to a term account of choice once the minimum deposit is reached.

Continual compounding raises the effective annual yield on all accounts. The nominal 7.50 percent interest on the four-year account offers an effective first-year yield of 7.9 percent. If the money is in a four-year account, the effect of compounding is considerable—$1,000 becomes $1,355.45 after four years.

Each year, new money is added, and the depositor must accept the then current rates. For example, if the rate went up on four-year money, he would make his annual contribution at the higher rate. He would make it at a lower rate if yields dropped.

Here are current savings bank yields in New York state:

7.90 percent annual yield on 7.50 percent a year, four-year term; minimum opening and transfer deposits $1,000.

7.08 percent annual yield on 6.75 percent a year, 2½-year term; minimum opening and transfer deposits $100.

6.81 percent annual yield on 6.50 percent a year, 1-year term; minimum opening and transfer deposits $100.

Residents of other states will have to check their local banks for available yields.

The savings banks are not the most aggressively run institutions in the world. When you go to set up a Keogh plan, be sure to allow plenty of time—particularly if you wait until the last minute. Keogh plans must be set up by the end of the year for which you wish to claim the deduction.

Certainly savings deposits are appropriate investments for Keogh plan and IRA money—even though the inflation rate is sometimes higher than the yield. This is money you are setting aside for retirement, not for speculation. Thousands of Keogh plan owners can hardly be blamed if they are bitter about the experience of their plans under the auspices of a mutual fund. We've already looked at the records of leading mutual funds over the five-year bear market. This chapter can hardly be pleasant reading for the Keogh mutual fund depositors. Most will have paid the mutual fund selling charges as well—up to 8½ percent.

Still, there will be investors who choose mutual funds and some will have good results. The mutual funds have routinized their sign-up techniques—like the savings banks.

GOING IT ALONE

You don't have to put your Keogh funds in a savings bank or mutual fund. You can run the investment portfolio yourself.

You'll need an arrangement with a broker. Most brokers have arrangements with banks or other outside trustees through which individual Keogh and IRA accounts are channeled. The arrangement does not limit the individual investor's freedom of selection and may even enhance it. As a practical matter and once the account is set up, the individual will find that dealing with the Keogh money is little different from dealing with other brokerage accounts.

The individual can invest in debt securities and in stocks listed on recognized exchanges. He can also invest in over-the-counter securities for which there is an active public market.

Certified Plans, Inc., of Newport Beach, California, is a nonbank trustee used by some brokers. The concern specializes in broker-Keogh plans and makes a special effort to make sure accounts meet federal requirements. The owner-client of a pension plan is notified directly of any changes in applicable law affecting his plan, and he receives periodic accounting. First Trust Corporation of Colorado is another specialist which offers trust services to Keogh plan owners through brokerage firms. And there are others. Question your broker to determine how good the service is. You want efficiency and quick reliable service.

It is quite a heady feeling for some Keogh planners—handling their own pension money. And it is probably too risky for some. It goes without saying that it is just as easy to lose pension-fund money as it is to lose money upon which you have already been taxed.

You would do well to limit your investments to relatively safe securities—corporate bonds of AA rating or better, for example. Since the income on these bonds will not be subject to tax in a pension account, you will do better with corporates than with lower-yielding municipal bonds of equal quality.

You may be able to earn substantial total returns through the purchase of discount bonds and preferred stocks (see Part IV), but be careful. The money you lose is precious. No Keogh or IRA assets, no fun in retirement.

NEVER TOO LATE

Most people think about Keogh and IRA plans at the last minute. If you don't believe that, walk into any savings bank on the last business day of December and you'll find a long line of individuals waiting to sign up for new plans just before the deadline.

The deadline, falling as it does just after the Christmas holiday, has been a problem for hard-pressed consumers. It is the worst possible time to raise several hundred or thousand dollars for a pension plan. But under the Pension Reform Act of 1974, there is relief. As long as a plan is set up by the end of December and a nominal deposit of, say, $25 is in place, the rest of the money can be added later. Quite a bit later.

The deadline for getting up the pension money is the extended due date for filing one's income tax return. Ordinarily, the tax return is due on April 15. But taxpayers can ask for and obtain an "automatic" extension of two months—to June 15. The final dollars for Keogh or IRA pensions must be in the plan by that same date.

27 · The Tax-Shelter Wrapper

A SUCCESSFUL Baton Rouge building contractor sold $405,000 of 4.5 percent tax-exempt bonds at an $18,000 loss and bought United States Government agency bonds with $375,000 of the proceeds. Ordinarily, the agency bonds with a pre-tax yield of 7.5 percent would produce much less net income to the contractor, since he was in a high tax bracket. (Yield on the municipals was $18,225 with no tax, but a taxpayer in the 50 percent bracket who received the $28,125 income on the U.S. Governments would have an after-tax yield of just $14,063.)

Why did the contractor switch? Because he knew that if he wrapped an investment annuity around the Government agency bonds, he would not pay current taxes on the income and thus, over time, the investment would be worth much more. For example, a man in the 50 percent tax bracket with $100,000 to invest at 8 percent would have $219,000 after 20 years and after the ravages of federal taxes. But on a sheltered basis—with full benefits of interest compounding—the same $100,000 would be worth $466,100 in 20 years.

Ultimately the taxes would have to be paid on the income. But they would ordinarily accrue after retirement—and at the lower rates usually associated with one's post-career years.

Among the attractions of the investment annuity wrapper is that the individual can maintain control over his capital—buy and sell securities as his investment instincts dictate. Ordinarily, the investor would not find stocks an attractive holding, since realized capital gains are taxable year by year under the special Internal Revenue Service rulings that make the annuity possible in the first place.*

* Nevertheless, hundreds of investors using the wrap-arounds have bought shares in mutual funds and pay the capital gains taxes as realized.

The pioneer in the business is First Investment Annuity Company of America, a small Valley Forge, Pennsylvania, concern. The equally small American Guarantee Life Insurance Company, of Portland, Oregon, began offering the annuities in 1975, and the Phoenix Mutual Life Insurance Company of Hartford, a major insurer with $1.7 billion in assets, is entering the lists.

The service comes at a price. First Investment charges initial premiums ranging from 4 percent on investments of the minimum $10,000 up to $250,000. The charges are scaled down to 1 percent for amounts over $1 million. There is also an annual "premium" of two-thirds of 1 percent of account value at year's end.

The annuities can be purchased either through a life insurance agent or a stockbroker licensed to sell annuities. Even if the policy is purchased from a non-broker life agent, the policyholder can select a broker of his choice to handle investments.

The assets must be registered in the name of a custodian approved by the annuity company. First Annuity and Phoenix Mutual are using Bradford Trust Company in Manhattan. FIAC also uses Wells Fargo Bank N/A on the West Coast.

Switches of securities, as, for instance, out of bonds and into money market funds, will be possible without penalty—unless you count custodian fees and transaction charges. Bradford charges a series of monthly fees for custodian work, ranging up to $10, and transaction fees of $15. Thus a switch involving both a purchase and a sale would cost $30.

Portfolios wrapped into investment annuities are available in most states, though New York and New Jersey are notable exceptions in the East. Easterners who reside in or maintain homes in Pennsylvania or Connecticut can obtain policies there. FIAC is hoping for approval in both New York and New Jersey.

Investment annuity wrap-arounds were available in the following states as this book went to press: Alabama, Alaska, California, Colorado, Connecticut, Delaware, Florida, Idaho, Illinois, Indiana, Iowa, Kansas, Kentucky, Louisiana, Maine, Maryland, Massachusetts, Michigan, Minnesota, Missouri, Montana, Nebraska, New

Hampshire, New Mexico, North Dakota, Ohio, Oklahoma, Oregon, Pennsylvania, Rhode Island, South Carolina, Tennessee, Texas, Utah, Virginia, Washington, Wisconsin, and Wyoming.

GROWTH PLUS*

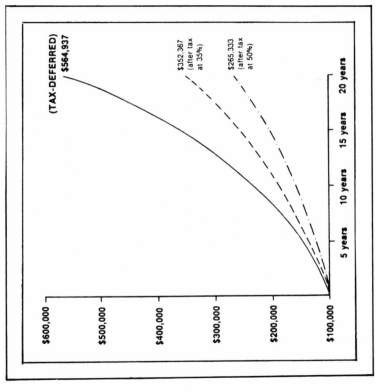

* Don't count on 10 percent a year. Most of those who do wind up with losses.
Source: First Investment Annuity Co. of America

The table on the next page assumes a more realizable 7½ percent growth rate.

$100,000 ANNUITY PURCHASE CONTRIBUTION

4% Initial Premium on amount invested
(4% on $96,154 = $3,846 IP)
0.75% Annual Premium
7½% Annual accumulation rate
No allowance for custodian fees

Accumulated Account Value at End of Year	Tax-Deferred Growth in an Investment	Non-Tax-Deferred Growth at Different Tax Brackets				
	35%	40%	50%	60%	70%
1	102,590	104,875	104,500	103,750	103,000	102,250
2	109,457	109,987	109,202	107,640	106,090	104,550
3	116,784	115,349	114,116	111,677	109,272	106,903
4	124,601	120,972	119,251	115,865	112,550	109,308
5	132,942	126,870	124,618	120,209	115,927	111,767
6	141,840	133,055	130,226	124,717	119,405	114,282
7	151,335	139,541	136,086	129,394	122,987	116,853
8	161,465	146,344	142,210	134,247	126,677	119,483
9	172,273	153,478	148,609	139,281	130,477	122,171
10	183,804	160,960	155,296	144,504	134,391	124,920
11	196,108	168,807	162,285	149,923	138,423	127,731
12	209,235	177,036	169,588	155,545	142,576	130,604
13	223,241	185,667	177,219	161,378	146,853	133,543
14	238,184	194,718	185,194	167,340	151,258	136,548
15	254,127	204,211	193,528	173,708	155,796	139,620
16	271,138	214,166	202,237	180,222	160,470	142,762
17	289,287	224,607	211,337	186,981	165,284	145,974
18	308,651	235,556	220,847	193,992	170,243	149,258
19	329,312	247,040	230,786	201,267	175,350	152,617
20	351,355	259,083	241,171	208,815	180,611	156,050
21	374,874	271,713	252,024	216,645	186,029	159,562
22	399,967	284,959	263,365	224,769	191,610	163,152
23	426,740	298,851	275,216	233,198	197,358	166,823
24	455,305	313,420	287,601	241,943	203,279	170,576
25	485,782	328,699	300,543	251,016	209,377	174,414
26	518,299	344,723	314,067	260,429	215,659	178,338
27	552,993	361,529	328,200	270,195	222,128	182,351
28	590,009	379,153	342,969	280,328	228,792	186,454
29	629,502	397,637	358,403	290,840	235,656	190,649
30	671,640	417,022	374,531	301,747	242,726	194,939

Source: First Investment Annuity Co. of America

Summing Up:
Rest and Rehabilitation

A STOCKBROKER I know, a previously successful glove executive, entered Wall Street in 1972—during the depths of what turned out to be the worst five-year bear market since the Great Depression.

He spent most of his first two years in the business trying to help clients repair the devastation of the bear market. Many were older investors; some were retired.

Characteristically, these investors had allowed their greed to control their saner instincts in the last great bull market—the go-go years of the late 1960s. Portfolio losses of 50 percent and more were not uncommon. For many, that speculative outburst was a last-gasp attempt to get rich quick. The broker—call him Mr. W—found it especially difficult to persuade the new clients to think realistically. They all thought they would break even if they just sat tight. Nobody likes to admit he or she has made a mistake.

True, many of the companies whose shares they held were still profitably in business. But the chances of stock recovery to anything like the speculative levels they had once attained were non-existent. True, there have been remarkable recoveries for particular companies after devastating losses, but such comebacks often take as long as 20 years.

Mr. W's problem was to convince his clients that it would be better to realize losses—at whatever cost—and put remaining dollars to work in sounder holdings. For many who were in advanced years or retired, this meant investing in quality, unexciting fixed-interest securities—corporate and Government bonds.

I might add that Mr. W survived in the business while thousands of those who played their clients' baser instincts are gone. It's not easy for a broker who has howled with the wolves to bleat like a lamb. But investors must learn to admit mistakes if they are to survive. For there comes a time—or times—in every investor's life when he must reassess his goals. Sometimes the time arises after a particularly successful series of investments in a roaring bull market. Unfortunately, however, few investors have the resolve to withdraw when they are ahead—even when they clearly see the dark clouds on the horizon.

For many more, however, the reappraisal comes too late—after staggering losses. I suggest that you make it a practice to reassess your investment strategy periodically, perhaps as often as yearly. You have no legal commitment to the stock market—or to any other market, for that matter. Question the condition of the markets you have invested in and try to arrive at the best future course for your financial security.

Remember, your goal is capital preservation in the first instance. Possible gains over and above the rate of inflation are secondary to keeping what you've got. Don't let your greedier instincts direct your investment strategy. You've got to buy cheap and sell dear to make money. Cheap is relative. It's too late if you call your broker after buying gobs of an obscure stock and tell him to sell and he says, "To whom?" A greater fool may not be around to bail you out.

Think about it. Perhaps it is time for you to withdraw from the markets now—claim those 7 percent returns available at the savings banks. You won't get rich and you might even fall behind in your race against inflation, but you'll still have your money. If you're young and have free capital, why then there's nothing to prevent you from reinvesting—when things improve.

• • • • • •